Taste of Truth

Awakening to Authenticity

Joe Stumpf

Copyright © 2025 by Joe Stumpf

All rights reserved.

No portion of this book may be reproduced in any form without written permission from the publisher or author, except as permitted by U.S. copyright law.

The Cinematic Experience

Don't just read the book—step inside it.

Each chapter of this book is being brought to life as a stunning visual meditation.

Filmed. Illustrated. Scored. Spoken.

A sacred blend of language and image. Now you're invited to experience it for yourself.

Scan the code and unlock private access to the Taste of Truth Video Library—a password-protected sanctuary where each chapter unfolds in a short film, created to move you beyond the page.

To enter, you'll be asked to share your name, email, and mobile number. This ensures we know who's walking with us. Once inside, you'll be welcomed with a selection of powerful chapters to view immediately—on any device, at your own pace.

One story. One breath. One truth at a time. Scan the QR code to begin your journey.

Contents

Welcome to the Taste of Truth — XIII

Taste 1: The Call to Depth — 1

Chapter 1. First Taste — 3

Chapter 2. The Knock at the Door — 5

Chapter 3. The Three Selves and the Choice to Change — 7

Chapter 4. The Imprint of Love — 10

Chapter 5. The Permission to Play — 12

Chapter 6. The Battle with Noise — 15

Chapter 7. The Wisdom in Stillness — 17

Chapter 8. The Price of Avoidance — 20

Chapter 9. The Invitation to Depth — 24

Chapter 10. Breaking Free from the Noise — 27

Chapter 11. The Body Remembers — 30

Chapter 12. The Intelligence of Release — 33

Chapter 13. The Books That Loved Me Back — 37

Chapter 14. One Thought Away — 41

Chapter 15. Who Rises Next? — 44

Chapter 16. Why Am I Here? — 47

Chapter 17. Cleaning the River — 50

Taste 2: The Unseen Architecture — 54

Chapter 18. The Voice Within — 56

Chapter 19. The Echo of the Unspoken — 59

Chapter 20. Breaking the Cycle — 61

Chapter 21. The Paradox of Seeking — 63

Chapter 22. The Illusion of the Map — 67

Chapter 23. The Power of Presence — 69

Chapter 24. The Projector Effect - Seeing Beyond My Own Lens — 71

Chapter 25. Seeing the Shadow — 75

Chapter 26. Integrating the Shadow — 76

Chapter 27. The Power of Not Knowing — 77

Chapter 28. The Consciousness Swap - Letting Myself Be Seen — 81

Chapter 29. The Cost of Speed — 84

Chapter 30. The Art of Presence — 85

Chapter 31. The Space Between — 86

Taste 3: The Disruptive Path to Mastery — 91

Chapter 32. The Art of External Disruption — 94

Chapter 33. The Art of Internal Disruption — 98

Chapter 34. The Silent Thief of Comfort — 102

Chapter 35. Motion as the Cure for Fear ... 105

Chapter 36. The Paradox of Disruption - Dancing at the Edge ... 108

Chapter 37. The Trap of Certainty ... 112

Chapter 38. Trusting the Unknown ... 115

Chapter 39. The Power of Disruptive Confusion ... 118

Chapter 40. The Art of Self-Disruption ... 121

Chapter 41. The Divine Reset ... 125

Chapter 42. The Grip and the Release ... 128

Chapter 43. The Play That Saves Me ... 131

Chapter 44. The Dance of Letting Go ... 137

Chapter 45. The Final Disruption - Becoming Nobody ... 143

Taste 4: Foundations for Practice ... 152

Chapter 46. The First Two Hours - A Ritual of Becoming ... 155

Chapter 47. The Breath & the Body: Listen to the Oldest Wisdom ... 160

Chapter 48. The Rhythm of Sleep & Eating for Aliveness ... 166

Chapter 49. The Ecology of Attention: What I Choose to Cultivate ... 171

Chapter 50. The Habit I Must Build & The Art of Devotion ... 176

Taste 5: The Architecture of Self ... 182

Chapter 51. Self-Esteem as an Immune System ... 186

Chapter 52. The Expansion of Joy ... 189

Chapter 53. The Inner Council - Who Sits at the Table? — 192

Chapter 54. The Inner Teacher - Listening for the Quietest Voice — 195

Chapter 55. The Riverbanks of Freedom - Balancing Structure and Flow — 198

Chapter 56. Living What You Believe - The Ethics of Self-Alignment — 205

Chapter 57. The Alchemy of Judgment and Curiosity — 211

Chapter 58. The Discipline of Curiosity — 216

Chapter 59. The Gravity of Motivation and the Fire of Intensity — 221

Chapter 60. The Power of the Pause — 225

Taste 6: Becoming - The Active Process of Transformation and Evolution — 228

Capter 61. The Future Me Already Exists — 230

Chater 62. The Chisel in my Hand — 233

Chapter 63. The Space Between Identities - Navigating Transitions — 237

Chapter 64. The Hesitation Before Becoming — 242

Chapter 65. Becoming the Future Me — 246

Chapter 66. The Art of Transformation - Releasing and Rebuilding — 249

Chapter 67. The Edge of Comfort - Living in Constant Expansion — 255

Chapter 68. The Weight of Truth — 262

Chapter 69. The Lightness of Being	266
Chapter 70. The Discipline of Stepping Into the Unknown	270
Chapter 71. Resolving the Inner Disturbance	277
Taste 7: Cultivate Vision - The Threshold of What Comes Next	**284**
Chapter 72. Questions for My Future Self	286
Chapter 73. What Would I Attempt If I Knew I Would Not Fail?	289
Chapter 74. The Decision That Shapes the Next Three Years	292
Chapter 75. The Courage to Transform: The Call and the Answer	297
Chapter 76. Cost of Half Commitments	302
Chapter 77. The Fire That Softens Me	305
Taste 8: Mastery & Wisdom	**308**
Chapter 78. The Tightrope Between Mastery and Surrender	310
Chapter 79. The Meta Principle: Owning My Category of One	314
Chapter 80. The Quiet Mastery of Becoming	320
Chapter 81. The Embodied Path - Breath, Food, and Movement as Devotion	324
Chapter 82. Learning to Become	329
Chapter 83. The Long Game of Becoming	334

Taste 9: Beyond the Self - Moving Into What Lasts   337

Chapter 84. The Nesting Dolls of Relationship Evolution   339

Chapter 85. The Disruptor's Way - Breaking Patterns to Grow   341

Chapter 86. The Five Stages of Business Growth   344

Chapter 87. From Success to Sacred - Transforming Work Into Purpose   347

Chapter 88. Leadership as a Cause - Building More Than a Business   349

Chapter 89. Purpose in Life Asking of Me   354

Chapter 90. Transcend and Include - Evolving Without Abandoning My Foundations   358

Chapter 91. The Art of Elegant Change - Finding My Riverbanks   362

Chapter 92. The Weight of What I Give   365

Chapter 93. What Do I Want the People Who Matter to Me to Say About Me When I'm Gone?   368

Taste 10: The Depth of Connection   371

Chapter 94. The Art of Presence   373

Chapter 95. Practicing Presence in Relationships   375

Chapter 96. Love as a Way of Being   377

Chapter 97. The Practice of Living with Love   380

Chapter 98. The Art of Appreciation   383

Chapter 99. The Courage to Open - Asking, Receiving, and Creating Safety in Connection ... 387

Chapter 100. The Orange Principle - Negotiating Interests, Not Positions ... 392

Chapter 101. The Work of Being ... 395

Taste 11: The Path Forward ... 399

Chapter 102. Meeting Others in their Becoming ... 401

Chapter 103. The Embodied Path of Integration ... 403

Chapter 104. The Only Time I Look Back ... 406

Chapter 105. The One Change That's Been Waiting for Me ... 408

Chapter 106. The Eagle's Flight - Trusting the Wind of Change ... 411

Chapter 107. The Chase and the Stillness ... 413

Chapter 108. The Power of Who - Surrendering the Need to Know ... 416

Chapter 109. The Art of Release - The Inner Work of Letting Go ... 420

Chapter 110. A Taste of Truth ... 422

Taste 12. A Taste of Home ... 426

Chapter 111. The Space Between Giving and Tending ... 428

Chapter 112. The Space Between Transactions ... 433

Chapter 113. The Space Between the Dance ... 439

Chapter 114. The Space Between Noise and Silence ... 443

Chapter 115. The Weight of the Unlived Life ... 447

Chapter 116. The Three Joes — 452

Chapter 117. Nothing Is Missing — 456

Chapter 118. The Seat of the Soul — 461

everything make sense. But truth does not operate within the confines of certainty. It lives in the questions we are willing to ask without needing an immediate answer. It exists in the raw, unfiltered moments where we stop performing and allow ourselves to be seen—by others, by ourselves, by something greater than both.

Truth arrives when we have exhausted our strategies for avoiding it.

If I had written this book ten years ago, it would have been different—more answers, fewer questions, more certainty, less wonder. If I had written it five years ago, it would have been different still—perhaps filled with techniques, methods, frameworks for capturing what cannot be captured. Even now, as I write these words, I know that truth is still unfolding. That I am still unfolding. That these pages are not an endpoint but a marker on a path that continues to reveal itself with each step.

But here's what I do know, without question:

Truth is not found in arrival. It is found in presence. In the willingness to be with what is, without flinching, without turning away, without numbing ourselves against what might be uncomfortable to see. In the courage to stand in the fire of our own awareness and let it transform us.

Taste of Truth - Awakening To Authenticity is an invitation.

Not just to read, but to experience. Not just to understand, but to awaken.

It is an invitation to step beyond the surface narratives we tell ourselves and into the depths of what has always been there, waiting for us. It is a guide through the architecture of perception, the unseen patterns that shape our lives, and the stories we carry—some inherited, some constructed, all deeply influential. It is about looking with new eyes at the ways we seek, the ways we hide, the ways we unknowingly hold ourselves back from what we claim to want the most.

And it is about finally understanding that the greatest barrier to truth has never been its complexity, but our resistance to its simplicity.

Welcome to the Taste of Truth

Truth is a living thing.

Not a static concept to be grasped, not a conclusion to be reached, not a doctrine to be memorized. It breathes, shifts, reveals itself in fragments—sometimes as a whisper, sometimes as a reckoning. And more often than not, it arrives in the spaces between what we thought we knew and what we are finally ready to see.

I've spent decades running from this understanding. Running toward knowledge, toward achievement, toward the next insight that promised resolution. Always moving, always seeking, always convinced that the answer was just ahead, around the next corner, in the next book, the next teacher, the next breakthrough.

But truth was never running ahead of me. It was running within me.

This book is not about truth as an abstract ideal. It is not about philosophical musings or distant contemplations. It is about the lived experience of truth—the kind that upends, unravels, and ultimately reconstructs us from the inside out. The kind that does not ask for our permission but instead burns away what is false until only what is real remains. The kind that sometimes feels like dying before you realize it's actually rebirth.

I have spent my life in pursuit of something just beyond my grasp. A deeper understanding. A clearer vision. A certainty that would finally make

I have spent years writing these pages, not as an expert who has mastered truth, but as someone who has wrestled with it, been broken open by it, and, at times, run from it. I have sought wisdom from every direction—books, mentors, experiences, failures, love, loss, silence. And in the end, the greatest revelations did not come from seeking more knowledge. They came from surrendering to what was already present.

There were days when I couldn't write because the truth I was touching was too raw, too close to the bone. Days when I had to put down the pen because what was emerging wasn't just words on a page but a mirror I wasn't yet ready to face. And that, too, was part of the journey—learning that resistance itself is a teacher, that avoidance holds its own wisdom, that the places we don't want to look are precisely where our liberation lies.

This book is not linear. It is not a step-by-step guide. It could not be, because truth does not arrive in sequence. It is a mosaic of insights, each chapter a reflection of a moment when truth revealed itself to me in a way I could no longer ignore. Some truths landed like a gentle realization; others came like a tidal wave, washing away everything I thought I knew. But all of them were necessary.

As you read, you may find pieces of your own story reflected back at you. You may recognize your own patterns, your own seeking, your own avoidance, your own longing. Some passages might pierce you with immediate recognition. Others might seem distant now, only to return to you months later with sudden clarity. And if you are willing, this book will not just be something you read—it will be something you feel, something you experience, something that shifts the way you see yourself and the world around you.

Because truth, real truth, is not meant to be merely understood.

It is meant to be lived. Embodied. Breathed into every cell until it becomes not something you know, but something you are.

And so I offer these pages not as a destination, but as a doorway. Not as answers, but as invitations to deeper questions. Not as an end to seeking, but as the beginning of finding.

Welcome to *Taste of Truth: Awakening to Authenticity*.

May it meet you exactly where you and may it call you forward into what you are becoming.

Joe Stumpf
Your Guide By Your Side

Taste 1: The Call to Depth

One day, without warning, the hunger for more became a hunger for meaning.

There is a moment—sometimes sudden, sometimes slow—when life stops being about what's next and starts being about what's underneath. A turning point where achievement gives way to authenticity.

At first, it feels like restlessness. A vague dissatisfaction that no accomplishment can fully quiet. The things that once excited you—the goals, the ambitions, the constant reaching—lose their grip. You begin to notice the spaces in between. The moments of silence that used to go unnoticed. The whispers beneath the surface of your thoughts.

It's not burnout. It's not boredom. It's something deeper. A shift in the center of gravity. A knowing that the way you've been moving through the world is no longer enough.

This is where depth calls you.

Not to a new project, a new plan, or a new pursuit. But to an entirely different way of being. A way of moving through life that isn't dictated by the external, but rooted in something far more stable—an inner knowing.

The mind will resist. It always does. It will convince you to chase one more milestone, to solve one more problem, to stay in motion just a little longer. Because stillness feels like surrender. Because stopping feels like losing.

But depth doesn't ask you to stop. It asks you to see.

To see beyond the surface of your life to what lies beneath. To recognize where you've been playing out the same patterns, mistaking motion for meaning. To acknowledge where you've been filling your days with noise, avoiding the questions that truly matter. To discern the difference between what you've been taught to want and what your soul is actually calling for.

This section is about that pivotal shift—the moment when external pursuit transforms into internal discovery. It's about the transition from seeking to knowing. From striving to arriving. From defining yourself by what you achieve to understanding yourself by what you are.

Because, at some point, the pursuit of more isn't growth. It's escape.

At some point, adding to your life doesn't make it richer—it makes it heavier.

At some point, you don't need another tool, another framework, another philosophy. You just need to stand still long enough to hear the truth that's already inside you.

In the pages that follow, you'll discover not just concepts but pathways—practical approaches to quiet the noise, release the weight of old stories, and attune to the wisdom that's been waiting for your attention. You'll learn to recognize the difference between the voice of your conditioning and the voice of your truth. You'll explore what it means to live not from your history, but from your imagination.

You already know. You've always known.

The only question left is—will you finally listen to the wisdom that waits beneath the noise?

Chapter 1. First Taste

The world doesn't just move—it hums.

A frequency beneath the surface. I don't just hear it—I feel it, like a second heartbeat. A signal I can no longer ignore.

It's not the noise of urgency. Not the static of distraction. It's something deeper—an undercurrent, a pulse rising just beneath the surface of things.

I feel it before I name it. A shift. A beckoning. The quiet awareness that what I once sought out there is now pulling me inward.

For most of my life, I've lived at the edge—sensing the curve before it bends, chasing what's next, always building, reaching, expanding. I built companies that scaled across continents. I created frameworks adopted by thousands. I pursued influence, impact, and recognition—always at the frontier of what's possible.

But now, the momentum has changed. The force driving me forward is no longer more, but deeper.

It's not retreat. It's refinement.

Aging isn't a narrowing, I see now. It's the accordion's second breath. First, the stretch—striving, proving, reaching. Then, the contraction—returning, distilling, deepening.

Not how far can I go? But how true can I be?

That's where I stand now. Not stepping back, not fading, but stepping fully into presence. Into creation that doesn't beg for applause. Into connection that sheds its scripts. Into a life led not by becoming, but by being.

For decades, I was the architect—raising frameworks, forging communities, and scaffolding growth for thousands. My hands shaped the structures. My voice carried the message. But what happens when the blueprints are set aside? When the need to build is replaced with the need to listen?

What happens when I stop trying to capture truth and start tasting it? When I trade the certainty of knowledge for the vulnerability of experience? When I release the compulsion to solve in favor of the courage to witness?

This isn't about answers. It's about the questions too stubborn to die.

What happens when a man—here, now, at this depth—stares into the truest mirror and doesn't blink? When he finally stands in the center of his own life, not as architect but as witness? When he chooses to taste truth rather than merely describe it?

This journey begins not with a destination, but with a deeper way of seeing. And it begins now.

Chapter 2. The Knock at the Door

There is a moment—sometimes subtle, sometimes deafening—when life knocks. Not a polite tap. Not a gentle whisper. But an undeniable, persistent rhythm against the walls of everything you've known.

It doesn't ask for permission. It doesn't care if you're ready. It comes when it comes.

At first, I ignored it. I was busy—building, striving, achieving. My life was full—full of ambition, full of momentum, full of the kind of success that quiets the deeper questions for a while. But only for a while.

Because the knock doesn't go away. It waits. It lingers. It finds you in the quiet spaces between accomplishments, in the stillness after the applause fades, in the moments when you realize that what you've built isn't the same as what you actually need.

For me, it started as a whisper, disguised as exhaustion—one that no amount of sleep could fix. 3 AM wake-ups filled with questions I couldn't answer. Days when my body felt like lead despite ten hours of rest. It showed up in the relationships that felt like home one day and a foreign country the next. It revealed itself in the gnawing sense that I had spent years mastering my time, but not mastering my focus.

I remember standing in my office one evening—awards lining the walls, inbox overflowing with opportunities, calendar filled with speaking engagements—when the knock became impossible to ignore. A hollowness spread through my chest, an ache so profound it made breathing difficult. All this success, all this recognition, and still something essential was missing.

I had always been the architect—constructing, designing, optimizing. But there comes a time when the scaffolding feels suffocating. A time when the question shifts from **What more can I build?** to **What is all this building for?**

It's a terrifying moment. Because it forces you to pause. To listen. And to ask yourself. **Is this the life I truly want, or just the one I know how to sustain?**

When you finally acknowledge the knock, everything changes. Not because your circumstances shift, but because your perception does. The mask of busyness falls away. The shield of achievement cracks. And beneath it all, you find the truth you've been avoiding that no external success can substitute for internal alignment.

The knock is always there, reverberating through the quiet moments, waiting for acknowledgment. The only question is—will you finally open the door and face what waits on the other side?

Chapter 3. The Three Selves and the Choice to Change

For most of my life, I thought of myself as a single, fixed identity—a "self" with clear edges, a core that never really changed. But I see it differently now.

We are always three selves at once:

PAST SELF – Clings to the story.

PRESENT SELF – Carries the weight.

FUTURE SELF – Knows the truth.

For years, I was feeding my future self the same script—the same patterns, the same limitations, the same unconscious loops disguised as certainty.

Then came the moment I could no longer unsee.

I was standing in a room I had built—literally and metaphorically. My office, overlooking the water, walls adorned with achievements: the awards acknowledging innovation, the framed book covers, the photographs with thought leaders and influencers. A business I had scaled to seven figures, a brand recognized across continents, a life I had meticulously designed according to every metric that should spell fulfillment. But something felt off.

Not broken. Not wrong. Just... hollow.

Like I was full of the wrong things. Like I had built the perfect machine, but somewhere along the way, I had misplaced the part of me that actually wanted to live inside it.

And I knew, in that moment, I had a choice.

Not a dramatic, reckless leap. Not a full destruction of what I had built. Just a simple, undeniable decision:

Would I keep living from my history, or would I start living from my imagination?

Because the past is strong. It is familiar. It is the weight in your bones that tells you what's possible, based on what has been. It is the voice that says, *This is who you are. This is what you do. Don't question it.*

But imagination is stronger. And I had been ignoring mine for too long.

That's when I turned inward, developing what I now call **Private-Work**—not just another productivity system or self-improvement technique, but a radical practice of questioning what I had accepted as reality. A disciplined approach to sitting with myself, honestly and deeply, to uncover what lies beneath the narratives I'd been living by. Not through force. Not through frantic effort. But through awareness, clarity, and a commitment to feeding the right future.

And so I asked myself:

- *What memories from my past are limiting my growth?* Those moments of rejection, failure, or loss that I've allowed to define what's possible for me.

- *What do I imagine is possible if I finally let them go?* The vision of myself unburdened by old wounds, free to create from a place of possibility rather than protection.

- *If my future self knocked on my door right now, what would they tell me?* The wisdom I already possess but haven't given myself permission to hear.

- *If I woke up tomorrow with zero attachment to the person I've been, what would I do differently?* The actions that fear has been keeping me from taking.

These questions became my compass, guiding me away from the well-worn paths of my history and toward the uncharted territory of what might be. Not as an exercise in wishful thinking, but as a profound recalibration of how I moved through the world.

The door to this transformation is already there, waiting. And all I have to do—is open it. Not to escape who I've been, but to finally become who I truly am.

Chapter 4. The Imprint of Love

There's a moment—so fleeting you might miss it—when love lands.

Not in words. Not in grand gestures. But in presence. In the way someone stays. In the way their eyes soften when they see you. In the way their arms lift—instinctively, without hesitation—to catch you before you even know you're falling.

I see it now, in my grandson, Dean Joseph.

The way my daughter and son-in-law meet him in every moment—every sound, every reach of his tiny hands, every burst of joy, every trembling frustration. They don't rush him through his experience. They don't turn away. They just meet him—completely, fully, without condition.

And I watch. And I wonder.

Because this is what love looks like when it arrives on time.

I didn't have that.

I don't say it with bitterness. I don't say it as blame. I say it as a fact—as the shape of a childhood spent in the orbit of a mother drowning in alcohol, buried beneath the weight of five children under five.

I have no memories of her playing with me. No warm laughter curling through my earliest years. No steady, gentle hands lifting me up.

I remember chaos. I remember the hunger of a child searching for something that wasn't there. And when love arrives late, you learn to fend for yourself. You learn to shrink your needs. You learn to be small enough to survive.

But love is patient. Even when it misses the moment, it finds another.

Because I also remember when my mother got sober. I remember the woman she became—the one who wrote with me, laughed with me, stood steady when I needed her. In her sobriety, she showed me that love could arrive later and still transform everything. That healing, while never erasing what was lost, can still create something new.

This realization has shaped my entire journey toward depth. For years, I chased achievement as a substitute for the love I didn't receive early enough. I built businesses, frameworks, and communities—all attempts to create externally what I hadn't fully developed internally: a sense of worthiness that didn't depend on performance.

Now I understand that the call to depth is, in many ways, the call to meet myself with the same love I witness between my grandson and his parents. To stop expecting validation from outside and start giving presence to what's within. To recognize that love—even when it arrives late—can still teach us how to return to ourselves.

And in that, I see the profound truth: **Love arrives in its own time.** Even when it isn't there when we first need it, it has a way of finding us. Not just in others, but in ourselves—in our capacity to finally meet our own experiences with the presence they've always deserved.

This is perhaps the greatest gift of watching Dean Joseph grow—not just witnessing love in action, but remembering that it's never too late to receive it, to give it, to become it. That depth itself might simply be another name for love that has finally found its way home.

Chapter 5. The Permission to Play

Breaking the pattern of trying to earn love.

My sister Jeannie and I have talked about this for years.

We laugh now—because we made it. Because we made something new. Because even though she never had children of her own, in so many ways, she raised me.

And because I learned, in my own way, how to break the pattern.

I see it in my daughters. I see it in the way I raised them—not perfectly, not without my own wounds seeping through—but fully. I see it in my grandson, Dean Joseph. I see it in my nephew Brian's children, Mia and Aurora, running wild and free on the beaches of New Zealand. I see it in the trust they have in their own worthiness—because the people who love them have made it clear: You matter.

Play is proof of love. Not forced. Not scheduled. Just the freedom to be ridiculous, to be weightless, to be alive.

When I am with children, I disappear into their world. Time ceases to exist. My mind quiets. There is no strategy, no calculation, and no need to shape or direct. There is only now. I become fully present—building sandcastles that the tide will take, creating voices for stuffed animals, dancing with abandon to music only children seem to hear. In those moments, I am not the architect, the strategist, the achiever. I am simply here, completely engaged in the joy of existence.

And maybe that's the truth I need to meet today.

I have always known that play is a form of love. But have I fully embraced that it is also a form of **presence**?

Because the truth is, I don't just love playing with kids—I love playing, period. In music, in movement, and in creative exploration without a predetermined outcome. And maybe I need more space for that. Not just in stolen moments. Not just when it's convenient. But as a way of being.

More dance. More spontaneous creation. More days where I am not the orchestrator of great ideas, but simply the man who laughs for no reason.

Because when I look at Dean Joseph, I see what happens when love meets a child in every moment. But when I look at myself, I see a man who is still learning that he, too, is allowed to be met in the same way.

That play isn't something I have to earn. That love isn't something I have to deserve by proving my worth. That I, even now, can let go into the lightness that is my birthright.

And if that is true—if I really let myself believe that—what might change?

What would it look like if I didn't just admire the way love is given to the next generation, but fully received it in myself? If I didn't just play with children, but allowed myself to become childlike again? If I stopped reaching forward for answers and simply danced inside the ones I already have?

Maybe that's my next evolution in this journey to depth. Not doing more. Not creating faster. Not achieving bigger.

But returning.

Back to joy. Back to play. Back to the boy I once was—the one who still lives inside me, waiting to be met with the presence he always deserved.

Play is not a luxury. It is proof that I am alive. And perhaps it is also the purest expression of the depth I've been seeking all along—not the depth of analysis or achievement, but the depth of full engagement with the present moment, unfiltered by expectation or fear.

This is the permission I now give myself: to play not as an escape from life, but as the fullest embodiment of it.

Chapter 6. The Battle with Noise

There was a time when I thought clarity was something I could wrestle into submission.

If I thought harder, analyzed deeper, sorted through the chaos long enough, the answer would rise—clean and whole—like a pearl pulled from the deep.

But some truths don't reveal themselves through effort. Some truths only surface in stillness. And stillness is harder than movement.

I learned this the way we learn most things—by doing the opposite until exhaustion set in.

For years, my mind was a snow globe, shaken by my own hands. Thoughts colliding, emotions swirling into storms, clarity buried beneath the blizzard of my own making. I filled my days with noise—ideas, conversations, work, distractions—because silence felt like surrender.

Because stopping meant **feeling**.

I used to believe that if I could just think enough, I could outmaneuver my own suffering. That the right sequence of thoughts would untangle the knots inside me.

But the mind is an unreliable narrator.

It recycles old fears. It warps reality to fit its stories. It searches the past for proof that the present will hurt just the same.

So, I kept trying to outthink my own pain. And every time I did, I only stirred the storm again.

Then, one day, I saw it for what it was:

The thoughts that tormented me weren't asking to be solved. They were asking to be **witnessed**.

Chapter 7. The Wisdom in Stillness

I don't remember the date—just the moment.

I had been running. Not physically, but mentally. Reaching, grasping, circling—always moving toward the next thing that might make me feel better. The next conversation, the next book, the next big idea that would finally solve the restlessness inside me.

I was sitting on my deck overlooking the Pacific, surrounded by notebooks filled with plans, strategies, insights—all the ways I was trying to think myself into peace. The sun was setting, painting the sky in deep oranges and purples, but I barely noticed it. I was too busy trying to solve myself.

And then, something inside me whispered:

"Put it down."

Not as a command. Not as an insight. Just a knowing, as clear and simple as the breath in my lungs.

So I did. I stopped. Right there, with the ocean stretching before me, I set down my pen. Closed my notebook. Took a full breath.

I let the weight of my thoughts exist without trying to fix them. I let the storm rage without running for cover.

And for the first time, I understood—

Stillness isn't emptiness. Stillness is where the truth rises.

The Seduction of Noise

Silence terrifies most people. We claim to crave peace, but we're conditioned for noise.

Distraction is easy. Picking up the phone, diving into work, numbing ourselves with habits we don't even recognize as numbing—easy.

Sitting with yourself? That's the hardest thing in the world.

Because the moment you stop moving, the mind starts talking. And it doesn't always say things you want to hear.

It reminds you of regrets. It brings up old wounds you thought you'd outgrown. It makes you question everything you've built.

So we keep ourselves busy—not because we have to, but because we don't know who we are without the motion.

I used to believe that if I could just think enough, I could outmaneuver my own suffering. That the right sequence of thoughts would untangle the knots inside me.

But the mind is an unreliable narrator.

It recycles old fears. It warps reality to fit its stories. It searches the past for proof that the present will hurt just the same.

So, I kept trying to outthink my own pain. And every time I did, I only stirred the storm again.

Then, one day, I saw it for what it was—

The Snow Globe I Shook With My Own Hands

I had spent years shaking the snow globe, hoping for clarity.

But clarity only comes when the storm settles.

Truth doesn't chase. It doesn't demand. It sits, patient and unyielding, waiting for you to be ready.

And when it arrives—

It will not come as a shout. It will not come as a grand revelation. It will come as a whisper.

"Put it down."

I've spent my life building. Building businesses. Building relationships. Building a version of myself that could stand against anything. Building defenses against the very vulnerability that might have set me free.

But now, the building feels less urgent.

Now, I want to know: What remains when I stop hammering? What's left when the scaffolding is removed? Who am I when I am not striving? What truths have been waiting beneath the noise of my constant motion?

I sit with those questions now. Not trying to answer them. Not trying to shape them into something presentable. Just listening. Allowing the silence to speak in its own language.

Because when the snow settles, the world doesn't disappear. It just becomes clearer.

And that clarity? That is the taste of truth—not acquired through effort, but revealed through surrender. Not found in addition, but in subtraction. Not arrived at through more thinking, but through the courage to finally be still.

The only question is— **Are you willing to put it down long enough to see what's been waiting for you all along?**

Chapter 8. The Price of Avoidance

I know where it started.

The early imprint. The absence of being met in those first formative years. A mother who—by no fault of her own—was drowning, overwhelmed, lost in alcohol and the relentless demands of five children under five.

I don't remember play. I don't remember mirroring. I don't remember the feeling of being fully held in my smallness.

And what doesn't get met, we learn to avoid.

The Cost of Self-Protecting

I have spent years working through this. I have built a life that feels whole, that feels expansive. I have learned how to **give** love in so many ways—to my daughters, my clients, my community.

But intimacy, true intimacy, requires receiving.

And I see, even now, the ways in which I still hesitate to let myself be fully gotten.

Am I choosing solitude? Or am I avoiding something?

The truth is—it's both.

The Window of Toleration

I have a narrow window.

The threshold of what I can hold before I need space.

Too much energy—excitement, stimulation, demand—and I pull away. Too little energy—stagnation, stillness, disconnection—and I retreat inward.

Between those two edges is where I feel most alive.

I see it in the way I structure my days—periods of intense connection followed by essential solitude. In how I can speak to hundreds, fully present and engaged, then need hours alone to recover. In how even the most loving relationships begin to feel like a weight against my chest after too much closeness, triggering an almost physical need to withdraw.

And I have spent years managing that space, refining my ability to regulate, to balance.

But how much of that is management, and how much of that is avoidance?

Have I, over time, repeated the same belief so many times that it's now just **true** for me?

And if so, what's the cost?

Because I know this cycle. The in and embrace, then out and retreat. The depth, then the disappearance.

And I don't want to keep building relationships that promise something they can't hold. I don't want to keep entering, knowing I will inevitably exit. I don't want to keep telling myself that solitude is always a choice when, sometimes, it's a shield.

A Different Rhythm

What I do want is to explore a different rhythm.

What would it feel like to be in a relationship—not just romantic, but in any form—without an exit strategy?

Without one foot resting in the comfort of my own space? Without the quiet, unspoken knowing that, if needed, I can leave?

What would it look like to trust that I can stay?

That I can be fully gotten—without the pressure, without the fear that it will become too much, too soon, too overwhelming?

And would I be willing to let love—real, sustaining, patient love—teach me how to widen my own window?

I imagine what it might feel like to remain present when the urge to withdraw first surfaces. To sit with the discomfort rather than escape it. To trust that the boundaries I need can exist without walls. To believe that I can be both connected and free, both seen and safe.

Longing as Proof of Aliveness

Because I can see that longing. I can feel it.

It's not a sign of lack. It's not something to escape.

It's proof that something in me is still alive, still stretching toward more.

And I owe it to myself to stop making that belonging conditional.

This is perhaps the deepest work of all—learning to stay present not just with others, but with myself. Learning to receive as freely as I give. Learning that the very discomfort I avoid might be the doorway to the connection I truly seek.

Because true depth isn't found in perfect self-protection. It's found in the courage to remain open, even when every instinct tells you to close. To trust that what you most fear—being overwhelmed, being consumed, being too much or not enough—might be the very illusion keeping you from the belonging you've always wanted.

The price of avoidance isn't just missed connections. It's a life that never fully arrives at itself.

Chapter 9. The Invitation to Depth

There comes a moment—quiet, subtle, almost imperceptible—when life stops simply happening to you and starts calling you forward.

It's not loud. It's not urgent. But it's undeniable.

Not a demand. Not a checklist. Not another mountain to climb.

But an invitation.

It doesn't arrive in the way you expect. It doesn't crash through your walls or shake you awake. It shows up between the noise.

In the way a conversation lingers in your mind long after it's over. In the space between breaths, between decisions, between the old version of yourself and the one waiting to emerge. In the brief silence that follows a laugh, when something real, something unguarded, sneaks through.

You don't always notice it at first. But once you do, you can't unsee it.

This is the moment of depth. The place where reflex becomes awareness. Where action turns to intention. Where the autopilot shuts off, and you realize—you've been invited to more.

Looking Through the Window of What's Possible

I imagine myself as a bird, hovering just beyond the window of my future self.

I see him inside. Not as he is now, but as he is becoming.

He is lighter. Unburdened by the weight of stories that no longer define him.

His presence is effortless, magnetic—not because he tries to be interesting, but because he is deeply interested.

He listens with his whole body, leaning in slightly, eyes focused, without the subtle distraction of formulating his response while others are speaking. He moves with intention, each action deliberate rather than reactive. He pauses before responding to difficult questions, comfortable in the silence that most rush to fill.

He is surrounded by people who are not merely existing, but expanding— **Learning. Unlearning. Relearning.** They gather not just for connection, but for transformation—sharing ideas, challenges, and insights without the need for masks or performance.

He is inside the flow of something greater than himself. Not grasping, but allowing. Not striving, but trusting. His day isn't structured around productivity metrics, but around presence. Time for stillness. Time for play. Time for deep work that emerges not from obligation, but from genuine curiosity.

And then, unexpectedly— I hear something.

Laughter.

The sound of easy conversation. The rhythm of ideas being exchanged. The music of connection without agenda.

And I feel it. That pull. That knowing.

I don't just want to watch him. **I want to become him.**

This vision isn't some distant fantasy or idealized projection. It's already forming in the moments when I choose depth over distraction. When I listen instead of waiting to speak. When I allow myself to be fully present rather than partially engaged in multiple directions.

The invitation to depth isn't asking me to become someone else. It's asking me to become more fully who I already am—beneath the noise, beneath the striving, beneath the patterns that have defined me but no longer serve me.

What I glimpse through that window isn't a different person—it's myself, freed from the weight of expectations, stories, and fears that I've carried for so long. It's what remains when I strip away the endless doing and settle into the simplicity of being.

And I realize now that the doorway to this transformation isn't something I need to find. It's something I need to accept. The invitation has always been there, waiting for me to recognize it not as a burden to shoulder, but as a gift to receive.

I don't just want to watch him. **I want to become him.**

And in this moment of recognition, I already have.

Chapter 10. Breaking Free from the Noise

But to enter that life, **I must leave something behind.**

The weight of old thoughts. The burden of emotions that no longer serve me. The habits of mind that keep me circling the same questions, searching for answers that have already expired.

For so long, I believed my feelings were facts. That if I felt something, it must be true. That anxiety meant danger. That doubt meant I was wrong. That restlessness meant I needed something more.

But I see now— Feelings are just the shadows of thoughts. They rise and fall with the stories I tell myself.

And if I can change the story, I can change the feeling.

Thoughts Are Just Salesmen

This is the work.

Not to fight my thoughts. Not to force them into submission.

But to choose them.

To recognize that thoughts are like door-to-door salesmen— They knock. They pitch. They try to sell me something.

But I am not obligated to buy.

I can let them knock. I can let them pass. I can open the door only to the ones that serve me.

I remember the morning I first truly understood this. Sitting in meditation, watching as the thought arose: "You'll never be enough." It came with such authority, such conviction—a salesman I'd bought from thousands of times before. But this time, instead of inviting him in, instead of arguing with him, I simply nodded and said, "Thank you for your offer. I'm not interested today."

And it changed everything.

Not because the thought disappeared. But because I realized I wasn't obligated to believe it.

The Choice to Step In

So, I stand at the threshold.

One foot in the life I have always known. One foot in the life that is waiting for me.

The familiar path is well-worn and comfortable in its predictability. It's the path where I listen to the same old stories, react to the same old triggers, and cycle through the same old patterns. It's the life where I remain the person I've always been—reliable, productive, successful by every external measure—but never fully free.

The new path is uncharted. It requires presence rather than habit. It demands that I question everything I've assumed to be fixed about myself. It asks me to trust what I feel rather than what I think. To listen to the wisdom of my body rather than the chatter of my mind. To allow rather than force. To be rather than do.

And **the invitation is clear**:

Will I stay in the noise, or will I step into depth?

Will I remain tangled in thoughts that no longer serve me, or will I release them and create something new?

Will I keep watching through the window, or will I walk through the door?

This is not a single decision, but a moment-by-moment choice. A continuous returning to what's real beneath the noise. A daily practice of asking: Is this thought serving me? Is this story true? Is this feeling guiding me toward depth or away from it?

The invitation is here. The future is already forming—not as some distant horizon, but as the natural unfolding of this very moment, when I choose awareness over autopilot.

And the only thing left to do—is step in. Not tomorrow. Not when I'm ready. Not when the conditions are perfect.

But now. In this breath. In this thought. In this choice, to finally hear the silence beneath the noise.

Chapter 11. The Body Remembers

It begins before thought.

A pulse beneath the surface. A sensation rising before the mind can make sense of it. A quiet knowing, deep in the bones.

The body keeps its own record.

Not as words. Not as logic. But as rhythm.

A tightening in the chest before a decision. A sudden stillness in the presence of truth. A heat that rises, unbidden, at the memory of something long buried.

Before the mind understands, the body already knows. And it knows when it's time to release.

The Road to the Unspoken

At 2:30 PM, I step into my car.

The road from Forestville to Sebastopol is familiar now, but it is never the same.

It is not just a drive. It is a passage.

A crossing from the weight of the thinking mind into something deeper—something wordless.

The trees blur past my window. The winding road carries me through vineyards and redwoods. With each mile, I feel my shoulders drop, my breath deepens, and my thoughts begin to quiet. I am no longer the architect, the strategist, the man of words. I am becoming something more primal, more honest—a body with a story to tell.

I arrive at the barn, the place where, every 90 days, I surrender to the practice of Soul Motion.

A place where movement isn't performance. It isn't choreography.

It is prayer. It is remembering.

But today, there is no group. No shared dance.

Only **Lysa Castro** and me.

Lysa does not tell me what to do. She does not instruct.

She witnesses.

Her eyes hold me without demand or expectation. Her presence creates a container strong enough to hold whatever might emerge. She stands in the periphery of the wooden floor, a guardian of the space between consciousness and release.

She holds space as my body speaks the things my voice has never known how to say.

Because some things— some wounds, some truths— live beyond words.

What the Body Holds

I have spent my life in pursuit of healing.

Therapy. EMDR. Plant medicine. Meditation. Writing.

Thousands of moments spent unraveling the imprint of what was done, what was absent, what was lost.

I've analyzed childhood patterns, reframed limiting beliefs, excavated memories, journaled insights, meditated through resistance—all the ways we try to think ourselves into wholeness.

And yet, for all of it, I have come to understand— There are places inside me that will not think their way into healing.

They have to be moved.

The wisdom of the body isn't something I was taught to trust. Like many men of my generation, I learned to live from the neck up—in thoughts, in plans, in words that could be controlled and measured. I learned to override sensation, to push through discomfort, to wear exhaustion like a badge of honor.

But the body remembers what the mind tries to forget. It holds the trembling that never happened, the tears that never fell, the rage that never found expression. It carries the weight of every moment we abandoned ourselves to survive.

And it waits patiently for the moment when we are finally ready to listen.

This is why I come to this barn. This is why I surrender to movement. Not to perform, not to achieve, but to finally let my body tell its truth. To let it shake loose what it has been holding. To let it dance its way into the healing that no amount of thinking could provide.

Because some wounds can only be released through motion. Some truths can only be spoken through the language of the body.

And I am finally learning to listen.

Chapter 12. The Intelligence of Release

The first time I stepped into this space, my body refused to rise.

I barely made it off the floor.

I remember the early sessions with Lysa—how my limbs resisted, how my chest felt weighted with concrete, how my breath caught in my throat. How my body whispered,

Not yet. Too much.

The pain wasn't just in my heart or my mind. It was in my bones.

The Memory Buried in the Body

A crib. A little boy, alone.

A diaper, soiled, sticking to his skin. A safety pin, open, stabbing into his thigh.

A mother—too lost, too overwhelmed, too absent to notice.

And the boy—me—screaming.

Not just because of the pain. Not just because of the pain.

But because even in his crying, he knew he wouldn't be met.

And my body collapsed into that knowing.

I remember the first time this memory surfaced during movement. How my legs gave way beneath me. How I found myself on the wooden floor, curled into myself, my fingernails scraping against the boards as if trying to claw my way out of the past. Tears streaming down my face, not from sadness, but from a primal recognition—this is where it began.

I scraped at the floor, at the weight of it all, at the part of me that had spent a lifetime believing I wasn't meant to be comforted.

Because what doesn't get met, we learn to avoid. And what doesn't get expressed, we store.

And the body—unlike the mind—does not forget.

From Surviving to Freeing

Even after all the therapy, even after all the tools, there were still pieces of me trapped in that crib.

Trapped in silence. Trapped in the belief that my pain was too much for anyone to hold.

But here, in this barn, on these Mondays, in this movement—something different happens.

I bring my pain to God through dance.

Not the dance of performance or technique. But the dance of surrender. Of honesty. Of allowing what has been locked inside to find its way out through motion.

I bring the things I cannot speak, the things too sacred, too raw, too untouchable to be reduced to language, and I let my body offer them up.

Sometimes, it's barely movement at all—a trembling, a shaking, a release of tension that has been held for decades. Sometimes, it's wild, uncontrolled, the expression of rage that has never had permission to exist. Sometimes, it's gentle, a swaying that soothes what has never been soothed.

And it changes me.

Not just in the moment, but in the way I move through the world. In the way I inhabit my own skin. In the capacity I now have to be present with sensations instead of numbing them. To trust the wisdom of my body instead of overriding it with my mind.

The Body Holds the Way Out

Because the truth is, the body holds everything.

The pain. The trauma. The years of silence.

But it also holds the way out.

It holds the intelligence of release. The wisdom of shaking. Of movement. Of rhythm.

It holds the capacity to clear what was once unbearable.

And that is why I dance.

Because some wounds don't heal through analysis. Some stories don't need to be retold in words. Some truths are meant to be moved through rather than dissected.

And for the first time in my life, I am no longer asking my body to carry what it was never meant to hold.

I am asking it to release.

And it is answering me—not with explanation, not with insight, not with understanding.

But with freedom. With presence. With the quiet knowing that what has been locked away can finally come home.

This is the intelligence of release—not to figure it out, but to let it go. Not to solve it, but to move it. Not to understand it, but to free it.

And in that freedom, I find myself.

Chapter 13. The Books That Loved Me Back

There are books that teach. Books that challenge. Books that arrive at exactly the moment you need them.

And then there are books that love you back.

I've surrounded myself with books my entire life. Not just as a student, but as a collector of meaning. As if, by gathering enough of them, I might someday gather enough of myself.

Some books were teachers, guiding me into new ideas like patient mentors. Some were companions, filling the quiet spaces when I didn't want to sit with my own thoughts. And some—only a few—felt like home.

I didn't always know the difference.

For years, I mistook knowledge for transformation. I thought if I read enough, learned enough, mastered enough frameworks, I would arrive—at wisdom, at peace, at some final resting place of knowing.

But books, like people, have limits. Some expand you. Some exhaust you. Some leave a mark. Some leave you empty.

And some, no matter how many times you turn their pages, cannot teach you the things you need to live.

The Books That Held Me

Some books were like old friends—reliable, steady, always waiting. They didn't change, but I did, and every time I returned, I saw something new in their pages.

Others were like lovers—intoxicating, impossible to put down, demanding to be consumed in a single breath. I remember nights spent with Rumi's poetry, with Frankl's "Man's Search for Meaning," with Rilke's letters—unable to stop, unwilling to break the spell, dawn finding me still turning pages, transformed.

Some felt like fathers, handing down rules, frameworks, discipline, and structure. The business books, the strategy guides, the manifestos on productivity and achievement—they shaped how I built my world.

Some felt like mothers, whispering warmth into the parts of me that longed to be seen. Mary Oliver's poetry, Pema Chödrön's gentle wisdom, and Annie Dillard's attention to the sacred in the ordinary—these nurtured what had been neglected.

And some were brothers—challenging me, competing with me, forcing me to see where I still had work to do. The books that made me uncomfortable, that confronted my privilege, that showed me where my thinking was too small or too safe.

And then there were the books that disappointed me. The ones I wanted to love, but that didn't love me back. The ones I expected answers from but only left me with more questions. The bestsellers that promised transformation but delivered only techniques. The spiritual guides that offered shortcuts to nowhere.

Books, like people, can only take you as far as they've been.

The Books I've Left Behind

There was a time when I hoarded books. Stacked high in my office, lined along my walls, scattered across every surface. I was afraid to part with them, as if letting go of a book meant letting go of a part of myself.

But some books, like some relationships, have served their purpose.

I've given away more books than I can count. Books that once meant everything, but now feel like remnants of a self I no longer am. Three full libraries donated—to universities, to prisons, to young leaders who might find in them what I once did.

There are books I've outgrown. Books that spoke to me at one stage of life, but now feel like echoes of a past I no longer need to revisit.

And then there are the books I will never part with—the ones that don't just hold ideas, but hold **me**.

Not because of what they taught me. But because of how they made me feel. Seen. Understood. Less alone in my questions, my struggles, my search for meaning.

When Books Become a Hiding Place

For a long time, I thought reading was a path to wisdom. And sometimes, it is.

But other times, books become an escape. A way to sit with profound ideas without ever embodying them.

I see it in myself—the tendency to reach for a new book instead of sitting with the discomfort of an unresolved question. The comfort of consuming ideas rather than the vulnerability of living them. The safety of intellectual understanding versus the risk of experiential knowing.

I used to believe that if I could just read the right book, I would change. Now I know—change does not live in pages.

At some point, the real work isn't in reading more. It's in **being more**. It's in putting the book down and stepping into your own unwritten story.

The Wisdom Beyond Books

I still love books. I always will. But I no longer believe they hold the final answer.

Because wisdom isn't found in what you read. It's found in what you do with it. In the risks you take. The conversations you have. The depth you allow yourself to feel.

It's found in the moment when a concept jumps from the page into your life. When an idea transforms from something you know to something you live. When a truth moves from your head to your heart to your hands.

Somewhere along the way, I stopped looking for the next book to change my life.

And I started living like someone whose life was worth writing about.

Maybe that's the only book that matters in the end—the one I'm writing every day, in real-time. The story told not in words on a page, but in moments of presence, courage, and love.

And the question is: **Am I living a story worth telling?**

Not for others to read. But for me to live.

Chapter 14. One Thought Away

For the longest time, I thought of happiness as a destination—A reward for good behavior. Something I'd reach one day.

I imagined it like a peak on the horizon—

Something just past one more goal,

One more achievement,
One more version of me that was finally enough.

Peace of mind wasn't something I lived in—

It was something that arrived in fleeting moments,

Like a gift from the universe after I had sufficiently earned it.

Then I heard the phrase: You are never more than one thought away.

No. It couldn't be that easy. It was too simple. Too clean. Too dismissive of the weight of real life.

I remember where I was when I first encountered this idea—sitting in a conference room, listening to a teacher whose life seemed so much simpler than mine. I nearly walked out. It felt like spiritual bypassing, like toxic positivity, like privilege disguised as wisdom.

I had lived a lifetime of sadness. A lifetime of joy. A lifetime of struggle, of triumph, of longing.

I had experienced genuine loss. Real heartbreak. The grinding weight of responsibilities that couldn't be thought away.

And if I was one thought away from happiness, then—

Had I been choosing suffering all along?

The question haunted me. It followed me home. It sat with me in the quiet moments, challenging everything I believed about the nature of happiness.

I resisted it at first—fiercely, defensively. I cataloged all the reasons why happiness couldn't be so accessible, so democratic, so available without credential or achievement. I listed all the legitimate reasons for my discontent, all the obstacles outside my control.

But the question remained. Slowly, I began to experiment with it.

Not as an attempt to bypass difficulty or deny reality. But as a genuine inquiry: What if my experience isn't determined by what happens to me, but by how I see what happens?

What if happiness isn't about controlling circumstances, but about releasing my grip on how things should be?

The more I sat with it, the more I realized it wasn't about choosing a better thought—it was about seeing that thought itself was the only thing separating me from what I sought.

It wasn't about forcing positivity or denying difficulty. It wasn't about pretending everything was fine when it wasn't.

It was about recognizing the nature of thought itself—how temporary it is, how fluid, how optional.

It was about noticing the space between stimulus and response, between circumstance and reaction, between what happens and what I make it mean.

Because the real shift isn't in choosing a better thought—

It's in realizing you were never trapped inside them to begin with.

There is a freedom that comes with this understanding. Not the freedom to control what happens, but the freedom to choose how we relate to it. Not the freedom from difficulty, but the freedom within it.

And in that space—that breath between what is and what we think about what is—lies everything.

Peace. Presence. The ability to respond rather than react. The capacity to see clearly rather than through the lens of old stories.

One thought away.

Not as magical thinking. Not as spiritual bypass. But as a profound recognition of where our experience actually comes from.

And in that recognition, everything changes—not because circumstances shift, but because we do.

Chapter 15. Who Rises Next?

I remember sitting in silence at Oneness Academy in India, absorbed in meditation, when someone asked the guru, Sri Bhagavan:

"Who are you?"

The room was electric with anticipation. Two hundred seekers from around the world, each holding their own answer to this eternal question. Each hoping for the revelation that would finally make sense of everything.

People began offering answers. Some profound. Some poetic. Some reaching toward the esoteric.

"I am consciousness." "I am divine awareness experiencing itself." "I am the witness beyond form."

The answers grew more elaborate, more conceptual, and more competitive in their spiritual sophistication.

And then Sri Bhagavan spoke, his voice soft but clear:

"You are a crowd. Whoever is rising in you now is who you are."

Silence.

I felt the words move through me, slow and heavy like a stone sinking to the ocean floor.

You are a crowd.

Not one self. Not one fixed identity. But a thousand shifting selves, rising and falling like waves.

The spiritual seeker. The devoted father. The ambitious builder. The wounded child. The critical judge. The compassionate friend. All present, all real, all me—but none permanent, none absolute, none the complete truth.

I looked around the room and saw the recognition rippling across faces. The relief. The challenge. The freedom in this simple observation.

Because if I am a crowd, then who I am in any moment isn't fixed or predetermined. It's emergent. It's responsive. It's chosen.

And in that moment, I understood—I get to decide who rises next.

When criticism comes, I can let the defensive self rise, ready with justifications and counterattacks. Or I can let the curious self rise, open to what might be learned.

When opportunity appears, I can let the fearful self rise, cataloging all the risks and reasons to hold back. Or I can let the courageous self rise, willing to step into the unknown.

When someone I love is suffering, I can let the busy self rise, too preoccupied with its own concerns to truly be present. Or I can let the compassionate self rise, capable of holding space without trying to fix.

No thought stays. No emotion lasts. I can choose which ones I follow.

And that choice? That is the most powerful thing in the world.

Not because it allows me to control what happens, but because it changes how I meet what happens. Not because it eliminates difficulty, but because it transforms my relationship to it.

This understanding has become my practice—not just in meditation, but in the moments that matter. In conversations. In decisions. In the small, seemingly insignificant choices that, together, create a life.

Who rises when I wake? Who rises when I'm challenged? Who rises when I succeed? Who rises when I fail?

And most importantly—who do I want to invite forward today?

Because I am a crowd. And whoever is rising in me now is who I am.

But who rises next? That's my choice.

Chapter 16. Why Am I Here?

13.8 billion years. All of time, unfolding, arriving here. So why am I still searching?

From the first explosion of light, from the dust that formed the stars, from the unfathomable unfolding of time—here I am.

So I ask, not as a philosophical riddle or a thought experiment, but as a real inquiry.

Why am I here?

Not in the abstract. Not in some grand cosmic sense. But right now. In this body. In this time. In this moment.

Why am I here, writing these words?

The Restless Mind

I breathe the question in.

I don't force it. I don't wrestle it into submission. I let it sit inside me like a stone resting on the riverbed, untouched by the current of my mind.

And I watch as the mind does what it always does.

It scans. It wanders. It searches for a way out.

Because there is a part of me—the monkey mind, the doubting mind, the restless mind—that always wants to be somewhere else.

That part tells me I should be in Texas, in Dubai, in Shanghai. Inside a book, inside a business plan, inside anything but here. It whispers of urgent emails unanswered, of opportunities missed, of a world racing forward while I sit still. It conjures images of more important work, more significant impact, and more valuable contributions I could be making elsewhere.

That part tells me I am not enough. That part latches onto distractions like a lifeline—scrolling, planning, analyzing, consuming—anything to keep me from fully being here. It seeks comfort in the familiar noise of productivity, in the illusion of control that comes with always doing, never being.

But I know better.

I know that being here is a practice. Not just physically, but consciously. A deliberate choice made again and again in each moment.

I could be in a thousand places at once—lost in my thoughts, consumed by noise, tangled in the endless, intoxicating swirl of 24/7 access to everything.

Or I could be here. Fully here. In this chair. In this room. In this breath.

I could turn down the volume on the world and listen for something quieter.

The Safari of Thought

My mind is a safari of thoughts—stories being regurgitated, memories being hashed out, loops repeating themselves to avoid what is real.

I watch them move across the landscape of my awareness—fears disguised as practical concerns, desires masked as noble ambitions, old wounds appearing as present dangers. Each thought invites me to follow, to identify, to become lost in its particular drama.

To avoid presence. To avoid the discomfort of not knowing.

But when I ask, Why am I here?—I expect an answer.

Not from my mind. Not from the noise. But from the deeper intelligence inside me.

From my wisdom mind. From my soul mind. From my God mind.

The part that knows beyond thinking. The part that recognizes truth, not through analysis but through resonance. The part that connects me to something larger than my individual concerns—to the vast web of life itself, to the boundless field of awareness in which all things arise and dissolve.

Why am I here today? Why am I here in this moment? Why am I here for this next breath?

And in the silence that follows these questions, something shifts. The urgency fades. The need to know relaxes. The search for meaning becomes meaning itself.

Because perhaps the answer isn't found in what I do or achieve or become.

Perhaps it's found in the simple miracle of being here at all—conscious, aware, alive at this precise moment in the unfolding of all things.

Perhaps I am here simply to be here. To witness. To receive. To offer the gift of my full attention to whatever this moment contains.

And in that presence—that complete, undivided attention—I find not the answer I sought, but the peace of no longer needing to ask.

Chapter 17. Cleaning the River

I am here to drop in.

Not to solve. Not to scramble. Not to map out the future.

I am here to imagine.

Because imagination exists without an outcome. Imagination is the love of the journey itself. Imagination is why I am here.

The River of Thought

I imagine my mind as a river.

Some days, it flows clean and clear—effortless, peaceful, steady. Ideas move through it naturally, reflections appear undistorted, the current carries me forward without resistance. On these days, my thoughts serve me. They illuminate rather than obscure. They connect rather than separate.

Other days, it's polluted.

A factory upstream dumps garbage into the water. Toxic worries. Manufactured fears. Endless distractions. And without even realizing it, I start orienting my whole life around the pollution.

I begin dodging the debris instead of cleaning the river.

I adapt to the contamination rather than addressing its source. I accept as normal what should never be normalized—a mind clouded by inputs that don't serve its natural clarity.

The Toxins We Absorb

The pollution doesn't always look like pollution.

It looks like:

- Mass media that feeds on outrage and division

- Social media that transforms attention into a commodity

- The constant feed of input that never allows for integration

- Urgencies that are not urgent but masquerade as essential

- Distractions masquerading as meaning, consumption disguised as connection

I let too much in.

I wake up and immediately check headlines, notifications, and markets—before I've even checked in with myself. I move through the day responding to external demands before I've connected to internal guidance. I end the day scrolling through other people's lives instead of reflecting on my own.

I let junk thoughts clutter my mind the way plastic clutters the ocean.

And suddenly—I don't feel clear anymore.

I don't feel present.

I feel like a man standing in a flooded river, desperately trying to grab onto something solid.

The Art of Cleaning the River

But I don't have to live this way.

I can be the steward of my own internal environment—just as Robert F. Kennedy Jr. fought for the Hudson River, cleaning up its contamination and restoring it to its natural state.

I can do that for myself. I can clean my mind the way he cleaned the water.

I can create boundaries around what I allow in—not from fear, but from discernment. Not from disconnection, but from a commitment to deeper connection. I can question the urgency of what demands my attention. I can distinguish between information and wisdom. I can recognize when I'm consuming out of habit rather than purpose.

I can remove the toxins of unnecessary noise. I can stop feeding myself distractions. I can clear the river.

Not through force, not through rigid control, but through conscious choice about what I allow to enter the stream.

The Power of Letting Go

I am not here for the White House. I am not here for Bitcoin. I am not here for the latest controversy, the latest crisis, the latest wave of manufactured urgency.

I am here for this moment.

For this breath. For the wisdom that exists beyond the noise. For the clarity that emerges when I stop looking elsewhere for what can only be found here.

And if I can let go of the unnecessary, if I can clear the river, if I can return to the purity of the stream itself—

Then I will have my answer.

And I will know, without question, why I am here.

The question dissolves not because I've found the perfect answer, but because I've removed what obscured the truth that was always there—beneath the noise, beneath the pollution, beneath the constant search for something more.

"If I clear the river, I won't need to search for why I am here. I will already be it."

Not as a concept to understand, but as a reality to live. Not as a destination to reach, but as the ground I already stand on.

The river, once cleared, doesn't need to ask where it's going. It simply flows.

Taste 2: The Unseen Architecture

Mapping the Inner World—Perception, Patterns, and the Stories We Carry

There is an entire world inside us, shaping our choices, our relationships, and the way we move through life. It is unseen yet ever-present—an architecture of beliefs, patterns, and inherited stories that operate beneath the surface, often without our awareness.

This journey is about making that world visible.

It's about stepping beyond the mirage of certainty, past the illusion of control, and into the raw truth of how our perceptions create our reality. It's about recognizing the shadows we cast, the echoes we inherit, and the cycles we unknowingly perpetuate until that singular moment of recognition when we finally see the pattern—and choose to break it.

We don't see life as it is—we see it as we are. We don't experience relationships in their purest form—we filter them through the stories tattooed on our souls, the wounds we've carried since childhood, and the identities we've meticulously constructed over decades. And herein lies the danger: we remain blind to our own blindness.

These chapters invite you into the sacred space between awareness and assumption. The exact point where perception transforms into projection. Where generational stories become silent scripts directing your life. Where the relentless desire to seek, to prove, to arrive at some final enlightenment keeps you trapped in the pursuit of something that has been yours all along.

Because seeking, despite its wisdom, is often the most elegant trap. A sophisticated method of avoiding stillness. A way of maintaining perpetual motion so we never have to face the question that terrifies us most: Who am I when I am no longer searching?

Here, we unravel that question to its core.

We explore what it means to release the maps we've followed blindly, to distinguish between inherited truth and chosen truth, to transcend the addiction to seeking, and step fully into the experience of being here. We examine how we grip life with white knuckles—whether clutching ideas, identities, or expectations—and how that desperate grip becomes the very thing that keeps what we desire most just beyond our reach.

This is about seeing with new eyes. Seeing where we cling when we should release. Seeing where we rush when patience is required. Seeing the spaces where we instinctively resist love, avoid intimacy, or maintain a calculated distance that feels safe but keeps us hollow. Seeing, perhaps for the first time, that our deepest struggles aren't imposed by the external world—but emerge from within.

And most profoundly, it's about what awaits us when we finally stop running.

Because the moment we cease seeking, we arrive. The moment we stop proving, we embody enough. The moment we release our grip, life begins to flow through us rather than against us.

This section isn't just about understanding these truths intellectually.

It's about feeling them in your bones.

Chapter 18. The Voice Within

There are two kinds of people in any profession. Those who do the work and those who are the work.

After decades of coaching real estate and mortgage professionals, I can distinguish between these two within moments of meeting them. One group approaches it as employment—a means to an end. The other? It pulses through their veins.

And I've lived both realities.

I remember the precise moment I realized I wasn't meant to merely sell real estate—I was born to teach others mastery. I wasn't in that seminar room to learn sales techniques. I was there to revolutionize how others sold.

It didn't arrive as a whisper. It crashed through me like thunder.

"Teacher. Be a teacher."

I listened without hesitation. Within weeks, I was selling seminar tickets during daylight hours and closing real estate deals after sunset. Exhausting? Absolutely. Exhilarating? Beyond words. And unmistakably right.

Because that's the truth about a calling—it doesn't request your attention. It commands it.

It doesn't knock politely or inquire about your schedule. It doesn't await permission or approval.

It demands. It insists. It arrives unannounced and refuses compromise.

When you hear it, you face only two choices: Step forward into your destiny or drown it in distractions until it becomes a distant echo.

The Cost of Ignoring It

I have witnessed this pattern countless times. People who know, in their marrow, what they are meant to create in this world... yet systematically avoid their purpose.

The noise they manufacture to silence their calling—the wrong career path, the strategic busywork, the cultivated self-doubt, the elaborate excuses. I've orchestrated these symphonies of avoidance myself.

And I know precisely what happens when I stop listening.

The creeping anxiety. The bone-deep fatigue. The persistent sense of misalignment that I can feel but not articulate.

Because when inspiration calls and I pretend not to hear—I slowly suffocate my own spirit.

What Am I Called to Now?

A calling isn't static. It evolves. It transforms.

Teaching, for me, has manifested in countless forms—seminars that filled auditoriums, books that circled the globe, coaching that transformed lives, and self-work that reconstructed my own identity. It continuously shifts shape. It relentlessly evolves. But it never vanishes.

And that consistency is how I know I'm still listening.

But what about those moments when I resist? When I silence that voice because it demands more courage than I feel ready to offer? When I let the seduction of comfort overpower the call to courage?

That's where the authentic tension resides. That's where suffering takes root.

The Hardest Question

So today, I ask myself without flinching:

What is calling me now?

Not what's practical or profitable. Not what's expected or easily explained. Not what feels familiar or safe.

What's true?

And am I willing to embrace it completely, regardless of the cost?

I strip away everything else—the obligations, the expectations, the distractions—and sit in silent communion with what remains.

Because I know intimately the cost of ignoring that voice.

And I know the indescribable reward of answering it without reservation.

So today, I stop all movement. I listen with every cell.

And I ask myself once more:

What is the voice within calling me to become and create? And am I finally ready to answer with my life?

Chapter 19. The Echo of the Unspoken

We inherit more than genetics. We inherit silences. The precise way a room suddenly stiffens when certain names are spoken. The weight of a sigh that lingers a moment too long. The careful pauses in family stories that never quite reach their endings.

I grew up without hearing direct stories about my mother's childhood. But I didn't need explicit narratives. Her stories lived in her body—in the tension that locked her jaw when certain topics surfaced, in the way she never spoke of her own mother with warmth—only duty. She was the child of alcoholics. And so was I.

Though she clawed her way to sobriety through sheer determination, though she sacrificed everything to break that generational cycle, the residue remained embedded in her nervous system. The visceral fear of losing control. The instinctive hesitance in love. The bone-deep belief that safety had to be earned through perfection rather than received as birthright. And I absorbed it all through osmosis.

Science now confirms what we've intuitively known—trauma alters DNA at the molecular level. What our ancestors endured becomes written into us—not just through stories but through cellular memory. This explains so much. Why I instinctively flinch at raised voices, even when directed elsewhere. Why I unconsciously scan rooms for emotional tension before fully entering. Why love, for decades, felt like something I had to continuously prove worthy of, rather than something I could simply inhabit.

These aren't merely my personal wounds. They are my mother's wounds. Her mother's wounds. The wounds of ancestors whose names I've never known but whose unhealed pain shaped my reality nonetheless.

Yet recognizing this inheritance isn't enough. The essential question remains: What will I do with these stories now that I see them clearly?

Chapter 20. Breaking the Cycle

I have daughters now. Grandchildren whose eyes reflect futures I'll never fully witness.

I think constantly about what passes through me to them—not just in conscious words, but in unconscious patterns they absorb without either of us recognizing the transmission. I wonder which wounds I've healed thoroughly enough that they no longer appear in their lives. I wonder which fears I've unconsciously clung to that might still reach them despite my most vigilant efforts.

Because this is the true nature of legacy. Not in assets. Not in property. Not in material possessions. But in patterns that shape how they experience being human.

My mother never played with me—her childhood taught her that vulnerability was dangerous. But I get on my knees and play with my grandson, Dean Joseph, watching joy transform his face.

My father was perpetually running, constantly striving, never arriving. But I am learning the revolutionary act of sitting still. Of staying present. Of allowing my unadorned presence to be enough.

These may appear as small adjustments. But they alter everything. Because the moment we break even a single thread in an inherited pattern, we fundamentally change the fabric of future generations. The moment we name a ghost haunting our family line, it loses its power over those who come after us. The moment we consciously stop repeating a cycle, it ceases being unconsciously passed down.

I cannot change where I come from. But I can transform what continues through me.

And perhaps this is the most sacred work of a lifetime. Not to resent our inheritance. Not to deny it. But to honor it by transforming it into something new.

To take the story I was given—and write a different ending that changes everything that follows.

Chapter 21. The Paradox of Seeking

I have spent my life seeking with relentless intensity. Seeking wisdom. Seeking love. Seeking understanding. Seeking to be seen, to be held, to be known at my core.

But seeking itself has become my most elegant trap.

Because the moment a seeker truly finds what they seek, they face an identity crisis.

Thomas Leonard once said something that shook my foundations: "The purpose of the seeker is not to find—because if the seeker actually found, it would no longer have a job."

And now I see with stark clarity: I have kept myself perpetually employed in the business of seeking.

I have architected an entire life around the pursuit, around the reaching, around the chase for something perpetually positioned just beyond my grasp. Not because I genuinely needed what I was chasing—but because the seeking itself became the cornerstone of my identity.

The Illusion of Arrival

For decades, I operated under the unconscious assumption that life was a linear sequence of accomplishments leading toward some ultimate destination.

The next insight. The next bestseller. The next transformation.

As if someday, I would cross some invisible threshold and finally arrive. As if fulfillment existed in some future moment, always positioned just beyond the horizon of now.

But what if home isn't a destination to be reached through effort? What if it's not something I discover through seeking but something I allow through surrendering?

What if I have already arrived at the exact place I've been searching for, and my only remaining task is to recognize where I stand?

Because if I stop seeking—if I release the compulsion to constantly reach for what comes next—then who am I without that familiar identity?

The False Refuge of Seeking

For years, seeking was my sophisticated refuge from stillness.

Because if I remained in perpetual motion, I could believe I was evolving. If I was evolving, I remained relevant. If I remained relevant, I felt safe in a world that frightens me.

But seeking is only necessary if I believe something essential is missing from this moment.

And what if nothing was ever missing? What if completeness has been my natural state all along?

Grieving the Seeker

My sister recently observed something that penetrated my defenses completely.

"You enter relationships intensely, and when they end, you seem more addicted to the grief than you ever were to the joy of the relationship itself."

Her words landed with the force of absolute truth.

Because grief, too, has been a form of seeking. Seeking validation. Seeking evidence that I invested authentically. Seeking the perverse comfort of longing because yearning has always felt more familiar than peace.

I have enacted this pattern in love. I have recreated it in business. I have repeated it in every domain where I've attached my identity to what I'm pursuing rather than who I already am.

And if I finally stop—if I no longer define myself by what I'm searching for—then who remains when the seeker dissolves?

The Softening into Receiving

This morning, I allowed myself to receive without effort or earning.

I received the sacred quiet of dawn before the world awoke. I received the golden light spilling across wooden floors. I received the profound, simple truth that I am enough in this precise moment, requiring no improvement or modification.

I don't need to seek it. I don't need to earn it. I don't need to prove worthy of it.

I simply need to let it in.

The Moment of Arrival

What if this is it?

Not asked in resignation or defeat.

But offered as liberation: "What if I have been frantically searching for something that has been mine all along?"

What if meaning isn't waiting in the next chapter but pulsing through the words I'm writing right now? What if peace isn't contingent on the next achievement but available in the precise moment I stop chasing? What if I have already arrived at my destination, and my only remaining task is to fully recognize where I stand?

Because the paradox reveals itself with perfect clarity—

The moment I stop running, I arrive. The moment I stop seeking, I find. The moment I stop trying to earn love, I realize I've been loved completely all along.

And perhaps, most revolutionary of all—

This recognition is enough to change everything.

Chapter 22. The Illusion of the Map

For years, I believed that knowing was identical to experiencing.

I convinced myself that with the right framework, the right strategy, the right mental model—I could master any domain of life. If I could map the territory with enough precision, I could somehow control it.

But a map is not the terrain it represents. A theory is not a lived experience.

And I learned this distinction through repeated collapse.

I spent decades constructing elaborate maps of reality. Business models. Relationship frameworks. Psychological constructs explaining human behavior.

I prided myself on understanding the architecture of success, of human connection, of meaning itself at a theoretical level few could match.

But intellectual knowledge isn't embodied wisdom. You can memorize every detail of a map showing the path to intimacy and still find yourself utterly lost in its actual landscape.

The first time this truth shattered my illusions was in love. I had studied every relevant text. I had mastered attachment theory, communication patterns, and the psychology of human connection.

I knew exactly how love worked—in theory.

But standing amid the wreckage of another failed relationship, facing the same patterns I had intellectually understood but emotionally reproduced, I finally grasped the humbling truth: Knowing how love works in concept is not the same as loving in practice.

Chapter 23. The Power of Presence

The territory of life is alive in ways no map can capture. It moves. It shifts. It refuses to be reduced to two dimensions on paper.

A map can show you where rivers flow, but it cannot let you feel the powerful current against your skin. A guidebook can describe a mountain trail's elevation changes, but it cannot replicate the burning in your legs as you climb toward the summit.

I see with clarity now—I invested years in preparation, planning, and structuring, believing that if I could only create perfect conditions, life would unfold according to my expectations.

But life isn't an itinerary to be followed. It is an untamed, gloriously unpredictable force that asks you to step into it—not from theoretical knowledge but from embodied presence.

The greatest teachers I've encountered weren't those with the most detailed maps of reality. They were those willing to get authentically lost in the territory of experience.

And perhaps that's the invitation that's been waiting for me. Not to master life through knowledge but to surrender to it through presence. Not to map reality with greater precision but to inhabit it with greater courage.

Because maps create the comforting illusion of certainty. They make us feel like we know exactly where we're going.

But the territory? The territory is where life actually happens in all its messy glory.

And I would rather be temporarily lost in something authentic than permanently certain about something that exists only in my mind.

Chapter 24. The Projector Effect - Seeing Beyond My Own Lens

I don't see the world as it is. I see the world as I am.

That's the uncomfortable truth I've spent decades avoiding.

Every interaction I experience is filtered through the lens of my own consciousness—my history, my beliefs, my unhealed wounds. I don't hear what's actually being said; I hear what I'm primed to expect. I don't see what's truly happening; I see what I unconsciously fear.

If someone pauses before responding to me, I automatically assume they're questioning my value. If someone creates space, I interpret it as rejection. If a business opportunity dissolves, I conclude I wasn't enough to make it happen.

I continuously project my ancient stories onto present realities. And in doing so, I severely limit what's possible in my relationships and work.

Because projections aren't objective truth. They are old psychological patterns masquerading as current reality.

And the greatest danger? I rarely recognize when I'm caught in this distortion.

The Difference Between Awareness and Assumption

For years, I believed myself exceptionally skilled at reading others.

I could detect the slightest hesitation in their voice. I could sense resistance before words were spoken. I prided myself on intuiting what others needed before they could articulate it themselves.

But was I truly perceiving them accurately? Or was I projecting my own unresolved narratives onto a blank canvas they happened to provide?

I reflect on past relationships with new eyes. The countless times I interpreted someone's silence as indifference—when it actually reflected their own fear of inadequacy. The moments I received hesitation as personal rejection—when they simply needed more time to process their own feelings.

How many magnificent possibilities have I walked away from because I saw threats where there was only human uncertainty?

How many times have I mistaken the reflection of my own fears for an accurate perception of another person?

Because the truth I can no longer avoid is this: I don't see others as they authentically are. I see them through the distorting filter of my own unexamined fears, my own recurring patterns, my own unintegrated shadow aspects.

The Moment I Saw It Clearly

Recently, I engaged in a deep conversation with a woman I deeply care for. I shared what I believed were profound insights, offering what I thought was connection, depth, and an opportunity to explore together.

And she sighed.

Just a soft exhalation. Nearly inaudible.

But that sound was enough to trigger everything.

Instantly, my mind flooded with assumed meaning: "She's exhausted by me. She's irritated. She thinks I'm overwhelming. She's merely tolerating my presence."

And then—with unprecedented clarity—I witnessed my projection happening in real time.

That sigh? It wasn't her rejecting me. It was my shadow speaking through her.

It was the voice of a young boy who once internalized his mother's exhaustion as personal failure. Who learned that an adult's exasperated breath meant he should make himself smaller, quieter, and less demanding.

And there it was—decades later—still controlling my perception, dictating my emotional response.

But this time, instead of blindly believing this interpretation, I paused.

I looked directly at her. I softened my defenses. And instead of reacting from that wound, I simply said:

"When you sigh like that, it triggers something deep in me. It makes me feel instantly dismissed."

She looked at me, genuine surprise in her eyes. "Joe, that had absolutely nothing to do with you. I'm just processing a difficult day."

In that moment of clarity, I recognized how much of my relational life has been shaped not by objective reality but by my own unconscious projections.

Bridging Into the Shadow

It's one thing to intellectually recognize that I project my internal world onto external reality. That I perceive through my own subjective lens.

It's an entirely different level of awareness to ask:

Where does that lens originate?

If I consistently experience the same painful patterns in relationships, business ventures, and intimate connections—then the common denominator isn't the changing cast of characters.

It's me and what lives in my shadow.

The essential work isn't simply altering how I perceive others. It's understanding what within me continues generating these distorted perceptions.

This is where surface awareness of projection must give way to deeper shadow work.

Because if I don't courageously examine what operates beneath my projections—if I don't confront the disowned aspects of myself that distort my vision—then I will continue living inside a reality largely of my own unconscious creation.

And I am finally ready to see beyond my projections into the unfiltered truth.

Chapter 25. Seeing the Shadow

The shadow moves faster than conscious thought. It speaks before your words form. It shapes your perception of reality before you even realize it's happening.

A loved one's sigh triggers ancient abandonment fears. A delayed response to a message spirals into certainty you've been forgotten. A momentary hesitation in someone's eyes becomes irrefutable evidence that you are fundamentally inadequate.

And the most dangerous part? You remain completely unaware of this process as it unfolds.

For decades, I believed I was responding to the objective reality happening around me. Now, I recognize the humbling truth—I was primarily responding to my own buried wounds projecting outward.

Carl Jung articulated this with perfect clarity: "Until you make the unconscious conscious, it will direct your life, and you will call it fate."

So today, I ask myself with unflinching honesty: Where is my shadow still silently directing my life's story?

Chapter 26. Integrating the Shadow

For most of my life, I waged war against my shadow aspects. I was determined to fix them. To erase them. To eliminate them completely from my identity.

But now I understand with clarity—the shadow is not my enemy requiring defeat.

My neediness, when fully embraced and integrated, transforms into an exceptional capacity for authentic connection. My fear, when understood rather than denied, becomes wisdom that protects what matters most.

The shadow isn't something to destroy through spiritual bypassing. It is something to integrate through courageous acceptance.

Because true self-mastery isn't about eliminating the aspects of myself that I find uncomfortable. It's about owning all dimensions of who I am with compassion.

And so today, I no longer run from my shadow. I no longer resist its presence. I no longer hide what I've deemed unacceptable. I turn directly toward what I've denied—and finally, I see myself completely.

Chapter 27. The Power of Not Knowing

There was a time when certainty felt like the ultimate achievement.

Certainty represented power. Certainty promised control in an unpredictable world.

In business leadership, in intimate relationships, in personal development—I operated from the belief that the more certainty I possessed, the safer I would remain.

If I could anticipate market fluctuations, I could maintain an advantage.

If I could predict the patterns in my relationships, I could preemptively avoid pain.

If I could define the future before it manifested, I could meet it fully prepared.

But certainty is a fragile fortress built on shifting sands.

The more desperately I clung to it, the more brittle my position became.

And I've gradually recognized a profound truth—what makes me truly powerful isn't what I know with certainty. It's what I'm willing to explore with curiosity.

Certainty Closes Doors—Curiosity Opens Them

In my real estate career, I was taught to position myself as the unquestioned expert—the one who possessed all answers before questions were even asked.

I learned to confidently predict market trends, forecast property valuations with seeming precision, and present myself as the ultimate authority whose judgment couldn't be questioned.

However, something unexpected emerged from this approach: The more certainty I projected, the less genuine connection I created with clients.

Because certainty closes doors to possibility. Curiosity opens them to exploration.

I recognize this pattern with perfect clarity now.

When I declare, "I know exactly where the market is headed," I might momentarily impress with supposed expertise, but I simultaneously shut down deeper conversation.

I terminate exploration before it has opportunity to reveal unexpected insights.

But when I say, "Here's what my experience suggests... What patterns are you noticing?" I create partnership instead of hierarchy.

I invite people into collaborative discovery. I transform from isolated expert on a pedestal to fellow explorer walking beside them through uncertainty.

And isn't that the relationship I truly desire?

I've never been satisfied merely being perceived as an authority figure. I want to be a transformative presence in people's lives.

I want relationships that breathe and evolve organically—not interactions constrained by rigid frames of presumed certainty.

The Illusion of Arrival

For decades, I unconsciously believed that complete understanding represented the finish line of growth.

That eventually, I would arrive at a state where everything made perfect sense. That healing meant achieving a place where I could definitively say: "Now I fully understand why events unfolded as they did, and now I'm completely free from their influence."

But authentic healing isn't about reaching neat conclusions. It's about developing comfort with perpetual not-knowing.

Not knowing with certainty why life unfolded in particular patterns.

Not knowing what challenges and opportunities await beyond the horizon.

Not knowing how long certain internal processes need to complete their natural unfolding.

Rather than resisting this uncertainty, I've learned to meet it with genuine curiosity rather than fear.

That's where true power resides. That's where transformation accelerates.

Because certainty anchors me in past limitations, but curiosity keeps me fully present to emerging possibilities.

Letting Go of the Need to Prove

This fundamental shift has transformed everything in my work and relationships.

I no longer feel compelled to prove I possess all answers to demonstrate value.

My presence itself carries value—precisely because I create space for the right questions to emerge naturally.

And what I've discovered through lived experience is this:

The people who trust me most deeply aren't those convinced I know everything with certainty. They are those who recognize I'll remain fully present with them while we navigate uncertainty together.

The clients who return year after year aren't primarily impressed by my expertise. They are drawn to how deeply seen, heard, and invited into the collaborative process they feel in my presence.

The relationships that have endured aren't constructed on rigid certainties or fixed beliefs. They thrive on a shared willingness to evolve beyond comfortable assumptions.

The Future Belongs to the Open

So now, I continuously ask myself:

Where else might I beneficially replace rigid certainty with genuine curiosity?

Where am I gripping too tightly to answers that no longer serve my highest development?

What new possibilities might emerge if I fully embraced the transformative power of not knowing?

Because if there's one thing experience has taught me with absolute clarity, it's this:

The future belongs to those who remain open in the face of uncertainty. And I intend to live with radical openness to whatever emerges.

Chapter 28. The Consciousness Swap - Letting Myself Be Seen

If I could momentarily exchange consciousness with someone else—if I could experience myself through their perception—would I even recognize the version of me they encounter? Would their experience of "Joe" bear any resemblance to my internal experience of myself?

I understand intellectually that no two people inhabit identical realities.

This isn't merely abstract theory—it's the fundamental principle that built my career.

I've mastered the art of entering others' perceptual worlds. I know how to meet people in their reality rather than mine. I know how to expand their frames to transform their experience. I know how to listen beyond surface words into the deeper territory where authentic meaning resides.

None of this represents new territory.

It's the element I navigate with practiced expertise.

But do I ever genuinely allow others to do this for me?

Or have I mastered seeing others so thoroughly that I've unconsciously avoided the vulnerability of being truly seen in return?

The Mirror I've Avoided

I reflect on countless people I've guided—how I've shaped their perceptions, beliefs, and life trajectories.

I've helped them navigate complex uncertainties, process their deepest fears, and step into expanded realities.

I've witnessed their breakthroughs, celebrated their transformations, and accompanied their evolutions.

But when have I genuinely allowed someone to guide me with equal depth?

When have I permitted myself to be deeply known—not as a teacher, leader, or authority, but as someone equally engaged in the messy process of becoming?

Because beneath my polished exterior, I hunger for genuine recognition.

I crave to be seen beyond my accomplishments, beyond what I create, beyond what I contribute.

I crave to be understood not just through my carefully chosen words but in the vulnerable silences between them.

I crave to be valued for my essence rather than my utility to others.

The Fear of True Visibility

Yet the prospect of such profound vulnerability unnerves me at my core.

What if I dislike what others reflect back about who I truly am?

What if I finally let someone in completely and discover they cannot hold the complexity of me?

What if, after decades of guiding others, I've lost the capacity to be guided in return?

The risk of allowing myself to be truly seen?

I might need to abandon carefully constructed narratives that have defined my identity. I might have to inhabit my own discomfort, acknowledge my own blind spots, and confront my own unfiltered truth without defensive strategies.

But the greater risk of continuing as I have?

I remain fundamentally isolated despite external success.

I continue performing as the lighthouse—eternally guiding others to safe harbor while never permitting myself to step onto solid ground.

I maintain people at precisely calculated distances—close enough to appreciate the structure I've built, yet never near enough to perceive the hidden fractures within it.

Stepping Out of the Tower

But I recognize this essential truth with new clarity:

If I never fully enter another's perceptual world—not as the observer studying them, but as the vulnerable one being witnessed—I will perpetually experience a profound loneliness beneath all external achievements.

Because the truth I can no longer avoid is this:

I deserve to be known with the same depth and compassion I've worked to know others.

And perhaps the crucial first step isn't waiting for someone exceptional to see me completely.

Perhaps the first step is granting myself permission to be fully seen without defensive armor.

So, I will begin now.

Chapter 29. The Cost of Speed

I move at an uncommon velocity. Faster than most people can comfortably track or process.

My cognitive patterns aren't linear sequences—they form interconnected webs of meaning. I perceive patterns and connections long before others register they exist.

And this represents both my greatest gift and my most significant limitation in connecting with others.

Because the truth I'm finally ready to acknowledge is this: People aren't actively resisting my insights. They're simply drowning in the wake created by my intellectual speed.

I have invested decades mastering language and communication. However, mastery without relational resonance eventually becomes isolating.

I have built influential empires with precisely chosen words. Yet, even with these outward achievements—authentic connection sometimes remains elusive.

Because clarity alone isn't always what others need most. Sometimes, they simply require space to process at their natural pace.

Chapter 30. The Art of Presence

The genuine challenge I face isn't further refining what I communicate. It's learning to enter others' metaphorical worlds before expecting them to enter mine.

It's developing the patience to stand still within their frames long enough that they feel truly met where they are. It's resisting the compulsion to lead with brilliance and intellectual sophistication and instead leading with receptive presence.

Because I now understand that slowing my pace isn't diminishing my capacities. It's creating space for others to genuinely access what I offer.

And perhaps that's the essential lesson I needed to learn: To meet people exactly where they are before inviting them to follow where I believe we could go together.

Because the most effective leaders don't merely possess profound insights—they understand precisely when and how to reveal those insights so others can fully receive them.

And today, I choose a different approach. I choose to reveal less initially. And listen more deeply.

Chapter 31. The Space Between

I've dedicated my professional life to mastering communication.

Persuasion that transforms.

Influence that inspires.

The precise rhythm of strategically placed silence.

I understand the architecture of compelling dialogue with a depth few can match.

And yet—

There are moments when my authentic voice disappears completely.

Not in professional contexts. Not during presentations. Not when I'm coaching, teaching, or guiding others.

But in moments of genuine intimacy.

The very domain where expression should flow most naturally—where truth should emerge without calculation, without strategy—is precisely where I sometimes find myself...

utterly silent.

The Pause That Matters Most

Viktor Frankl articulated a profound truth that shaped my approach to life:

"Between stimulus and response, there is a space. In that space is our power to choose our response. In our response lies our growth and our freedom."

I have not only internalized this principle—I've built methodologies around it. I embody it in my work.

I understand how to leverage the strategic pause—to create heightened meaning, to direct attention precisely, to allow important concepts time to fully land.

But there exists another category of pause entirely.

The kind not rooted in strategic communication.

The kind not calculated for specific effect.

The kind that emerges when something raw, authentic, and unfiltered rises from depths I rarely access—and I find myself without practiced response.

Because certain moments don't call for persuasive technique. They don't require guidance, reframing, or masterful language.

They simply demand presence.

And genuine presence cannot be manufactured through skill. It cannot be strategized in advance. It cannot be rehearsed to perfection.

It requires simply being fully here, without protective armor or performative identity.

The CrossFit of Intimacy

I understand what it means to train at the absolute limits of human capacity. I know what it means to push my physical body to the very edge of possibility.

At age 60, I transformed myself into one of the fittest men on the planet. I qualified for the CrossFit Games against competitors decades younger. I made what seemed impossible not just possible but actual.

And then—

I pulled back before the final harvest of that effort.

Not by accident or circumstance.

But because, at some unconscious level, I wasn't fully prepared for what winning would mean.

Was it fear of success? Was it unconscious resistance? Or did my deeper wisdom recognize that victory would have directed my life toward destinations I wasn't truly aligned with?

And now I find myself wondering with new clarity...

Is vulnerability in intimacy my next CrossFit-level challenge?

Is staying fully present, receiving without deflection, opening completely—without retreating into intellect, without strategic communication, without rehearsed responses—the arena I'm truly meant to master next?

Because I can feel the truth of it resonating through me.

There are relationships that offer something profound, something life-changing, something sacred beyond words.

And my instinctive response?

Step back. Create distance. Regain control.

Not because I don't desire genuine connection. Not because I don't recognize its value.

But because authentic intimacy demands something I haven't fully developed—the capacity to be completely present without the armor of expertise.

Not intellectually strong. Not persuasively brilliant. Not masterfully in control.

Just vulnerably, imperfectly present in the raw truth of the moment.

Leaving Before the Harvest

This pattern reveals itself with unmistakable clarity.

Not just in competitive achievement. Not just in business ventures. But most significantly in love.

I have built remarkable empires. I have generated extraordinary wealth, community, and movements that transform lives.

And yet—

At pivotal moments, I have stepped away before the deepest rewards materialized. Not from failure or incapacity but from some instinctive withdrawal when genuine vulnerability was required.

And now, I must ask myself the question that changes everything:

What would it mean to stay fully present when everything in me wants to retreat to safety?

Not just in professional projects, not just in business ventures, but in the sacred territory of authentic intimacy.

What would it mean to allow love to arrive in its complete form and remain steadfastly present to receive it without defensive strategies?

Because perhaps, just perhaps—

This represents my ultimate challenge. My most essential test of courage.

To trust fully in the unfolding moment. To trust myself within that unguarded vulnerability. To find my authentic voice—not the one that persuades through strategy, but the one that simply speaks unvarnished truth without calculation.

Because in that sacred space between stimulus and response—

Isn't that precisely where love in its purest form becomes possible?

And I am finally ready to inhabit that space without retreat.

And this time, I will remain present regardless of what emerges.

Taste 3: The Disruptive Path to Mastery

Mastery is not a destination. It is a rhythm, a continuous interplay between order and chaos, certainty and surrender, structure and reinvention.

It is a path not of perfecting but of disrupting—of breaking patterns before they harden, of allowing what no longer serves to fall away, of stepping boldly into the unknown without a promise of safety.

This section is about that process. The art of recalibrating. The courage to sit in the discomfort of change. The willingness to question everything—even the very strategies and beliefs that have brought success in the past.

When Mastery Becomes a Cage

For years, I built frameworks that provided clarity. I constructed systems, disciplines, and routines that made my work predictable and my influence replicable.

And then something shifted.

I began to see the cost of over-identifying with what I had built. I saw how mastery, when held too rigidly, can become a cage.

At 3 a.m., staring at the ceiling of my hotel room after a wildly successful event, I felt it—a hollowness that no amount of external validation could fill. I had become the person they expected me to be. My own creation had begun to constrain me.

Mastery is not about controlling outcomes. It is about meeting each moment with full presence. It is about staying fluid—disrupting patterns before they stagnate, leaning into the tension between discipline and play, and letting go of what has served its purpose so that something new can emerge.

The Disruptor's Dilemma

We don't just build structures—we become them. We don't just repeat habits—we become them.

The very thing that once gave us freedom can begin to feel like a leash.

A method that once felt alive starts to feel like a formula.

A system that once expanded you, starts to contain you.

A belief that once served you begins to limit you.

The danger isn't failure. The danger is getting too good at something and becoming trapped by it.

I've felt this in my bones. The moment I mastered the keynote formula that drove standing ovations, it began to feel mechanical. The moment my company reached the financial goals I'd set, I felt myself growing restless with the very model I'd perfected.

So, the question is:

Am I holding mastery too tightly? Have I stopped asking better questions? Where in my life have I mistaken certainty for wisdom?

Because true mastery is not found in gripping. It is found in knowing when to release.

The Dance of Structure and Surrender

In these chapters, you will see what it means to disrupt from within. To dismantle old frameworks. To question the illusion of certainty. To embrace the power of discomfort—not as something to be avoided, but as an essential part of growth.

You will find the paradox of structure and surrender— how true mastery is not found in controlling but in knowing when to let go.

You will see the dance between:

- Intention and spontaneity

- Deep focus and expansive awareness

- Preparation and the courage to begin before you feel ready

And at the heart of it all, you will find this truth:

Mastery is not about perfection. It is about alignment.

It is about knowing when to refine and when to disrupt.

It is about choosing, again and again, to wake up— to step beyond what is comfortable, to lean into the edges, and to trust that the greatest transformations happen not when we control but when we let go.

The Real Reward of Mastery

This is the disruptive path to mastery.

It does not offer guarantees. It does not offer certainty. It does not offer a neat, predictable ending.

But it does offer something far more valuable: Freedom.

Chapter 32. The Art of External Disruption

Breaking Industry Norms, Reinventing Frameworks

Disruption is my native language. It always has been.

I've built my career on seeing what others don't, on spotting the cracks in an industry's foundation before anyone else even notices the ground shifting. It's why I've never been interested in just playing the game—I'd rather change the rules entirely.

But disruption is not about destruction. It's about reinvention. It's about breaking what no longer serves, not for the sake of breaking it, but to build something better.

The world rewards those who master the existing system. But it remembers those who reinvent it.

The Illusion of Best Practices

For decades, I watched real estate agents, mortgage professionals, and business leaders worship at the altar of "best practices." They followed scripts, repeated formulas, copied what worked before, and called it mastery.

But here's the problem: Best practices are just past practices. What worked yesterday is rarely what will create breakthroughs tomorrow.

And yet, people cling to what they know because it's familiar.

I remember sitting across from Howard, a successful real estate agent by anyone's measure. Twenty years in the business. Respectable numbers. A comfortable life.

"I've been making cold calls for two decades," he told me. "Some days, I hate it, but that's just what works in this business."

The certainty in his voice was absolute. And utterly wrong.

The first time I started teaching referral-based business, people told me it wouldn't work. "Cold calling is the only way," they said. "You can't build a business without chasing leads."

I ignored them. And in doing so, I built one of the most successful referral-based training companies in the world.

Six months after our conversation, Howard called me. "I haven't made a cold call in three months," he said, voice cracking. "My business is up 47%. I've been miserable for twenty years for nothing."

Because disruption isn't about proving the old model wrong. It's about creating a new model so undeniable that people forget the old one ever existed.

How I Break Patterns on Purpose

I don't disrupt for the sake of being different. I disrupt to create something better.

And over time, I've learned the difference between reckless destruction and strategic disruption.

Reckless destruction burns bridges. Strategic disruption builds new ones.

Reckless destruction fights the old. Strategic disruption renders the old irrelevant.

Reckless destruction operates from ego. Strategic disruption operates from vision.

When I disrupt an industry, I don't come in swinging blindly. I come in with a blueprint for what should exist—and I make it real.

Disrupting from Within

The biggest mistake people make when they want to be disruptors? They think they have to burn everything down from the outside.

But the truth is, real disruption happens from within.

Amazon didn't destroy retail. It reinvented how we buy. Tesla didn't kill the car industry. It forced it to evolve. Netflix didn't kill Blockbuster. Blockbuster killed itself by refusing to adapt.

And in the same way, I never set out to "destroy" traditional sales and marketing—I set out to make them irrelevant by offering something far more powerful.

When I introduced the concept of By Referral Only to the real estate industry, I didn't attack cold calling. I simply created a system where it became unnecessary. I didn't fight against the old way—I built something that made the old way obsolete.

Because the best disruptors don't fight the existing system. They build a new one and invite people in.

The Next Industry That Needs Disruption

Right now, the world is shifting faster than ever. AI is rewriting how we create, how we work, and how we connect. And as always, there are two types of people:

Those who fight to preserve the old system.

Those who lean into the disruption and shape what's next.

I know which one I choose. Because the future does not belong to those who defend the past. It belongs to those who dare to build what's next.

What industry will you disrupt? What "best practice" will you render obsolete? What framework are you building that will make the old way irrelevant?

The opportunity is waiting. The only question is whether you'll take it.

Chapter 33. The Art of Internal Disruption

Dismantling the Ego, Rewriting Personal Identity

I am not who I was five years ago.

Or even last year.

And if I am, then I am failing.

Because the same way I disrupt industries, I must disrupt myself.

The hardest truth I've learned? The greatest threat to my own evolution is my attachment to who I used to be.

The Ego's Death Grip

The ego loves stability. It craves certainty. It wants to be seen, validated and understood.

And the bigger my platform became, the more I felt its grip tightening.

I had built an empire. I had a name people recognized. I had a role—a leader, a teacher, a guide.

And that's the problem. I had become too attached to the very identity I had worked so hard to create.

I remember standing backstage before a keynote to 5,000 people. My introduction video played on massive screens—highlighting my accomplishments, my insights, and my impact. The audience applauded before I'd even said a word.

And in that moment, I felt it—the golden cage I'd built for myself.

Because if I am the leader, the teacher, the guide... Then who am I if I step off the stage?

The Fear of Letting Go

I used to fear losing relevance. That if I stopped speaking, if I stopped producing, if I stopped leading, the world would move on without me.

But here's what I see now: The world is always moving on. The question is whether I will evolve with it.

I don't need to be the same person I was last year. I don't need to cling to an old version of myself just because it once worked.

The true masters are not the ones who cling to their legacy. They are the ones who reinvent themselves before the world forces them to.

Disrupting My Own Patterns

I have disrupted my own thinking more times than I can count. Each time, it felt like a small death.

Because when I let go of an old identity, an old way of being, it does feel like a loss.

Letting go of being the "sage on stage" meant embracing a quieter, deeper form of leadership.

Letting go of needing validation meant finding value in my own presence, not in the applause.

Letting go of control meant trusting that my work, my relationships, and my life would unfold exactly as they needed to—without my constant interference.

Last year, I walked away from a seven-figure opportunity because I knew it would keep me tethered to an old version of myself. My team thought I was crazy. My accountant questioned my sanity. But something deep within me knew it was time to evolve.

And the biggest lesson? Every time I disrupted my identity, something better took its place.

The Most Dangerous Thought in the World

If I ever catch myself thinking:

"I already know who I am."

"I already know how this works."

"I've figured it out."

I know I'm in trouble.

Because the moment I believe I have arrived is the moment I stop growing.

The moment I hold too tightly to my identity—whether as a leader, a creator, or a thinker—is the moment I stop evolving.

And if I stop evolving, I become obsolete.

The Only Identity That Matters

So now, I hold my identity loosely.

Not because I don't care who I am. But because I trust that I am always becoming.

I am not the person I was last year. And a year from now, I hope I have the courage to be someone new again.

Because real mastery isn't about defending who I was. It's about becoming who I am meant to be next.

And that—more than anything—is the disruption that matters most.

Ask yourself: What version of yourself are you clinging to that's preventing your evolution? What identity have you outgrown but still wear like an old, familiar coat? What would be possible if you released yourself from who you've been?

The greatest act of courage isn't standing your ground. It's having the wisdom to release it.

Chapter 34. The Silent Thief of Comfort

How Staying Safe Steals the Life We Were Meant to Live

Comfort is a liar. It tells me I'm safe. That I'm doing fine. That I'm right where I need to be. And it is the single most seductive force in the world.

For years, I mistook comfort for success. I built systems, routines, and habits that shielded me from unnecessary friction. I mastered efficiency. I optimized my work, my relationships, and my business—made everything predictable, controlled, and repeatable.

And in doing so, I unknowingly built myself a cage.

Because the real danger in life is not failure.

It's stagnation.

Comfort Doesn't Mean You're Winning—It Means You've Stopped Playing

We weren't meant to live easy lives. We were meant to live full lives.

And a full life requires friction.

Friction is what strengthens muscle. Friction is what sharpens intelligence. Friction is what transforms an idea into a movement. Friction is what turns a relationship from surface-level to soul-deep.

Without friction, we don't just stop growing—we shrink.

I see it in business: The moment a company stops innovating, it starts dying.

I see it in relationships: The moment two people stop challenging each other, they start drifting apart.

I see it in myself: The moments when I've been the most "comfortable" were the moments when I was the least alive.

I remember the year my business hit eight figures. Everything worked. My team was solid. My systems were smooth. My reputation was established.

And I was bored out of my mind.

Not because I didn't appreciate what we'd built. But because comfort had become a thief, quietly stealing my aliveness while I was busy celebrating stability.

How Comfort Steals Our Greatest Potential

Comfort doesn't announce itself as a problem. It doesn't show up as a warning sign.

It shows up as ease.

"I don't need to push myself today."

"I've already done enough."

"I'll start tomorrow."

And then one day, tomorrow doesn't come.

One day, I wake up and realize I've been in the same place for far too long. One day, I see that the life I thought was stable has actually been shrinking, closing in on itself. One day, I realize:

I didn't choose stagnation—comfort chose it for me.

And the worst part?

I never even noticed it happening.

Where in My Life Have I Made a Home Out of Comfort?

I ask myself this all the time:

Where have I stopped pushing myself?

Where have I started believing my own excuses?

Where am I choosing comfort over the possibility of something greater?

Because I already know what comfort feels like. I already know what happens when I choose the easy path.

But what if I chose differently?

Last year, I signed up for Kokoro—a 50-hour military-style crucible training designed by Navy SEALs. I was twice the age of most participants. It defied all logic. It would break my comfortable routines. It would demand more than I thought I could give.

And it was exactly what I needed.

Because in that brutal experience, I found something comfort could never give me: the realization that I am capable of more than I believed possible.

What if, instead of making my life easier, I made my life bigger?

That is the real question.

And that is where the next chapter begins.

What areas of your life have become too comfortable? Where are you avoiding necessary friction? What expansion is waiting for you beyond the borders of what feels safe?

Remember: Comfort isn't the prize. It's the consolation.

Chapter 35. Motion as the Cure for Fear

Why Action is the Only Way Forward

There is a simple truth about fear:

Fear only grows in stillness.

When I sit in uncertainty, my mind creates monsters. It builds worst-case scenarios, amplifies doubts, invents reasons why I should wait—why I shouldn't take the risk, why I should hold back just a little longer.

And the longer I wait, the worse it gets.

Because fear doesn't live in action.

It lives in hesitation.

Fear is Never the Problem. Stagnation Is.

Most people think fear is the enemy.

It's not.

Fear is natural. Fear is a signal that something matters. Fear means I am at an edge, standing in front of something unknown.

The real problem isn't fear.

It's the pause that follows fear.

Because hesitation is what kills dreams.

It's the pause before saying yes. It's the second-guessing before making the call. It's the endless overthinking before taking the leap.

Hesitation is where the mind creeps in and builds a cage around possibility.

And the only way out?

Move before the cage locks.

I remember the night before launching my first major business. All the doubts flooded in at once. Who was I to create this? What if it failed? What if people rejected it? What if I wasn't ready?

That hesitation nearly paralyzed me. But instead of giving in, I did something simple but decisive—I clicked "publish" on the website.

One action. No turning back.

And by morning, the first clients had already signed up.

The Confidence Myth

For years, I believed confidence was what I needed in order to act.

I thought that once I felt ready, once I had proof, once I had more certainty—then I would take the leap.

But I had it backward.

Confidence is not the requirement for action. Action is the requirement for confidence.

Confidence is not a feeling that shows up first. It is something I earn by moving. It is something I build by stepping into the unknown and realizing, over and over again, that I can handle it.

I've seen it in myself, in my students, in my friends: The moment we take the first step—before we feel ready—everything shifts.

When Sarah, one of my mentees, was terrified of public speaking, she didn't wait until she felt confident to begin. She booked her first speaking engagement before she'd written a word of her talk. She moved first, and confidence followed. Today, she commands stages across the country.

The Only Question That Matters

Fear will always be there. Doubt will always be there. Uncertainty will always be there.

The only question is:

Will I let it stop me?

Because if I wait until I feel ready, I will wait forever.

But if I move—

Even while afraid,

Even while unsure,

Even while doubting myself—

I win.

Because motion beats fear. Every. Single. Time.

What step have you been hesitating to take? What dream is waiting for you to move? What fear would dissolve if you simply took action today?

Remember: You'll never feel fully ready for the things that matter most. Move anyway.

Chapter 36. The Paradox of Disruption - Dancing at the Edge

I have lived my life at the edge of disruption.

I've disrupted industries. I've disrupted mindsets. I've disrupted my own identity—sometimes with precision, sometimes with force.

I know, in my bones, that transformation happens at the boundary of discomfort.

I saw it when I walked away from one life to build another. I saw it when I challenged an entire industry to rethink its foundation. I saw it when I trained for Kokoro, testing my body and mind beyond anything I thought possible.

Every major breakthrough has come from stepping into the unknown, choosing growth over safety, expansion over comfort.

And yet, when it comes to my most personal spaces—when it comes to vulnerability, love, and my own willingness to be deeply seen—do I hold myself to the same standard?

Or do I, at times, resist disruption when it threatens the structures I've built within?

The Comfort Trap

Discomfort is the doorway to expansion. I know this. I teach this. I embody this.

But comfort has a way of seducing even the most self-aware among us.

In business, I know how to dismantle stagnant thinking with a single well-placed question. I can challenge someone just enough to crack their framework wide open, revealing possibilities they never considered. I can introduce the kind of tension that forces a shift without breaking them.

But am I willing to let that happen to me?

Am I willing to let someone else gently disrupt me—not as a mentor, not as a guide, but as a human who still has work to do?

Last spring, a close friend asked me a question that shattered my composure: "You help others transform, but who helps you? Who do you allow to see your unfinished edges?"

I had no answer. And in that silence, I saw the truth—I had become an expert at creating disruption but had insulated myself from experiencing it.

Because the real challenge isn't just knowing the power of disruption. It's allowing myself to be disrupted.

Where Am I Holding On Too Tightly?

There is a paradox here.

I have built structures—routines, beliefs, ways of operating—that have served me well. They have created the life I now live.

But what happens when those very structures start to confine me?

What happens when the identity I've created—the one that has given me success, influence, and impact—becomes the very thing that needs to be questioned?

What truths have I avoided facing? What patterns in my life need to be shaken? What would happen if I let go of the parts of me that no longer serve who I am becoming?

Stepping Into the Uncomfortable Question

I ask myself right now:

Where in my life am I resisting disruption?

Because I know the answer.

It's in the places where I crave certainty. It's in the moments where I choose control over surrender. It's in the relationships where I hold back instead of leaning in.

For me, it's been in my reluctance to be a beginner again. To put myself in spaces where I'm not the expert. To allow myself to be messy, unpolished, and unfinished in front of others.

I've made my name being polished. What would it mean to let others see me struggle?

And I know what happens when I release my grip.

That's where transformation lives.

So today, I step into the uncomfortable question. I let it reshape me. I let it take me beyond where I've been before.

Because if disruption is the key to growth, then I must allow myself to be undone.

And that is the next edge.

What edges are you avoiding? Where are you resisting the very disruption that could transform you? Who do you allow to challenge your most deeply held assumptions about yourself?

Remember: The master doesn't just create disruption. The master welcomes it.

Chapter 37. The Trap of Certainty

Why the Illusion of Control Keeps Us Small

For most of my life, I chased certainty.

I believed that if I could map out the future, control the variables, and eliminate risk—then I would be safe. Then, I would be at peace. Then I could finally relax into my life.

So, I built businesses with precision. I created strategies that reduced chaos. I shaped my world into something predictable.

And for a while, it worked.

Until it didn't.

Because certainty is a lie.

Certainty Feels Like Freedom—Until You Realize It's a Cage

We tell ourselves that certainty keeps us safe. That if we can just figure it out, just get it right, then we will be free.

But certainty is not freedom. It is a slow, quiet suffocation.

Certainty tricks us into believing that safety lies in the known. That if we plan ahead far enough, control every variable, we can eliminate risk.

But risk is never eliminated—only avoided. And the cost of avoiding risk? The loss of aliveness.

Everything truly alive—love, growth, creativity—exists beyond certainty.

Love is uncertain.

Growth is uncertain.

Art is uncertain.

New beginnings are uncertain.

And yet, they are the only things that make life worth living.

I once spent two years meticulously planning the perfect business model. Every variable accounted for. Every scenario mapped out. Every risk mitigated. The plan was bulletproof.

And then reality intervened. The market shifted. A pandemic hit. Everything changed overnight.

All those spreadsheets, all those contingencies—useless in the face of a world that refused to follow my script.

What saved me wasn't my planning. It was my ability to pivot when the plan failed.

The Hidden Cost of Control

There is a moment in every person's life when they realize they are not in control.

For some, it comes as a sudden shock. A loss. A failure. A disruption that shatters the illusion.

For others, it creeps in slowly. The quiet realization that no matter how well they plan, life moves on its own terms.

And that moment is terrifying.

But what I've learned is this:

The tighter we grip, the more we suffer.

Control is exhausting. It keeps us locked in a battle against reality, trying to force life to obey our expectations.

And the moment we let go, something unexpected happens:

We breathe.

Because life was never meant to be controlled. It was meant to be experienced.

And the sooner we recognize that, the sooner we truly start living.

What are you trying to control that might actually be controlling you? Where has your pursuit of certainty become a prison? What would be possible if you embraced the inherent uncertainty of being alive?

Remember: The need for certainty is the mind's attempt to protect us from life. But life, in all its beautiful uncertainty, is exactly what we're here for.

Chapter 38. Trusting the Unknown

How Uncertainty Invites Us Into Expansion

I used to resist uncertainty. Now, I see it as an invitation.

Uncertainty is not a void. It is a doorway.

And what's on the other side? Everything I've ever wanted.

Why Everything I Wanted Lived in the Unknown

I used to believe that not knowing was dangerous.

I thought that if I didn't have the answers, I was at risk. That if I didn't have a plan, I was failing.

But then I looked back.

And I saw the truth—

Every great moment in my life came from stepping into uncertainty:

I didn't know what would happen when I left my old career.

I didn't know what would happen when I launched my first business.

I didn't know what would happen when I said yes to love, to risk, to adventure.

But I moved anyway.

I remember the day I decided to write my first book. I had no publishing deal, no guarantee it would ever see the light of day. Just an idea that wouldn't let me go.

Three hundred early mornings later, that manuscript would become a bestseller and open doors I couldn't have imagined. But none of it would have happened if I'd waited for certainty.

And that's the difference between those who stay stuck and those who expand:

The ones who expand trust the unknown before they have proof.

Leaning Into Trust When There Are No Guarantees

Trust is not something we wait to feel. It is something we choose.

And that choice changes everything.

When I trust myself, I don't need certainty.

When I trust life, I don't need guarantees.

I step forward, not because I have all the answers, but because I trust myself to find them along the way.

And that is the real gift of uncertainty: It forces us to trust.

Trust that we are capable. Trust that we will figure it out. Trust that even if we fall, we will rise again.

Because life is not about knowing. It is about becoming.

And becoming requires stepping into the unknown.

What's Waiting in the Unknown?

Right now, there is a place in my life where I am resisting uncertainty. A decision I am delaying because I don't have a guarantee. A risk I am avoiding because I don't know how it will unfold. A leap I am afraid to take because the outcome is unclear.

But what if, instead of fearing uncertainty, I welcomed it? What if I saw it as my ally, not my enemy? What if I trusted that the unknown is not empty—but filled with everything I have been waiting for?

Because I know this: The best things in my life were once unknown.

The greatest relationships.

The biggest opportunities.

The most profound transformations.

All of them began in uncertainty.

And if I had waited for certainty, I would have missed them all.

So today, I make a new commitment: I will not wait for certainty. I will step forward without guarantees. I will trust that whatever is on the other side of uncertainty is exactly what I need.

Because the future does not belong to those who grip the past. It belongs to those who trust themselves enough to let go.

What uncertainty are you resisting right now? What leap are you afraid to take? What would change if you trusted yourself enough to move without guarantees?

Remember: The unknown isn't empty space. It's where everything you want is waiting.

Chapter 39. The Power of Disruptive Confusion

Why Confusion is the Catalyst for Breakthroughs

People don't change because they are told to. They don't shift because they read an insight or hear a truth. They shift because something disorients them just enough to make them pause.

That pause—those few seconds where the mind searches for meaning—

That's where transformation happens.

I have used this instinctively for years. I call it the confusion technique—the art of disrupting expected patterns just enough to create a reset.

It's in the unexpected silence after someone asks a question—when I let the tension stretch instead of filling it with words.

It's in responding to a transactional request with a question so deep it forces the other person to step outside their script.

It's in breaking my own predictable patterns—forcing myself into uncertainty, not because I enjoy discomfort, but because I know it is where I grow the most.

Confusion is not something to be feared. It is something to be designed. It is something to be leveraged.

Why Confusion Unlocks the Mind

Most people don't live in curiosity. They live in certainty.

And certainty is what keeps them stuck.

When someone is certain—about how business works, about who they are, about how relationships unfold—there is no room for transformation.

But when I introduce a level of productive confusion, everything shifts.

A client who "knows" exactly why they're struggling suddenly questions their own narrative.

A team member who is stuck in routine thinking suddenly sees a new angle.

A friend who has been trapped in a cycle of limiting beliefs suddenly finds a new doorway.

I remember working with Marcus, a successful entrepreneur who was convinced his business problems stemmed from his marketing strategy. He had it all figured out. He just needed me to validate his analysis.

Instead of agreeing, I asked him, "What if your marketing isn't the problem at all? What if it's working perfectly to create exactly the business you secretly believe you deserve?"

The confusion on his face was immediate. Then came the silence. Then, finally, the revelation—he had been limiting his own growth out of a deep-seated belief that he didn't deserve more success.

The key is not to provide clarity too soon.

When I let someone sit in the discomfort of not knowing, their mind does something powerful—it begins to search.

And in that searching, breakthroughs happen.

The Role of Disruptive Questions

When I coach, I don't give answers. I give questions that break assumptions.

"What if the thing you're avoiding is the thing that would save you?"

"What if you stopped trying to solve the problem and just allowed it to be?"

"What if the story you're telling yourself about this is completely wrong?"

People expect solutions. But solutions keep them comfortable.

What they need is disruption. Because only in that space do they start thinking for themselves.

What certainties are you clinging to that might actually be limiting you? Where could a little productive confusion create a breakthrough? What assumptions about your life might need disrupting?

Remember: Clarity is useful, but confusion is transformative. Learn to welcome both.

Chapter 40. The Art of Self-Disruption

Allowing Ourselves to Be Confused, Broken Open, and Transformed

I have spent a lifetime disrupting others. But am I willing to let life disrupt me?

Confusion is easy when I'm the one creating it. I can introduce tension in a conversation, ask a disruptive question that makes someone rethink their path, or dismantle a belief system with one well-placed insight.

But what happens when confusion finds me? When I am the one being undone?

Because real transformation isn't about making others uncomfortable. It's about allowing myself to sit in discomfort without rushing for clarity.

Why We Fear Our Own Confusion

We like to believe we are in control. That we understand who we are, how the world works, and what the future holds.

But then life happens.

A loss. A failure. A revelation so disorienting it shakes everything we thought we knew. A moment when the scaffolding of certainty collapses, and we are left standing in the rubble of what we once believed.

And in that moment, we have a choice:

Fight to hold onto the old narrative.

Or surrender to the breaking open.

Most of us resist. We seek quick explanations, scramble for meaning, and try to force the broken pieces back into place. Because sitting in the unknown—without a plan, without an identity, without the safety of certainty—feels like death.

But what if that's exactly the point?

Last year, I lost someone I loved deeply. In the aftermath, nothing made sense. My frameworks for understanding life, for making meaning, for finding purpose—they all failed me.

And my instinct was to fight it. To force clarity where there was none. To rebuild the foundation before the dust had even settled.

But something in me knew better. It whispered: "Stay here. Don't run from this breaking. Let it teach you."

So I did. For months, I let myself be confused. I let myself not know. I let myself be broken open by grief.

And what I found in that confusion wasn't weakness—it was a depth I had never known before.

The Gift of Being Broken Open

Every major transformation in my life began as confusion. Not clarity. Confusion.

The moments when I didn't know who I was anymore. The moments when the old way stopped working, but the new way hadn't arrived yet. The moments when I thought I had lost myself—only to discover a deeper version waiting underneath.

Because here's the truth: Confusion isn't a sign that something is wrong. It's a sign that something is changing.

It is the space between identities. It is the dissolving of an old self before the new one has fully formed. It is the death before the rebirth.

And the deeper the confusion, the bigger the transformation.

Why We Must Let Go of Understanding

For most of my life, I believed understanding was power. If I could just figure it out, then I could fix it. Then, I could move forward.

But I've learned something else: Sometimes, the fastest way to clarity is to stop searching for it.

Understanding is not required for transformation. Only surrender is.

The moment I stop demanding answers, something unexpected happens: The answers reveal themselves.

Not because I forced them. Not because I worked for them. But because I made space for them to emerge.

When my business faced its greatest crisis, I spent weeks frantically trying to understand what went wrong, analyzing every variable, and seeking explanations that would ease my anxiety. The more I grasped for understanding, the more exhausted and confused I became.

Finally, in complete exhaustion, I surrendered. I stopped trying to understand and simply said, "I don't know, and that's okay."

Within days, solutions began to appear—not from my frantic analysis but from the quiet space that opened up when I stopped demanding immediate answers.

The Questions That Break Me Open

When I feel myself gripping for control, I ask:

Where am I still clinging to an old identity?

Where am I seeking certainty instead of allowing expansion?

What if I stopped trying to solve this and just let it be?

And then, I listen.

Not to my mind, which wants to rush ahead. Not to my fear, which wants to retreat. But to the still, quiet voice underneath it all—the one that already knows.

Because transformation is not something I achieve. It is something I allow.

And the moment I surrender to it—truly, fully, without resistance—I become something new.

What confusion are you rushing to resolve that might actually be transforming you? Where are you demanding understanding when surrender might serve you better? What would happen if you allowed yourself to not know—even just for a little while?

Remember: The greatest clarity often comes not from figuring things out but from letting things be.

Chapter 41. The Divine Reset

Why Disruption is an Invitation, Not a Punishment

For most of my life, I have been a builder. I built businesses. I built systems. I built frameworks to make sense of chaos.

Mastery was my pursuit—mastery over my mind, my habits, my work, my relationships. I learned to predict, structure, refine, and optimize.

And in that pursuit, I created stability.

But then something unexpected happened. The very structures I built to support my growth became the things that began to limit it.

Because mastery without disruption is stagnation. And certainty without space for the unknown is a cage.

It took me years to realize this truth: What I resist breaking is often the very thing breaking me.

Why Disruption is Sacred

Disruption is not random. It is not chaos for the sake of destruction. It is a reset. A recalibration. A divine clearing.

It shows up as:

The business model that no longer works the way it used to.

The relationship that is forcing me to evolve beyond my comfort zone.

The inner knowing that whispers, "This isn't it anymore."

It is the moment when something breaks apart, not to punish me but to make space.

Three years ago, the business model that had served me for a decade suddenly collapsed. Revenue dropped. Programs that had always filled now sat half-empty. The formulas stopped working.

My first response was panic. My second was determination—I would fix it, force it back into place, and make it work again.

But the harder I pushed, the more resistance I felt.

Until finally, I heard it—the quiet invitation beneath the chaos: "Let it break. Something new wants to be born."

Breaking as an Opening

I have seen this in my own life. The moments when everything felt like it was falling apart—when I resisted, fought, tried to hold it together—

And yet, in hindsight, those were the moments when something greater was trying to emerge.

The collapse of an old way of doing business made room for a new way of serving.

The loss of an identity I clung to allowed a deeper version of myself to rise.

The breaking of expectations freed me from stories that no longer fit.

And I see now—

Disruption is not something happening to me. It is something happening for me.

When I finally stopped fighting the collapse of my old business model and surrendered to the breaking, a new vision emerged—one more aligned with who I was becoming, not who I had been. The reset wasn't destroying my work; it was evolving it.

What if Disruption is a Blessing?

What if the discomfort is not a problem? What if the falling apart is not a failure? What if the uncertainty is not a void—but a doorway?

Because the truth is—

Everything I have ever deeply wanted was waiting on the other side of what I refused to let go of.

The question is not—

"Why is this happening?"

The question is—

"Am I willing to see the gift in it?"

Where in your life is disruption trying to create space for something new? What are you desperately trying to hold together that might need to come apart? What wisdom might be hiding in the very breakdown you're trying to avoid?

Remember: The breaking is never the end of the story. It's the beginning of a better one.

Chapter 42. The Grip and the Release

Why We Hold On Too Tightly—And What It Takes to Let Go

I used to believe strength was about holding on. Holding on to certainty. Holding on to control. Holding on to what I had built.

But now I see—

Strength is not about gripping. It is about knowing when to let go.

Why We Grip

We grip because we are afraid. Afraid that if we loosen our hold, we will lose something important. Afraid that if we stop trying to control, we will fall apart.

And so we grip—

To our old identities.

To our outdated beliefs.

To our stories of how life is supposed to be.

But what if the very thing we are holding onto is what's holding us back?

I've gripped tightly to relationships long after they stopped serving growth. I've clung to business models that no longer aligned with my values. I've held onto beliefs about who I am even when they became too small for who I was becoming.

The fear of the unknown keeps our fingers locked around the familiar, even when the familiar has become a prison.

The Cost of Holding Too Tight

I have seen this in my own life—

The moments when I gripped so tightly to a vision, a plan, a way of being that I suffocated the very thing I was trying to nurture.

In business, I once refused to let go of an old model—even when it was clear the world had changed.

In relationships, I held on to patterns of proving and performing—rather than surrendering into being seen.

In personal growth, I resisted change because it felt like losing myself—when, in reality, it was the path to finding a deeper version of myself.

Because holding on doesn't create safety. It creates resistance. And resistance blocks flow.

I remember the moment when I finally released my grip on a long-held belief about success. For years, I measured my worth by external metrics—revenue, audience size, and recognition. I white-knuckled that definition, even as it drained my joy and disconnected me from my purpose.

The day I let it go—truly, fully released it—I felt a weight lift that I hadn't even known I was carrying. Something new could now flow in.

What it Means to Truly Let Go

Letting go does not mean passivity. It does not mean surrendering to life. It means surrendering into life.

It means saying—

"I don't have to control this."
"I don't have to force this."
"I don't have to grip."

It means trusting the natural unfolding of things rather than trying to bend them to my will.

And the paradox is—

The moment I stop gripping, life begins to flow.

The Practice of the Release

I ask myself:

Where in my life am I holding too tightly?

What would happen if I loosened my grip, even just a little?

What if, instead of forcing an answer, I allowed it to reveal itself?

Because letting go is not an event. It is a practice.

And every time I choose release over resistance, something unexpected happens—

I feel lighter.

I feel freer.

I feel... alive.

What are you gripping too tightly right now? What story, belief, relationship, or expectation might be asking for a gentler hold? What would happen if you opened your fingers just a little and allowed some space?

Remember: The tighter you grip, the less you can receive. Sometimes, the greatest act of courage is simply to open your hands.

Chapter 43. The Play That Saves Me

How Play Disrupts Patterns, Unlocks Mastery, and Balances Structure with Spontaneity

There was a time when I thought play was something you earned. Something reserved for after the work was done. A reward for being disciplined, meeting expectations, and proving myself worthy of rest.

Play was a vacation—not a vocation.

It wasn't until much later—until I had lived enough, lost enough, and learned enough—that I realized:

Play is the work. It's not something I need to earn. It's something I need to live inside of.

Play as the Ultimate Pattern Disruptor

Disruption is what keeps us evolving. Disruption is what forces growth.

But not all disruption has to be painful. Some of it can be playful.

Play isn't just about fun. It's about breaking patterns. It's about loosening the grip on control. It's about seeing things from angles we hadn't considered before.

And here's the paradox—

The more structured we become, the more rigid our thinking. And the more rigid our thinking, the more likely we are to miss the breakthrough that's trying to emerge.

Play shakes things loose. It disrupts stagnation. It opens new pathways. It tricks the mind into learning without resistance.

I see this clearly now—

The moments of greatest innovation in my life didn't happen when I was locked into a plan. They happened when I was playing inside the unknown.

The unplanned detour in a conversation that sparked a life-changing insight.

The willingness to abandon an agenda in a meeting that led to a completely new way of thinking.

The times I followed curiosity rather than expectation and discovered something I never would have sought on purpose.

The greatest disruptor isn't just intensity—it's lightness.

I remember the creation of one of my most successful programs. After months of meticulous planning that led nowhere, I scrapped everything and invited a small group of friends to simply play with possibilities together. No agenda. No expected outcome. Just exploration.

In that playful space, the entire framework emerged in two hours—more innovative and aligned than anything my careful planning had produced in months.

The Dance of Structure and Spontaneity

Mastery requires both discipline and flow. Too much structure? You suffocate. Too much chaos? You lose direction.

The sweet spot? Enough structure to give stability. Enough play to allow expansion.

It's the same in dance. There is footwork—but within that framework, there is freedom. There is technique—but what makes it art is the improvisation within it.

I've learned that the moments of true mastery don't happen when I grip too tightly to a process. They happen when I trust the structure enough to let go inside of it.

Play is not the opposite of discipline. Play is what makes discipline sustainable.

Where I Forgot to Play

For years, I ran on achievement. Metrics. Numbers. Results.

Play felt like a waste of time. Something for people who weren't serious about impact.

But now? I see that the most impactful people I know are the ones who play the most.

Not because they don't work hard. But because play keeps them from burning out.

They don't just think their way to solutions. They move. They experiment. They explore. They laugh their way into breakthroughs.

And that's the shift—

When play becomes part of the process, mastery becomes inevitable.

The Role of Play in Relationships

Play doesn't just disrupt business—it disrupts connection. The strongest relationships in my life are the ones built on play.

Because play creates safety. Play creates lightness. Play allows people to show up as they are rather than as who they think they're supposed to be.

The moments I've felt closest to people? Not in the structured, serious conversations. Not in the moments of proving or teaching.

But in the in-between moments—

The inside jokes.

The spontaneous laughter.

The silly detours in conversations that led to the deepest truths.

Because without play, connection becomes transactional. And the moment something becomes just another transaction, it starts to die.

Play keeps it alive.

My longest partnership nearly ended before we discovered this truth. We had become so focused on optimization, goals, and improving our relationship that we'd forgotten how to simply enjoy each other. The moment we prioritized play again—actual, purposeless, joyful play—everything began to heal.

Mastery Requires Novelty

Here's what I've come to understand—

The brain thrives on patterns, but it also thrives on novelty.

If I repeat the same routine, the same approach, the same way of thinking for too long—

My mind stops expanding.

But if I introduce just enough novelty, I stay engaged. I stay sharp. I stay alive inside my own work.

Play is structured novelty. It's how I make sure I'm still evolving. It's how I keep my work, my relationships, and my own mind alive.

Playing My Way Into the Future

I don't build from a blueprint. I build from wonder.

And I see it now—

Every time I've allowed play to lead, I've stepped into something bigger than I imagined.

By Referral Only didn't come from following a rigid business plan. It came from playfully rethinking how trust and business intersect.

The Medivations project didn't happen because I strategized it for months—It happened because I experimented with AI and let it take me somewhere new.

PrivateWork didn't start as a system. It started as a curiosity, a question, a willingness to see where the conversation could go.

Everything that has worked in my life has had an element of play.

And now, I ask myself—

Where am I gripping too tightly?

Where am I clinging to old structures instead of playing my way into new ones?

What would happen if, instead of strategizing my way into the future, I danced into it instead?

The Only Question That Matters

At the end of all of this—

When the books are written,

When the businesses are built,

When the goals are met—

The only thing that will have truly mattered is this:

Did I love well?

Did I play enough?

And if I can say yes to both—

Then I'll know I did it right.

Where in your life have you forgotten to play? What work feels heavy that could be lightened through playfulness? How might you introduce more wonder and less striving into your pursuit of mastery?

Remember: The master at anything was once willing to look foolish. Play isn't separate from the path—it is the path.

Chapter 44. The Dance of Letting Go

Mastering Detachment—Why Letting Go is the Highest Form of Control

Letting go isn't an act of force. It isn't about severing or turning away. It's a movement—a dance.

I've spent a lifetime learning when to grip and when to release. And I see now—

Mastery isn't about knowing how to hold on. It's about knowing when to let go.

The Illusion of Control

For most of my life, I thought control was the key to success. If I could just control outcomes, control my emotions, control my environment—

Then I'd be safe. Then I'd be powerful. Then I'd be free.

But here's the paradox—

The tighter I gripped, the more I lost. The more I controlled, the more life slipped through my hands. The more I resisted change, the more I suffered.

Control, I've learned, is an illusion. We don't own the outcomes. We don't own other people's decisions. We don't even own the direction of our own lives as much as we'd like to think.

What we do own?

How we respond to change.

How we adapt to uncertainty.

How we move inside the letting go.

Because true power isn't in controlling the dance. True power is in knowing how to move with it.

My most painful lessons in this came from trying to control the uncontrollable. I once spent two years attempting to force a business relationship that wasn't aligned. No matter how much I strategized, communicated, or adjusted, it remained a struggle.

The day I finally let go—not with resentment, but with acceptance—everything shifted. Within weeks, a perfect partnership appeared, one that would have remained invisible had I continued clinging to what wasn't working.

The Leap Between Vines

I think of a monkey in the jungle, swinging from vine to vine. He doesn't just let go randomly. He releases only when he knows he has another vine to grab.

And in that split-second moment—between letting go and catching the next vine—

He is weightless. Suspended in midair. In free fall.

That is the moment of trust. The moment of surrender. The moment of pure, absolute faith.

And I ask myself—

Where in my life am I still clinging to the vine?

What am I gripping so tightly that it's keeping me from my next leap?

What would happen if I trusted the free fall?

Because I've seen it again and again—

The life I want is always waiting on the other side of what I refuse to let go of.

Recalibrating the Formula

For decades, I lived by a formula—

Vision

Strategy

Relentless execution

And it worked. It got me here.

But now I ask—

Is it still working?

Because letting go isn't just about release. Letting go is about recalibrating.

Is my vision still aligned with who I'm becoming?

Are my strategies still serving me—or have they become a cage?

Am I gripping an identity that no longer fits?

Because mastery isn't about rigid control. Mastery is about adaptation. And sometimes, the highest form of wisdom is knowing when to stop pushing.

The Backward Step—Finding Freedom in Detachment

There's a practice in Zen called the backward step. It means pulling back—not out of fear, not out of avoidance—

But to create space.

Space to see clearly. Space to detach from identity. Space to let go of the need to prove anything.

I ask myself—

Who am I without my work?

Who am I without the need to be needed?

Who am I if I stop gripping so tightly to what I've built?

And the answer? I don't need to know.

Because letting go isn't about having a new plan. Letting go is about allowing space for the next thing to emerge.

Last year, I took a three-month sabbatical—no work, no creating, no teaching. Just space. People asked what I would do after. I had no answer. For the first time in decades, I allowed myself to not know, to fully detach from my professional identity.

In that emptiness, in that not-knowing, something unexpected happened. A vision for the next evolution of my work appeared—not from striving but from stillness.

The Space Between the Notes

Music isn't just made of sound. It's made of silence. The spaces between the notes. The pauses that give meaning to the rhythm.

And I see now—

I've spent much of my life trying to fill every gap. To be useful. To be valuable. To be the one with answers.

But what if the most profound thing I could offer... was silence? Was space? Was trusting the pause?

Because control says, "I need to fix this." But mastery says, "I need to let it breathe."

Leaving Before the Harvest

This is the pattern I see in myself—

Not just in business. Not just in fitness. But in love.

I have built empires. I have created wealth, impact, and community. But at times... I have stepped away just before the deepest reward arrived.

Not out of failure. Not out of lack. But because something inside me feared the stillness after the achievement.

What happens after you win? What happens after the mountain is climbed? What happens after you get everything you want?

For some, it's celebration. For others—

It's discomfort.

Because if I let myself fully receive, Then what? Then who am I?

That is the real edge. That is the real dance. To not just create—

But to stay.

To sit inside the success. To not run when intimacy deepens. To not retreat when something good is fully arriving.

I see this pattern clearly now. The way I've left relationships just as they deepened. The way I've pivoted businesses right at the moment of their maturation. The way I've abandoned projects right before completion.

The art isn't just in the creation. It's in the staying. It's in receiving the full harvest of what I've planted.

The Master Knows When to Release

I used to think mastery meant control. But now I see—

Mastery is fluidity.

The master knows when to hold the note. And the master knows when to let it resolve.

So I ask myself—

Where am I still gripping?

Where am I still forcing?

Where am I still afraid of the free fall?

Because the real movement begins when I release. And the moment I let go... I am free.

Where are you still attempting to control the uncontrollable? What are you clutching that wants to be released? What would become possible if you trusted the space between letting go and what comes next?

Remember: You don't need to know what's next in order to release what's now. Trust the dance.

Chapter 45. The Final Disruption - Becoming Nobody

The Mastery of Release, the Freedom of Letting Go

I have spent my life building.

Building businesses that transformed industries. Building frameworks that redefined possibility. Building strategies that others claimed couldn't work until they did. Building influence that shaped generations. Building reputation that opened doors before I knocked. Building mastery that became its own currency.

Building myself into something substantial, something unassailable, something undeniable in a world that prefers the comfortable mediocrity of the known.

And for decades, this approach succeeded beyond what most would dare imagine.

I didn't merely disrupt the game—I reinvented it entirely. I perceived shifts in markets before others sensed the tremor. I moved decisively while others deliberated. I didn't follow trends that already existed—I created currents that others eventually recognized as inevitable.

But after enough seasons of success, after enough summits conquered, I began to feel the weight of it all settle into my bones.

Not the familiar weight of failure or setback.

But the unexpected weight of being *somebody*.

The relentless weight of being the leader everyone turns to. The mentor who must always have the answer. The architect of ideas that others build their lives upon. The lighthouse that cannot flicker.

The crushing weight of holding it all together while making it appear effortless.

The revelation I never anticipated—the disruption that blindsided me completely—was that the ultimate disruption was never about breaking industries or markets. It was never about reinventing business models or challenging accepted practices.

The final disruption was always about dismantling myself.

The Final Pattern to Break—The Grip of Identity

I have dedicated a lifetime to disrupting others' limiting patterns. Asking the questions they avoided. Shattering assumptions they didn't realize were cages. Pulling them into uncharted territory where true growth begins.

But what happens when I am the one gripping too tightly to what is familiar?

When I am the one resisting the call to evolution?

When I am the one desperately clinging to a version of myself that no longer contains what I'm becoming?

I reflect on the times I disrupted systems from the outside in—By Referral Only that transformed how real estate functioned. PrivateWork that revolutionized coaching. Medivations that pushed mindfulness beyond recognition. AI-driven self-coaching that made transformation accessible at scale. I systematically broke obsolete models, architected something more aligned with truth, and witnessed thousands of lives transformed as a result.

But I also recognize the times I disrupted from the inside out—The raw crucible of Kokoro that stripped away everything but essence. The terrifying unknown of fatherhood that humbled everything I thought I knew. The years dedicated to pushing my physical body to its absolute limits, then deliberately pulling back to discover an entirely different kind of strength hidden within stillness.

And now, I sense another seismic shift approaching. Something fundamental. Something that cannot be avoided or postponed.

A voice in the deepest silence asking with unnerving clarity:

What becomes possible if you release the need to be somebody?

What awaits when you finally stop gripping the identity you've constructed?

Not from resignation or retreat.

But from profound, unshakable trust in what lies beyond the constructed self.

The Moment You Realize Control is the Illusion

Control is what architected the first empire. The systems. The structures. The carefully calibrated processes.

However, control is also what eventually made success feel like a beautiful prison.

Control is what enabled me to master the external game by every conventional metric. But it's also what led me to question whether the game itself was worth the continuous cost of playing.

I see now with absolute clarity that I've invested years holding on with white knuckles.

Holding on to systems I created that others now depend upon. Holding on to a name that opens doors but constrains who I can become. Holding on to expectations that once drove me but now limit where I can go. Holding on to rhythms of work and life that no longer align with what my spirit requires. Holding on to the intoxicating feeling of being irreplaceable.

But here's the truth that masters rarely reveal:

True mastery isn't about perpetual refinement toward perfection. Mastery is about recognizing precisely when to release your grip.

The authentic leap isn't found in continuously building something new atop what already exists. The authentic leap manifests when you allow what has completed its purpose to end without resistance.

Because certainty feels like protection, but it silently becomes the most elegant cage ever designed.

I witnessed this pattern in business—when I clung too tightly to models that had served their purpose. I experienced it in relationships—when I tried to engineer outcomes instead of allowing natural momentum. I felt it most acutely within myself—when I resisted the inevitable evolutionary shifts that were already underway beneath my awareness.

And without exception, in every single instance, the moment I finally surrendered control...

The next chapter wrote itself with an elegance I could never have engineered.

The Ego's Last Defense—The Fear of Disappearing

There is a primal reason we hesitate at this threshold.

We don't actually fear taking decisive action. We fear who we might become when we are no longer anchored to the version of ourselves we've invested decades constructing.

It is the existential fear of disappearing completely.

If I am no longer the recognized leader, then who remains? If I am not the industry disruptor, then what purpose do I serve? If I cease the relentless pursuit of mastery as I've defined it, then what gives my existence meaning?

I recognize now that these aren't questions demanding intellectual answers. These are questions to be released entirely.

Because what if the ultimate aim was never to become somebody of consequence?

What if the highest expression of mastery is to dissolve so completely into the present moment that no separate self remains?

To disappear entirely into the work without needing recognition. To vanish into pure movement without performer or audience. To merge so completely with life itself that no boundary remains between experience and experiencer.

I've glimpsed this state in rare, transcendent moments.

In the darkest hours of Kokoro training, when my body had nothing left to give, but something beyond my individual self continued moving forward. In moments of pure dance, when I stopped performing movements and instead allowed rhythm to move through me without resistance. In the depths of meditation, where the boundaries I mistook for identity revealed themselves as convenient fictions.

These were the moments when I gripped absolutely nothing.

No fixed identity. No hidden agenda. No desperate need to be seen as anything at all.

Just pure movement. Just complete presence. Just the simplicity of being without the exhausting narrative of becoming.

The Moment of Release

So now, I ask myself the question that changes everything—

What emerges when you finally release the last thing you're gripping?

What happens when you stop clinging to even the identity of mastery itself? What awaits when you step into the next chapter without needing to know its contents in advance? What becomes possible when you no longer need to be anybody at all?

Because I know the answer with bone-deep certainty.

When I finally let go completely—I become everything.

I become free from the constraints of a single identity. I become light enough to move in any direction life requires. I become genuinely open to whatever is trying to emerge through me rather than from me.

And so do you.

The Final Invitation—Where Are You Still Holding On?

So now, I extend this invitation directly to you—

Where are you still gripping with unconscious desperation? What are you still trying to control beyond what's actually within your power? What identity, what belief, what attachment are you clinging to that's subtly preventing your next evolution?

And what would happen if you simply... let go?

Because freedom was never found in the desperate grip of control. Freedom was always waiting in the counter-intuitive act of release.

And in that singular moment—when you stop clinging to who you think you should be, stop proving your worth to those who cannot truly see you, stop resisting what's already underway—

You will recognize with stunning clarity that you were already free.

You just had to open your hand and let go.

The Ego's Last Defense—The Fear of Disappearing

There is a primal reason we hesitate at this threshold.

We don't actually fear taking decisive action. We fear who we might become when we are no longer anchored to the version of ourselves we've invested decades constructing.

It is the existential fear of disappearing completely.

If I am no longer the recognized leader, then who remains? If I am not the industry disruptor, then what purpose do I serve? If I cease the relentless pursuit of mastery as I've defined it, then what gives my existence meaning?

I recognize now that these aren't questions demanding intellectual answers. These are questions to be released entirely.

Because what if the ultimate aim was never to become somebody of consequence?

What if the highest expression of mastery is to dissolve so completely into the present moment that no separate self remains?

To disappear entirely into the work without needing recognition. To vanish into pure movement without performer or audience. To merge so completely with life itself that no boundary remains between experience and experiencer.

I've glimpsed this state in rare, transcendent moments.

In the darkest hours of Kokoro training, when my body had nothing left to give but, something beyond my individual self continued moving forward. In moments of pure dance, when I stopped performing movements and instead allowed rhythm to move through me without resistance. In the depths of meditation, where the boundaries I mistook for identity revealed themselves as convenient fictions.

These were the moments when I gripped absolutely nothing.

No fixed identity. No hidden agenda. No desperate need to be seen as anything at all.

Just pure movement. Just complete presence. Just the simplicity of being without the exhausting narrative of becoming.

The Moment of Release

So now, I ask myself the question that changes everything—

What emerges when you finally release the last thing you're gripping?

What happens when you stop clinging to even the identity of mastery itself? What awaits when you step into the next chapter without needing to know its contents in advance? What becomes possible when you no longer need to be anybody at all?

Because I know the answer with bone-deep certainty.

When I finally let go completely—I become everything.

I become free from the constraints of a single identity. I become light enough to move in any direction life requires. I become genuinely open to whatever is trying to emerge through me rather than from me.

And so do you.

The Final Invitation—Where Are You Still Holding On?

So now, I extend this invitation directly to you—

Where are you still gripping with unconscious desperation? What are you still trying to control beyond what's actually within your power? What identity, what belief, what attachment are you clinging to that's subtly preventing your next evolution?

And what would happen if you simply... let go?

Because freedom was never found in the desperate grip of control. Freedom was always waiting in the counter-intuitive act of release.

And in that singular moment—when you stop clinging to who you think you should be, stop proving your worth to those who cannot truly see you, stop resisting what's already underway—

You will recognize with stunning clarity that you were already free.

You just had to open your hand and let go.

Taste 4: Foundations for Practice

The Sacred Architecture of Everyday Discipline

I've spent decades chasing transformation. What I've discovered is both humbling and profound: no life is shaped by what is wished for or imagined. We become what we practice—day after day, moment after moment—until those practices become the very architecture of who we are.

This truth arrived for me not in a moment of triumph but in surrender. I had built empires of ambition, constructed visions of who I might become, yet found myself returning to the same patterns, the same limitations, and the same barriers.

Until I understood: transformation doesn't happen in the grand gestures. It happens in the quiet moments between breaths. In the small choices we make when no one is watching. In the disciplines we return to, not because they're easy, but because they're necessary.

This section isn't about rigid formulas or perfect systems. I've tried those. They crumble under the weight of real life. Instead, what I offer are rhythms—ways of moving through each day that sharpen the mind, refine the body, and align the spirit with something deeper than achievement.

Practices that elevate not just what we do, but who we become in the process.

Discipline as Liberation, Not Limitation

I used to fear discipline. I saw it as restriction—the narrowing of possibilities, the closing of doors. I believed freedom meant boundlessness, limitless options, and the absence of structure.

I was wrong.

True freedom, I've learned, isn't found in the absence of boundaries. It's found in the presence of foundation.

The rituals we choose daily are the ones that define us forever. They are the choices we return to, the commitments that shape a more intentional, embodied, and fully alive existence:

The way we meet the morning before the world makes demands
The breath we take when everything feels too heavy
The nourishment we choose when no one else is watching
The movement we embrace even when resistance whispers "later."
The presence we cultivate in a world designed for distraction

These are not small things. They are everything. They determine how we meet challenge, how we navigate uncertainty, how we create not just moments of clarity, but a life built upon them.

I know this because I've lived both sides. I've experienced the slow dissolution that comes from undisciplined days—the fog that settles, the energy that scatters, the purpose that blurs. And I've known the crystalline clarity that emerges from aligned practice—when what I do aligns perfectly with who I am becoming.

The Practice Begins With Truth

Before I could build new practices, I had to face a harder truth: the gap between who I claimed to be and how I actually lived.

I said health mattered, yet I negotiated with sleep. I valued presence yet reached for distraction. I spoke of purpose yet surrendered to urgency.

The practices I share are born from this reckoning—from moments of profound honesty about where I was and where I needed to go. They weren't designed in theory but forged in the crucible of personal transformation.

These chapters are an offering—an open door into the kind of mastery that does not happen by accident but by design. They aren't perfect. They carry the imprint of my own struggle, my own resistance, my own journey toward alignment.

But they work. Not because they're revolutionary but because they're true.

If you are here, you are ready. Not because you've solved everything, not because you've eliminated all weakness, but because you're willing to begin where you are.

Step in. Step fully.

The practice begins now.

Chapter 46. The First Two Hours - A Ritual of Becoming

I have spent a lifetime refining my mornings, not out of discipline alone but desperation. I discovered long ago that without these sacred first hours, the day owns me rather than I the day.

These first two hours aren't just blocks on a calendar. They are:

The threshold between who I was yesterday and who I choose to be today. The sanctuary where I remember what matters before the world tells me what should. The foundation upon which everything else either stands strong or crumbles under pressure.

Lincoln said, "If I have to chop down a tree, I'll spend 50 minutes sharpening my axe." I say: if I am to create, lead, teach, love, and serve with the fullness of who I am, I must spend these first hours sharpening my mind, body, and spirit. Not as luxury, but necessity.

Meeting Myself Before the World Does

There was a time when I woke to immediacy—to emails, demands, the voices of others echoing in my mind before my feet touched the floor. I lived reactive days, wondering why clarity remained elusive, why purpose felt distant.

Now, before the world asks anything of me—before I answer to clients, to friends, to the constructs of my own ambition—I sit at my altar. This altar isn't ornate; sometimes, it's simply a corner of a hotel room, a chair by a window, or the edge of my bed. But it is where I return to something deeper than my name, my roles, my work.

It is where I listen to the part of me that doesn't shout but whispers. The part that doesn't seek but knows.

Here, my Medivation begins. Over 700 mornings, I have crafted and recorded these meditations, these visualizations, these reflections. They are more than words into a microphone. They are the architecture of my inner world, the scaffolding that holds me when everything else feels uncertain.

Each morning, I gather source material:

- A phrase that lingered as I drifted to sleep
- A passage from a book that wouldn't let me go
- A conversation that still echoes in my mind
- A question I've been avoiding

I don't force the words. I wait for them to find me. I sit with them. I breathe into them. I listen for the frequency beneath the syllables—the feeling tone that must accompany them if they are to reach beyond intellect into the body, where real transformation happens.

Then, I match the music. The music isn't background noise—it's the soul of the message. It gives weight to the silence between sentences. It allows the words to land not just in the mind but in the places beyond thought where meaning is felt before it's understood.

I refine. I adjust. I listen again. Then—and only then—I release it into the world. This is my devotion. Not a task on a list, but the way I sharpen the axe of my soul each day.

The First Domino of Sovereignty

I have learned, sometimes painfully, that I am the best in the world at what no one else can do for me:

Breathing for me. Thinking for me. Moving for me. Creating for me.

No one else can live these first two hours for me. No one else can make me intentional. No one else can make me awake. No one else can make me conscious. These are sovereign acts that cannot be outsourced or delegated.

If I get these first two hours right, everything else follows with a different quality. The first step in alignment leads naturally to the next. The first domino falls, and the path reveals itself not through planning but through presence.

The Negotiation With Resistance

Some mornings, Resistance waits for me at the edge of my bed. I know its voice intimately now.

"Stay a little longer," it whispers. "You've earned it."

It's persuasive. It knows my patterns, my vulnerabilities, and the exact tone that will make inaction seem reasonable, even necessary.

But I have trained myself to negotiate differently.

"Fine," I tell it. "After my feet hit the floor. After one sun salutation. After three squats. Then I'll decide."

And by then—the battle is already won. Not through force but through motion.

Resistance wants inertia. It wants to hold me in the limbo of indecision. But movement—even the smallest gesture in the direction of intention—shatters resistance more effectively than willpower ever could.

I do not ask myself if I feel like doing my morning ritual. I simply do it. And in that doing, I reclaim my sovereignty one breath, one movement, one moment at a time.

The Morning as Sacred Threshold

There is something holy about the morning—that first breath before the world rushes in, that space where yesterday is complete and today is still unfolding.

This is the threshold—the moment before anything has happened, where everything is still possible.

For years, I have honored this space. The morning is my place of renewal, where I return to myself—where I remember who I am before the demands, the expectations and the roles I play for others take shape. It is where I consciously choose who I will be today, rather than letting circumstance decide.

There was a time in my life when I didn't understand the power of beginnings. I thought momentum was something you built once, and then it carried you forward indefinitely.

But life does not move in a straight line. Growth is not a single decision—it is a daily recommitment. And the most powerful thing I have learned is this: Every day is a chance to begin again, not from where we fell, but from where we stand.

Reclaiming Each Day

Every morning, I wake up and reclaim my life.

There are no guarantees that the day will unfold as I expect. There are no promises that I won't face challenges, resistance, or setbacks.

But what I do have—what I always have—is the power to begin. To step into the day with awareness. To choose my thoughts before they choose me. To direct my energy rather than reacting to whatever comes.

This is what makes the ritual of beginning again so powerful: It is not about waiting for perfect conditions. It is about deciding, right now, that I am willing to engage fully with whatever lies before me—not because it's easy, but because it's mine.

The Price of Waking Up

There is a risk in everything.

The risk of not establishing this morning practice is clear: I move through the day less awake, less present, and less powerful. I lose the edge of self-mastery. I surrender to reaction rather than creation.

But there is also a risk in doing it: I can't go back to unconscious living. I can't unknow what happens when I start my day awake, intentional, and aligned.

And maybe that's the greatest risk of all—To wake up fully... To never again be able to sleepwalk through life... To know exactly how much is possible when we begin each day by reclaiming our sovereignty.

What's Next?

I have spent 52 days writing myself into greater awareness and deeper alignment.

But the real question is not what's next—It's who I choose to be next.

Who am I when I sharpen the axe of my soul every morning? Who am I when I refuse to let Autopilot Joe run my life? Who am I when I wake up knowing I am the best in the world at being me?

That is my question for today. And tomorrow. And every day after that.

Spill the ink. Drop the pen. The first two hours are waiting.

Chapter 47. The Breath & the Body: Listen to the Oldest Wisdom

The first thing I did when I arrived in this world was inhale. The last thing I will do before I leave is exhale.

And in between—breath has carried me through every moment. Yet, how rarely I have stopped to honor it.

For years, I chased success. I chased clarity. I chased time. I pushed forward—always moving, always doing, always seeking.

But what if the greatest clarity, the deepest wisdom, and the truest presence have been with me all along? What if they have always existed in the simplest, most fundamental rhythm of my life—breath?

The Forgotten Language

I inhale—slow, deep, expanding beyond what feels natural, filling every space within me. My heart quickens slightly, my mind sharpens, and my body awakens from the mild trance of shallow breathing.

This is what it feels like to receive. To allow. To welcome. To open.

I exhale—longer than the inhale, a deliberate release. A surrender. A letting go. My body softens, my mind clears.

This is what it feels like to give. To empty. To trust. To create space for something new.

Breath is the foundation of everything.

Without food, I can live for weeks. Without water, days. Without breath? Minutes.

And yet, for years, I unconsciously deprived myself of this gift. I let my breath become shallow, rushed, an afterthought—rather than a practice, a communion with my own aliveness.

The Training: Breath as Power

I remember the training. The discipline.

The electrical tape over my mouth during sleep, forcing my body to adapt, strengthen, and learn. The discomfort at first. The resistance. The struggle to rewire old patterns.

Until one day—it wasn't a struggle anymore.

It was power.

My VO2 max increased. My endurance improved. My clarity sharpened.

And it wasn't magic—it was breath. The same breath available to me all along, now harnessed, directed, honored.

Could it be that my breath has always held the key to my resilience, my focus, and my ability to endure? Not as metaphor, but as literal, physical reality?

The Three-Breath Reset

I close my eyes.

I empty my lungs completely. Empty, up, out, down, empty. Again.

Three deep breaths.

I feel the reset. I feel my body align. I feel my mind settle.

The snow globe clears, and all that remains is wisdom.

Breathing is not passive. It is the most intentional act I can engage in.

It detoxifies. It resets. It fuels.

It prunes away distractions, silences the noise, and makes space for insight.

Three breaths. Available anywhere. At any time. The simplest, most portable practice of presence I have ever found.

The Body Never Lies

There is a language older than words. It speaks in sensation, in breath, in the quiet pull of intuition. It doesn't argue. It doesn't explain. It doesn't try to convince.

It simply knows.

For most of my life, I have trained myself to listen. To pay attention to the subtle shifts inside me—the micro-adjustments my body makes before my mind catches up.

At 68, I am in the best shape of my life. Not because I push harder—but because I have learned to hear what my body is saying before it has to shout.

I call it split-second awareness—the moment I feel something shift inside me, and without hesitation, I translate it into action.

It's the instant I sense fatigue and step back. The moment I feel expansion and lean in. The flicker of knowing before thought arrives.

This is my practice. My body, my teacher.

Five Practices of Embodied Wisdom

The body does not think in words. It speaks in rhythm, in sensation, in flow. So, my daily disciplines are not about controlling the body—they are about tuning into its intelligence.

1. Breath: The First Signal

Before my mind wakes up, my breath is already speaking.

If I wake and my breath is short, I know something in me is holding back. If I breathe deep and easy, I trust the path ahead.

Before any decision, before any movement, before I open my mouth to speak—I listen to my breath.

It tells me everything.

2. Sleep: The Unconscious Whisper

I do not wake up and check my phone. I wake up and check my dreams.

Sleep is not just recovery—it is conversation. It is where the body integrates what the mind cannot process during waking hours.

If I wake up restless, I ask: What is unfinished? If I wake up clear, I ask: What is ready to begin?

My unconscious speaks to me at night. And I have trained myself to listen.

3. Nourishment: Eating What Aligns

I do not eat for fuel. I eat for alignment.

Food is not just calories—it is information, energy, vibration.

When I eat, I ask: Does this expand me or contract me? Does this bring clarity or dullness? Does this move me toward my future self or further from it?

At 68, my body is lean, strong, and awake—not because of a diet, but because I listen.

4. Movement: The Body's Natural Language

The mind thinks—but the body moves.

When I dance, when I walk, when I lift, when I stretch—I am not exercising. I am communicating with my body.

Strength training reminds me that I am capable. Dancing reminds me that I am free. Walking reminds me that clarity is found in motion, not in thought.

Movement is meditation. It is the practice of getting out of my head and into my life.

5. Stillness: The Deepest Listening

There is wisdom that only arrives in silence.

I sit in solitude—not to escape the world, but to hear what the world is trying to tell me.

Stillness is where I meet my future self. Stillness is where I hear the next step before I know what it means. Stillness is not passive. It is active receiving.

And when I create space for it, my body delivers exactly what I need to know.

The Body as Compass

Carl Jung said, "Until you make the unconscious conscious, it will direct your life, and you will call it fate."

This is what the body does—it makes the unconscious conscious.

A tightening in the throat before we speak a hard truth. A flutter in the gut before we step into something unknown. A weight on the chest before we acknowledge what is no longer ours to carry.

The body knows. The body knows. The body knows.

And now—so do I.

I listen without hesitation. I move when it says move. I rest when it says stop.

Because my body is not just my vehicle—it is my compass.

And it will never lead me astray.

Chapter 48. The Rhythm of Sleep & Eating for Aliveness

There is a rhythm to all things. The waves pull in, then retreat. The seasons change in their perfect cadence. The sun rises, then falls. The heart beats, expands, and contracts. Everything in nature pulses between activity and rest.

And yet, I have spent so much of my life resisting this rhythm. Pushing instead of pausing. Grinding instead of restoring. Forcing instead of allowing.

I have stolen from myself, borrowing energy I did not have as if my body were a credit card I could swipe endlessly without consequence. But the debt always comes due. Fatigue. Fog. Irritability. The slow erosion of clarity, creativity, and presence.

The Surrender to Sleep

For years, I believed sleep was something I could negotiate with, that I could outsmart it, cut corners, and push through. But I see now—sleep is not an obstacle to move around. It is the very foundation of everything.

I sit with this realization.

What happens when I let my future self take the pen? What happens when I surrender to the rhythm I was always meant to follow?

I inhale deeply, filling my lungs, my cells, and my mind. I exhale slowly, releasing tension, resistance, and the belief that I must always be "on." The moment I exhale, I feel the truth settle in.

Sleep is my restoration. Sleep is my recalibration. Sleep is where my mind clears, my body heals, and my spirit resets.

I imagine the version of me who sleeps deeply and fully. The version that respects the sacred act of restoration. What does he know that I have forgotten?

He knows that everything is better when well-rested. He knows that focus sharpens, emotions stabilize, and energy multiplies. He knows that sleep isn't just for the body; it is for the mind, for the soul, and for the future self who needs clarity to build what is next.

I see him standing before me. His eyes are clear. His breath is steady. He moves with ease, with a quiet power, with the kind of confidence that comes from being fully charged instead of constantly depleted.

I ask him—what is between me and the deep sleep I desire?

He points to the habits I have built that betray my best intentions. The glowing screen in my hand late at night. The restless mind that refuses to slow. The caffeine I use to fuel momentum instead of surrendering to rest. The belief that I must do more, be more, prove more—before I can rest.

And then I see it.

My present self has been resisting the very thing my future self is built upon: renewal.

Because rest is not idle. It is not wasted time. It is not weakness.

Rest is power.

My future self is waiting for me to honor this. To train myself in sleep the way I have trained in movement, breath, and discipline. To approach rest not as an afterthought but as a practice.

I make a decision.

I choose to end the day with intention, just as I begin it. I choose to close my eyes and trust that the work is done. I choose to let go, to let sleep carry me, to let renewal shape me.

And when I wake, I will wake as him.

My future self.

Rested. Clear. Ready.

What is possible when I devote a larger portion of my awareness to sleep?

Everything.

Eating for Aliveness

I am not a doctor, a scientist, or a nutritionist. But I am something far more important—I am the only one living inside this body. And I have spent a lifetime testing, refining, and listening.

Every bite I take is casting a vote. Either for energy, clarity, and longevity—or for fatigue, fog, and regret.

The simplest truth is this: some foods give me life, and some foods steal it from me.

I sit with this truth. I let it settle into my body. What happens when I choose aliveness?

I think about the moments when I have felt truly vibrant—when my body was strong, my mind was clear, my spirit was steady. Those moments were not random. They were earned. They were the result of a thousand small choices stacked upon one another like bricks building the foundation of my future self.

And yet, I have also known the weight of poor choices. The sluggishness, the fog, the frustration. I have watched myself reach for food that numbs rather than nourishes. I have justified, delayed, and promised myself that tomorrow, I would be better.

But my future self does not live in tomorrow. He lives in this moment, in this decision, in this bite.

I close my eyes and listen.

What does my future self desire?

He desires clarity. Strength. Energy that sustains, not spikes and crashes. He desires a body that feels like home, not a burden to be carried. He desires ease, not struggle.

And he reminds me—it's not about perfection. It's about intention.

Food is not just fuel. It is instruction. Every meal is a message to my body, a conversation with my future self.

I ask myself—what do I want that message to be?

I breathe deeply and remember: I do not need rules. I need awareness.

I do not need to count calories. I need to count the cost of unconscious choices. I do not need to follow a diet. I need to follow how I feel. I do not need to deprive myself. I need to honor myself.

There is no universal blueprint. No one-size-fits-all. There is only the deep listening to what my body already knows.

I ask myself again: what is between me and my most alive self?

I see the patterns. I see the stories I have told myself about food. I see the ways I have used it as comfort, as a reward, as an escape.

And I see something else—I see my power to choose differently.

My future self stands before me—clear-eyed, strong, fully alive. He is not judging me. He is not disappointed. He simply asks: Are you ready to wake up?

I nod.

I choose food that is real, whole, and vibrant. I choose to slow down, to savor, to be present. I choose to let go of guilt, of judgment, of all-or-nothing thinking.

Because this is not about discipline. This is about devotion.

To myself. To my energy. To my future.

I place my hands on the table, look at what is before me, and ask: Will this bring me more life? Will this honor the person I am becoming?

If the answer is yes, I eat with gratitude. If the answer is no, I let it go with love.

Because I know now: aliveness is not a diet. It is a decision. And my body already knows the way.

Today, I listen. Today, I choose life.

Chapter 49. The Ecology of Attention: What I Choose to Cultivate

Attention is currency. The most valuable thing I own isn't my time, my knowledge, or my experience—it's my attention. It is what I choose to see, what I choose to engage with, and what I choose to nurture.

And yet, the world is built to steal it.

I've learned that attention is not something I have—it's something I train. It is a living ecosystem, constantly shaped by what I feed it, where I direct it, and what I allow to occupy its space.

When I give my full, undivided attention to something, it thrives. When I fragment it, spread it too thin, or let distractions pull me away, everything suffers.

I know what it feels like to be here—fully engaged, fully present, fully alive. And I know what it feels like to be elsewhere—my body in one place, my mind in another, my energy scattered.

The difference is everything.

What Deserves My Undivided Attention?

There is a moment before distraction—a flicker of awareness. A pause before I reach for my phone. A breath before my mind scatters. A decision before I let something meaningless pull me away from something essential.

That moment is the difference between a life of presence and a life of reaction.

When I ask myself, What deserves my undivided attention?—it is not a question of time. It is a question of devotion.

Not all work is equal. Not all conversations are equal. Not all moments are equal.

Some things are worth everything I have. Some things don't deserve a single second more.

So I ask:

What, if I gave it my full attention, would change everything? What, if I ignored it, would cost me something I can never get back? What, if I devoted myself to it fully, would unlock something extraordinary?

The answer is never about urgency. It is always about meaning.

Focus is a Decision

Attention is not passive. It is a choice. Every day, I decide:

Will I be present in this conversation, or will I check my phone? Will I stay in this creative flow, or will I let my mind wander? Will I give my full self to my work, my relationships, and my own growth—or will I let myself be pulled in a thousand directions?

Some people don't make this choice consciously. They let the world decide for them. They let notifications, emails, algorithms, and distractions dictate where their energy goes.

But I know better. I know that if I do not choose what gets my attention, someone else will.

The greatest work of my life has come not from doing more but from choosing better.

The Garden of My Mind

I am the gardener. My thoughts are the seeds. My mind is the soil.

Somewhere along the way, I forgot just how much power I have over what grows here.

For years, I have tended to this garden—pulling weeds, planting ideas, watering beliefs, pruning habits. Some have flourished, some have withered. Some have taken deep root without my consent, growing wild in the shadows of my subconscious. Others I have deliberately cultivated and nurtured with care and intention.

But today, I stand in my garden with new awareness.

I ask myself:

What am I still watering, even though it no longer grows? What am I unconsciously cultivating? And what do I need to plant instead?

Because there is no neutrality in the subconscious. It absorbs everything.

If I speak to myself in frustration, my subconscious believes it. If I reinforce stories of lack, they will continue to manifest. If I operate on autopilot, my life will reflect it.

But the reverse is also true.

If I speak to myself with kindness, my subconscious will shape itself around that love. If I reinforce stories of abundance, I will see more of it. If I move through my day with conscious intention, I will reshape my reality.

So today, I take back control of what I plant.

I choose to stop watering what depletes me. I choose to cultivate habits that align with the person I am becoming, not the person I have been. I choose to edit my rituals—not just to remove what does not serve me, but to replace it with something better.

What Stays, What Goes

There are habits that serve me. They stay.

My morning practice. Sitting at my altar. Meditating. Letting silence fill the space before the world rushes in.

My physical movement. The way my body tells me the truth before my mind does. The way sweat, breath, and rhythm recalibrate me.

My creative work. Writing. Speaking. Building. Creating from a place of deep connection.

My devotion to learning. Every book, every conversation, every exploration of a new idea that expands my world.

My generosity. The way I give, not just with money, but with presence.

And then there are the habits, routines, and rituals that no longer serve me. They go.

The constant checking of the external. Email. Messages. Social media. The illusion that something urgent "out there" is more important than what is present in here.

The small, daily self-betrayals. Saying yes when I mean no. Ignoring the whisper of intuition. Postponing the things I know bring me peace.

The justification of exhaustion. Allowing "being busy" to substitute for being fulfilled.

The subtle self-judgments. The quick criticisms I pass over—but my subconscious absorbs fully.

I cannot control every thought that passes through my mind. But I can control which ones I nurture.

Tending to My Garden

I close my eyes and imagine myself standing in the garden of my mind.

I see the flowers that are thriving—the parts of me deeply rooted in truth, love, and power. I also see the weeds—small, tangled thoughts that, if left unchecked, will choke out what I most want to grow.

So today, I take action.

I pull the weeds. The limiting beliefs. The unconscious patterns. The things I do because I always have rather than because they serve me now.

I plant new seeds. Thoughts of possibility. Routines that energize me. Rituals that elevate me.

I water what matters. My time, my energy, my presence—poured intentionally into what brings me joy, not what simply fills space.

And I recognize that growth takes time.

I don't need to change everything in a day. I don't need to rip up my entire garden in a moment of frustration. I only need to begin.

One small shift. One new choice. One adjustment toward the light.

Because in the end:

I am not my habits. I am not my routines. I am not my rituals.

I am the gardener. And I decide what grows.

Chapter 50. The Habit I Must Build & The Art of Devotion

Regret as the Fuel for Change

Regret whispers at the edges of my awareness—not for what I have done, but for what I have not yet committed to. It is not the bold mistakes or the reckless attempts that haunt me. It is the hesitations, the postponed decisions, the unfulfilled intentions.

There is something I must do. A habit I must build. Or I will wake up one day, look back, and ache for having let it slip away.

The question is not whether I should build it. The question is: Why haven't I already?

Facing the Hard Truth: What Will I Regret?

I imagine myself at 100 years old, looking back at this moment.

What is the thing I wish I had done every single day? What will I ache for, knowing I had the time but not the discipline?

Will I regret...

Not carving out sacred time each morning for silence—to hear what only stillness can reveal?

Not fully embodying my physical health, building a body that carries me effortlessly into old age instead of one I have to battle against?

Not letting myself truly love, keeping an arms-length distance from the kind of closeness that would demand all of me?

Not documenting my life—not just through ideas, but through presence, engagement, and contribution?

I don't fear failure. I don't fear judgment. I fear waking up one day and realizing I had the time, I had the ability, and I let the moment pass.

Breaking the Loop: What Needs to Change Today?

If I continue doing what I've always done, I won't just keep getting the same results—I'll reinforce the pattern until it becomes even harder to undo.

So, I decide today:

What is my prompt? The signal that tells my brain, It's time. No negotiation. No avoidance.

What is my new routine? The habit I will repeat until it becomes automatic.

How will I reinforce this so that it becomes who I am, not just something I do?

Because here's the truth: I don't want to try to build this habit. I want to become the person who just does it.

Self-Mastery and the Absence of Regret

Self-mastery isn't about willpower—it's about alignment. It's about creating a system where I don't have to keep choosing—the habit is chosen once and then simply lived.

The version of me that has already built this habit exists. The question is—do I step into him?

Warren Buffett said: "Chains of habit are too light to be felt until they are too heavy to be broken."

The heaviest regrets aren't the big, dramatic failures. They are the small, daily decisions not to show up for myself.

So here it is—the truth I must say now before it's too late:

I will not let regret be my teacher. I will not be the person who had all the time and let it slip through his fingers. I will make this habit part of me now.

Because my future self—the one looking back at this moment—will thank me for it. And when that moment comes, I will know:

I did not waste this.

The Art of Devotion: Choosing One Discipline

I used to believe mastery was an all-or-nothing pursuit. That discipline meant rigid adherence to an impossible standard. That transformation required fixing everything at once.

But I see now—true mastery is not about conquering everything. It is about devotion.

The tightrope walker does not stay perfectly balanced. He adjusts. Micro-movements. Tiny shifts. Moment to moment.

Mastery is not about holding still—it is about staying in relationship with the movement itself.

And today, I choose just one.

One discipline. One breath. One step forward.

Because mastery is not about volume—it is about depth.

The Keystone Habit

I close my eyes. I breathe. I listen.

What is my keystone?

The five disciplines—breath, sleep, eating, meditation, and movement—are not separate. They are spokes on the same wheel. Each one turns the others.

But there is always one that calls louder than the rest.

One that—if honored—sets all the others in motion.

I listen. What is my body asking for? What is my mind craving? What is my soul gently nudging me toward?

I hear it clearly now.

Movement as Prayer

Movement is not just exercise. It is an expression of aliveness.

When I move, I do not just strengthen my muscles—I soften my resistance. When I move, I do not just burn calories—I burn away stagnation. When I move, I do not just increase endurance—I increase my capacity to feel.

Movement is a conversation with life itself. It is an offering. A prayer. A signal to my future self that I am willing to show up, that I am devoted to the process, and that I am listening.

Some days, movement is sweat, strain, the pounding of feet against the earth, and the fire in my lungs. Other days, it is stillness—the deep, subtle work of sitting in perfect posture, letting my breath move instead.

Today, my movement is breath-led, heart-guided. A dance with gravity.

One Simple Devotion

I make a decision.

I will not sit for more than 20 minutes at a time. A timer will remind me. When it rings, I will rise. I will stretch, sway, shift, reset.

I will take three short walks—no more than ten minutes each. Not to get anywhere, not to achieve, but just to be in my body, to feel the earth beneath my feet.

I will pay attention to how I move—not just in the gym, not just in structured time, but in the micro-moments—how I stand, how I breathe, how I hold myself in space.

This is my devotion for today. One thing. One focus.

The Power of One

I once believed transformation had to be grand and dramatic. But it is never the sweeping change that reshapes a life.

It is the tiny, consistent, intentional choices made every day.

One discipline today. One percent better. One promise kept.

I whisper to my future self:

"I am here. I am listening. I am in motion."

And my future self whispers back:

"I see you. Keep going."

Now, close your eyes. Breathe deeply.

What is your one? What is your devotion today?

Taste 5: The Architecture of Self

Building the Inner Structures That Support Growth

Before anything can rise, it must be rooted.

Before a bridge can bear weight, before a house can offer shelter, before a life can expand—it must be structured from within.

I've spent decades building—businesses, relationships, influence, legacies. I've measured my life through milestones, numbers, achievements that others could see and applaud. But beneath every trophy, every accolade, every moment of external validation, something deeper was at work:

The unseen architecture of self.

Because no matter what I construct in the external world, it will only be as strong as the foundation inside me. The structures I've built have collapsed before, not because they weren't engineered brilliantly, but because I hadn't yet built myself to hold them.

So I ask myself now, with unflinching honesty—

What are the structures that truly hold me steady? What invisible frameworks shape my thoughts, my choices, my identity? Am I constructing from truth, from alignment, from integrity—or am I building on borrowed beliefs, fragile assumptions, outdated blueprints that were handed to me but never questioned?

And perhaps the most sobering question I've finally found the courage to ask— What have I built that cannot hold the weight of who I am becoming?

Building Up or Excavating Down?

For much of my life, I believed growth was about adding. Stacking more knowledge, more discipline, more success onto the framework of who I already was. The more I acquired, the stronger I would become.

But now I see it differently. With clarity that cuts to the bone.

Growth isn't always about building up. Sometimes, it's about tearing down.

Sometimes, it's about dismantling the scaffolding that no longer serves me, stripping away the unnecessary, the conditioned, the inherited. I've spent years of my life maintaining structures that were never mine to begin with—expectations inherited from my father, standards absorbed from mentors, limitations I accepted as truth because I heard them spoken with authority.

Because real self-worth isn't something I manufacture—it's something I uncover beneath the rubble of who I thought I needed to be. Real confidence isn't something I accumulate—it's something I remember when I stop trying to be someone I'm not.

And the truth is, no matter how much I build, if the foundation beneath me is cracked, the weight of it all will inevitably collapse.

I have seen this in my own life. Felt it in my bones.

The moments when external success couldn't hold the weight of internal doubt. The times I chased achievement as if it would make me whole—only to feel the same emptiness on the other side of it. The years I spent strengthening the structure of my business while neglecting the structure of my self until both began to crumble under the weight of the lie.

So now, I turn inward with a ferocity that terrifies the parts of me still clinging to the old ways.

This is not about what I build, but what builds me. Not about the empire I create, but the architecture of self that determines whether I am built to hold it—or whether it is slowly crushing me.

The Frameworks That Shape Us

Self-esteem—not as a fragile ego to defend, but as an immune system that protects, strengthens, and stabilizes. I've watched mine falter in boardrooms where I should have stood strongest, and seen it rise unexpectedly in moments of complete surrender.

The inner council—the many voices inside me, the ones that push, doubt, create, hesitate—and learning how to orchestrate, rather than suppress, them. I've spent too many years letting only the loudest voices—the achiever, the critic—run the show, while neglecting the quiet wisdom of other parts of myself.

The balance of structure and flow—the paradox of discipline and freedom, knowing when to build strong walls and when to open doors. I've lived at both extremes and felt the cost of each. The rigidity that suffocates creativity, the formlessness that dissipates power.

The power of belief—understanding that every thought I repeat becomes a brick in the architecture of my mind. I've built prisons with my thoughts, and I've built cathedrals. The difference wasn't in circumstance but in what I chose to believe about myself.

The necessity of pause—because in the space between action and reaction, between stimulus and response, is where I shape the self I am becoming. In those breaths between moments, I've found myself either strengthening old patterns or forging new ones.

The Real Work

There was a time when I thought my work was about achievement. When I measured my worth by metrics and milestones.

Now I know, with bone-deep certainty: My real work is about alignment.

Because in the end, success isn't just about what I build. It's about whether I am built to hold it. Whether the external creations of my life are reflections of my truest self, or elaborate distractions from it.

And that—more than anything—determines whether what I create will enrich me or deplete me, whether it will last or crumble, whether it will fulfill me or leave me hollow.

Chapter 51. Self-Esteem as an Immune System

"What if my self-esteem isn't something to build, but something to uncover?"

There was a time when I thought self-esteem was something I had to manufacture. That if I worked hard enough, achieved enough, performed well enough, I would construct a version of myself that was finally solid, impenetrable, beyond doubt. I collected accomplishments like armor, thinking they would protect me from the vulnerability of being truly seen.

I was wrong. Catastrophically wrong.

Self-esteem isn't built through achievement. It's protected. It's strengthened. It's uncovered from beneath the layers of conditioning, the early whispers of not enough, the moments where I absorbed the world's judgments as my own. It was there all along, before the world taught me to question it.

If my physical body has an immune system that shields me from external threats, why would my sense of self be any different?

A strong self-esteem does not mean I never feel doubt—it means that doubt does not infect me. It does not spread through my entire being, does not take root in every decision, does not turn into the paralysis that has kept me frozen at critical moments of my life. A weak self-esteem, though? It means every criticism lingers for days, echoing in my mind at 3 AM. Every rejection festers into evidence of my fundamental unworthiness. Every moment of uncertainty spirals into a story of inadequacy that feels more true than any accomplishment.

And I've lived both extremes. I know the difference in my body, not just my mind.

I know what it feels like to be solid, unshakable, trusting my own knowing even when the world pushes against it. To stand in a room of doubters and hold my truth without defensiveness or apology.

And I know what it feels like to be fragile—to walk into a room and immediately scan for approval, to hold my words back for fear they will be misinterpreted, to shrink just a little when met with resistance. I've given presentations to thousands while a voice inside whispered I wasn't enough, made decisions that affected hundreds of employees while secretly fearing I was a fraud.

I know the version of me that moves freely, untethered from the weight of needing to be liked. And I know the version of me that hesitates, waiting for permission that will never come, holding back the fullness of who I am because I'm afraid it's too much.

And so I ask myself, with ruthless honesty—how strong is my self-esteem immune system right now?

Not in theory. Not in philosophy. Not in the motivational quotes I post. But in the way I live. In the way I move. In the way I wake up and take my first breath of the day.

Am I bracing for impact? Or am I open to experience? Am I reacting from old wounds? Or am I grounded in present truth? Am I outsourcing my worth to metrics and opinions? Or do I already know who I am, regardless of performance?

Because the difference between survival and stability, between fragility and resilience, between self-doubt and self-trust is not found in some external achievement or validation.

It is found in the inner architecture of how I hold myself. How I speak to myself when no one is listening. How I treat myself when I fail. How I honor or dishonor my own boundaries.

And if self-esteem is my immune system, then today—I strengthen it. Not by doing more, but by undoing the beliefs that have weakened it.

Chapter 52. The Expansion of Joy

"How long can I allow joy before I sabotage it?"

For years, I thought happiness was something to chase. Something that existed in some mythical future state, once all the conditions were perfect.

I thought it was a prize, something earned, something I had to work toward. That when I reached a certain level of success, or built the right kind of life, or aligned all the external pieces just so—then I would finally feel it. Then I would be allowed to rest in it.

But joy does not work that way. And I've paid dearly for not understanding this sooner.

Because every time I reached a place where I should have felt content—where I had every reason to exhale, to relax, to trust the goodness of my own life—I felt something else creeping in.

Restlessness. Discomfort. A whisper in my mind saying, This won't last. You don't deserve this. The other shoe is about to drop.

And before I knew it, I was disrupting my own peace. Picking fights in relationships that were going well. Piling more work onto my plate when I'd earned a break. Finding some new way to prove my worth, to maintain momentum, to stay moving so I never had to sit still long enough to actually feel my own happiness.

It took me years to see the pattern. Decades, if I'm honest.

That the problem wasn't that I hadn't reached happiness—it was that I didn't know how to hold it. That I felt unsafe in joy.

That I had trained my nervous system for struggle, for survival, for striving—but I had never trained it for ease, for pleasure, for peace.

That I could endure pain, outlast hardship, push through resistance—but I could not simply let myself be happy without also preparing for it to disappear. Without also feeling that I needed to earn it anew each day.

And so I ask myself, with a tenderness I am still learning—how long can I allow joy before I sabotage it?

How long can I sit inside my own life, fully present, without looking for the next thing to fix? How long can I let things be good without anticipating their unraveling? How long can I feel loved without questioning if I deserve it?

Because holding joy is a practice. One that my driven, achievement-oriented self resists in ways both subtle and obvious.

And maybe that is the next threshold of mastery for me—not learning how to push through, but learning how to stay inside what I once feared was too good to last. Not learning how to strive harder but learning how to receive more deeply.

Maybe my work is not to fight for joy. Maybe my work is to stop fighting joy when it arrives.

Because if I cannot sit with happiness without running, then what exactly have I been running toward? What future state am I imagining that would finally allow me to rest, if not this one?

And so today—I stay. Today—I let joy settle in my bones without trying to rush it out the door. Today—I expand my capacity to feel good.

Not just for a moment. Not just until I find the next problem to solve. But for as long as I will allow myself to hold it. Which means confronting the part of me that believes I am only valuable when I am striving, only worthy when I am achieving, and only safe when I am preparing for the worst.

Today, I practice staying in joy until joy becomes the foundation, not the exception.

Chapter 53. The Inner Council - Who Sits at the Table?

"If I am not one voice but many, how do I listen deeply to them all?"

I used to think I was just one person. One voice. One mind. One coherent, consistent self.

But when I sit in stillness, when I quiet the external noise and listen deeply, I hear them. The council. The gathering of selves inside me. Some voices I have known for years—the strategist who sees ten moves ahead, the builder who turns vision into reality, the protector who scans for threats before they materialize. Others I have silenced, ignored, buried beneath ambition and movement.

They sit at the table of my consciousness, whether I acknowledge them or not. Whether I hear them or not. Whether I honor them or not.

There is the achiever, who moves with relentless urgency, who speaks in deadlines and objectives, who whispers, "More. Keep going. Never stop. Never enough." I know his voice intimately—it's gotten me far, but at what cost?

There is the critic, sharp-eyed and merciless, who finds every flaw before the world has the chance to, who tightens his grip whenever I come too close to uncertainty or vulnerability. I've let him run the show for too long, mistaking his harshness for clarity.

There is the wounded child, still waiting for permission, still bracing for rejection, still wondering if he is truly welcome here. I've spent decades pretending he wasn't there, pushing forward while he stood frozen in time, carrying the weight of early hurts I refused to feel.

There is the philosopher who steps back from the fray, questions assumptions, observes rather than reacts, and reminds me that the game I am playing is not the only game there is. I've often dismissed him as impractical, yet he sees what my ambitious self misses.

There is the creator, who wants nothing to do with structure or strategy or deadlines—who just wants to make, to explore, to spill ideas onto the page with no agenda beyond truth. I've silenced him when his wildness threatened my carefully constructed plans.

There is the one who longs for silence, who waits for me at the altar every morning, who does not speak in words but in breath, in presence, in the slow, deliberate exhale of knowing. I've rushed past him countless times, too busy to pause, too driven to be still.

I have spent years letting some voices dominate. Letting the achiever run the show, letting the critic keep me "sharp," letting the wounded child hide in the corner, unseen and unheard. But what happens when I give them all a seat? When I listen to the voices I've silenced?

What happens when I stop letting one voice define me?

Because I have been all of them, at different times, in different measures, I have been the one who pushes beyond limits and the one who retreats in fear. I have been the one who builds empires and the one who burns it all down when it feels empty. I have been the one who loves without condition and the one who disappears when vulnerability feels too threatening.

And if all of them are me, then who is the one listening?

That is the real question. The question that changes everything.

The one who listens is not any single voice. The one who listens is the chair at the head of the table. The one who listens is the stillness before the decision. The one who listens is the awareness that I am more than any one part of me—I am the space that holds them all.

I used to let my loudest voices run my life. The ones that spoke with urgency, the ones that demanded to be heard, and the ones that promised safety through control. Now, I do something different.

I call the council to order. I let every voice speak, especially the quiet ones that have been waiting years to be heard. And then, before I move forward, before I act, before I decide—I ask:

Who is truly leading today? Which voice am I following? Which self am I embodying?

Because if I do not choose consciously which voice to follow, the old patterns will choose for me. The familiar pathways, carved deep by repetition, will become the default.

And I refuse to be ruled by voices that no longer serve the man I am becoming. I refuse to let the critic's fear drown out the creator's wisdom. I refuse to let the achiever's drive silence the mystic's knowing.

Today, I listen to them all. And then I choose, with clarity and intention, which voice will lead.

Chapter 54. The Inner Teacher - Listening for the Quietest Voice

"What does the wisest part of me know that I have not yet accepted?"

There is a voice inside me that does not shout. That has never shouted, even when I needed its guidance most desperately.

It does not argue. It does not fight for dominance the way my achiever does, the way my critic does, or the way my strategist does.

It waits. Patiently, endlessly, it waits.

It waits in the moments between thoughts. In the breath between sentences. In the pause before I answer a question that I already know the truth to but hesitate to speak because of what it might cost me.

For years, I ignored it. Not because I couldn't hear it—but because I wasn't ready for what it would say.

Because the inner teacher does not tell me what I want to hear. It tells me what I already know, deep in my bones, but have not yet had the courage to accept or act upon.

It is the voice that said, "You are no longer meant to be in this place," long before I admitted it to myself. It is the voice that whispered, Let go, long before I loosened my grip on the relationship that was beautiful but complete. It is the voice that knew when a business had served its purpose, when a chapter was closing, and when the next step would require me to walk alone for a while.

I did not always listen. Often, I actively silenced it.

I stayed in places longer than I should have, forcing enthusiasm for work that no longer lit me up inside. I held on to things that were already finished, relationships where love remained but growth had ceased. I argued with myself, pretended not to know what I knew, and filled the silence with movement and noise and distraction so I wouldn't have to hear what the quiet voice was telling me.

But the inner teacher does not go away. It cannot be permanently silenced.

It does not force. It does not beg. It simply waits for me to become quiet enough to hear it again.

And the moment I get quiet enough, the moment I stop filling every empty space with noise, with strategy, with the constant movement that keeps me from feeling what needs to be felt—it is there. As it always has been.

So I ask myself, with a humility that once would have felt like weakness: What is it saying now?

If I could strip away all the shoulds, all the expectations, all the calculations of what makes practical sense—what does my deepest knowing tell me about the path ahead?

Because that is the voice I must follow if I want to live a life of authenticity and purpose.

Not the loudest. Not the most persuasive. Not the one that promises safety or certainty. But the one that speaks with quiet, unwavering certainty from the center of who I am.

The one that knows before my mind has caught up. The one that sees around corners my strategic thinking cannot imagine.

And when I hear it—when I finally have the courage to listen—the only question left is:

Do I have the courage to follow where it leads? Even when it asks me to let go of identities I've carried for decades? Even when it guides me toward uncertainty? Even when it requires me to disappoint others to honor myself?

This is the precipice I stand on now. The edge between the life I've known and the life that awaits if I listen to the quietest voice.

Now we're back inside the work. This is the voice. This is the excavation. What's landing? What needs to shift?

Chapter 55. The Riverbanks of Freedom - Balancing Structure and Flow

I have lived at both extremes.

I have built structures so rigid they became cages, their bars invisible until I tried to move freely within them. I have followed flow so recklessly I lost my footing, mistaking chaos for freedom until I found myself unmoored.

And somewhere between those two—between discipline and surrender, between structure and fluidity—I have found the space where I can breathe. Where I can create. Where I can fully become.

A river without banks is a flood, destructive in its formlessness. A life without boundaries is chaos; energy dissipated without direction. Yet a life with too many rules is suffocation, vitality crushed beneath the weight of shoulds and musts.

I have spent years designing frameworks. For my business—systematic approaches that built eight-figure success. For my body—training protocols that pushed physical limits. For my relationships—clear agreements that defined expectations. For my mind—practices that focused scattered attention into laser precision.

And yet, for all my mastery in building structure, I have also felt the quiet exhaustion of being trapped inside my own creation. The subtle deadening that comes when discipline hardens into rigidity.

Because sometimes the very things I build to support me become the things that define me. The systems I create to serve me begin to own me instead.

And there is nothing more dangerous than forgetting that I am more than what I build. That I am the builder, not the building.

When Structure Becomes a Cage

There was a time when I thought success meant control.

Control over my time. Control over my work. Control over how others saw me. Control over outcomes that were never truly mine to determine.

I created routines that ensured my output. Systems that guaranteed my effectiveness. Schedules so optimized that spontaneity became an interruption rather than an opportunity. I knew how to make things work with ruthless efficiency.

But something in me resisted. Something deeper than my strategic mind.

It wasn't loud at first—just a whisper beneath the productivity. A hesitation before I sat down to write according to schedule. A subtle exhaustion in conversations I once loved. A feeling in my body that said, this is working, but it isn't alive.

I had built a structure so strong that I left no room for evolution. No space for the unknown. No allowance for the parts of me that couldn't be optimized or measured.

And the cost?

I stopped listening to what was emerging. I stopped feeling the natural rhythms of creativity and rest. I stopped trusting anything that couldn't be planned or predicted.

Because structure, when it is not allowed to breathe, becomes a prison.

It tells you that the way you've done it is the way you must always do it. It tells you that momentum is more important than presence. It tells you that there is too much at stake to question the path you're on. It whispers that deviation means failure.

And that is the most dangerous belief of all.

Because the truth is, the path must always be questioned. It must be allowed to evolve as I evolve. It must bend with the seasons of my life.

So, I did what terrified me. I broke my own rules.

I let myself wander without agenda. I said no to opportunities that once would have defined success. I stopped forcing myself to follow structures that no longer fit the man I was becoming.

And in that space, something shifted. Something opened.

I realized that structure should never be about control. It should be about supporting what is most alive in me at any given moment.

When Flow Becomes Distraction

But there is another side to this truth.

Because the opposite of control is not freedom—it is drift. It is aimlessness mistaken for liberation.

I have had seasons where I resisted all structure in the name of authenticity.

I told myself I was living in flow. I told myself I was following inspiration. I told myself I was giving myself space to evolve beyond rigid systems.

But the truth, when I finally had the courage to see it?

I was avoiding commitment. I was evading the depth that only comes through focused devotion.

I was keeping my options open not because I was free but because I was afraid.

Afraid to anchor into something that required depth. Afraid to choose one path and close the door to another. Afraid to be held accountable—to be responsible—to be fully in something rather than skimming the surface of everything.

There were days I let this resistance keep me from writing when the blank page felt intimidating. Keep me from training when my body craved comfort over growth. Keep me from deepening relationships that deserved more from me than sporadic attention.

And I learned something essential:

Flow without direction is not freedom. It is distraction disguised as liberation.

Without structure, I float rather than swim. Without structure, I lose the depth that only comes from repetition, devotion, and showing up even when I don't feel like it. Without structure, inspiration remains a fleeting visitor rather than a cultivated presence.

I was mistaking openness for avoidance. I was calling my fear of commitment "spontaneity."

So, I came back to structure, but differently this time.

Not to the old, rigid way. Not to the inflexible systems. But to a structure that held me without suffocating me. To boundaries that protected what mattered without blocking what needed to enter.

I began carving out time—not to force productivity, but to deepen presence. I began protecting my energy—not to shut people out, but to give fully where it mattered most. I began honoring discipline—not as control, but as devotion to what truly matters.

Because structure is not the enemy of my authentic self. It is the foundation that allows authenticity to express itself powerfully.

And flow is not the absence of structure. It is the energy that moves within the structure, the current that brings it to life.

I need both. The container and what it contains. The banks of the river and the water that moves within them.

The Discipline of Boundaries

There was a time when I thought boundaries were walls. That they existed to keep things out to create separation.

That saying no was shutting people out. That protecting my energy was selfish. That prioritizing my needs would diminish my impact rather than enhance it.

But what I see now is this:

Boundaries are not restrictions. They are declarations of what matters most.

They are the way I say: This is what I value. This is what I will protect. This is what I will give myself fully to because it deserves nothing less than my full presence.

Boundaries are not about separation. They are about wholeness. About integrity in the truest sense of the word—the state of being undivided.

Because without them, I do not belong to myself. I become fragmented, scattered across too many commitments, and diluted across too many priorities.

I have learned to hold my own edges with both firmness and compassion.

To stop giving from depletion. To stop proving my worth through over-commitment. To stop stretching myself so thin that there is nothing left of me to give to what matters most.

Because when I say yes to everything, I am fully present for nothing. I offer the world a diminished version of myself rather than the full force of my presence and gifts.

And I refuse to live that way anymore. I refuse to confuse busyness with purpose or accessibility with impact.

Where I Stand Now

So, where do I stand now? What have I learned in the tension between structure and flow?

I wake up early—not because I have to, not because some productivity guru prescribed it, but because I know that my best thinking happens before the world wakes up before the demands of others shape my attention.

I write—not because I am chasing an outcome or building a platform but because I am committed to my own excavation, to uncovering truths that lie beneath the surface of my conscious mind.

I move my body—not because I fear losing something, not because I'm chasing some ideal physique, but because I know the cost of stagnation, because movement is how I process emotion, because strength in body creates strength in spirit.

I protect what matters with fierce intention. I allow what wants to move through me with open hands.

Some days, I follow a plan with precision. Some days, I burn the plan and follow something deeper, something that cannot be scheduled but must be honored when it appears.

This is the balance. This is the work.

To build the banks so that the river can flow freely without dissipating. To create the structure so that inspiration can move with direction rather than scattering. To trust that I will not lose myself in either extreme.

This is what I know now:

Freedom is not the absence of structure. Structure is not the absence of freedom.

Real freedom is knowing when to hold firm and when to let go. When to maintain boundaries and when to dissolve them. When to follow the plan and when to follow the soul's unexpected promptings.

And today, as I stand at the edge of what is next, I ask myself with both pragmatism and intuition:

Where do I need more structure to channel my energy? Where do I need more flow to revitalize what has become rigid?

Because I know that the answer will shape everything that comes next. It will determine whether I build a life that looks impressive but feels empty or one that may appear simpler from the outside but pulses with authenticity from within.

Chapter 56. Living What You Believe - The Ethics of Self-Alignment

I used to think beliefs were private—something that lived in my head and shaped my inner world but remained separate from the reality around me.

But the truth is, beliefs leak. They shape my choices, my words, my posture, and the energy I bring into a room. They define what I allow, what I accept, what I expect, and what I create.

A belief is not just a thought I hold. It is a thought that holds me. That shapes me. That either expands or contracts the possibilities I can perceive.

And if I say I believe something, but my actions tell a different story, the dissonance is unbearable. Not because of what others might think but because I can feel it in my body. In my breath. In the subtle tension that accumulates when I am out of alignment with myself.

I feel it when I speak words that don't align with my core truth. I feel it when I make a choice that betrays what I know is right for me. I feel it when I justify an action that serves my convenience over my integrity.

And I feel it most acutely when I look in the mirror and realize— I am not yet fully living what I claim to believe. That there is still a gap between my highest values and my daily choices.

The Architecture of Belief

A belief is just a thought I keep thinking. And the more I repeat it, the more solid it becomes—like a river carving a canyon into stone. What begins as a trickle becomes a gorge over time.

But not all beliefs are conscious. Not all beliefs serve me. Not all beliefs were deliberately chosen.

Some were inherited, passed down like old furniture—worn, outdated, yet still taking up space in my mind because I never questioned if they belonged there.

Some were formed in moments of pain—a single failure, a single rejection, a single wound that whispered, Never again. And without examining it, I let that whisper become a wall that limited what I believed was possible.

Some were shaped by survival—the things I told myself to make sense of what I didn't understand, to protect myself from what felt threatening, and to navigate a world that seemed unpredictable.

And so the work is not just to ask, What do I believe? But Where did this belief come from? Is it mine? Did I choose it consciously? And is it still true for the person I am becoming?

The Friction of Misalignment

There have been moments in my life where I said I believed in something—claimed it as a core value, even preached it to others—but my actions exposed the gap between declaration and embodiment.

I said I valued presence, yet I filled my days so full there was no space for stillness, no margin for the unexpected, no room to simply be rather than do.

I said I valued deep relationships, yet I kept people at arm's length, afraid to be fully seen, afraid to be vulnerable, afraid to let anyone close enough to see the parts of me that didn't match the carefully crafted image.

I said I wanted to live freely, yet I clung to the familiar because it felt safer than stepping into the unknown, clung to identities that no longer fit because they were at least predictable.

Every time I said one thing but did another, I could feel the friction. Not as guilt. Not as shame. But as an invitation.

An invitation to close the gap. To let my actions rise to the level of my beliefs or to have the courage to admit that perhaps I didn't truly believe what I claimed to.

Because there is a kind of peace that only comes from knowing—I am who I say I am. I live what I say I value. My outer world reflects my inner truth.

And when it doesn't, I have the awareness to notice, the honesty to admit it, and the courage to realign.

Integrity is a Practice, Not a Destination

For a long time, I thought ethical living was about perfection. About never making the wrong choice, never slipping, never failing, never contradicting myself.

But now I see—it is not about never falling. It is about noticing when I have fallen and standing back up. It is not about never straying from my values but about returning to them with greater commitment each time I wander.

Integrity is not a rigid standard I must meet at all times. It is a practice. A daily refinement. A commitment to recalibrate when I drift off course.

I have made choices I regret. I have acted in ways that were out of alignment with my deepest values. I have taken the easy road when the right road required more courage, more discomfort, more truth.

But the question is not, Have I lived perfectly? The question is, Am I willing to return to alignment? Am I willing to own when I have strayed? Am I willing to keep refining, again and again, as I grow and as my understanding deepens?

This is the practice. This is the work. This is the journey that never ends but simply becomes more nuanced, more conscious, and more embodied over time.

The Weight of an Unquestioned Belief

Some beliefs are chains, not truths. They are limitations I accepted without examination, restrictions I imposed on myself without realizing I was the one holding the key.

I have held onto beliefs that kept me small. Beliefs that said I had to earn rest. Beliefs that said love was conditional on performance. Beliefs that said I was only as valuable as what I produced. Beliefs that said vulnerability was weakness.

And the hardest part wasn't believing them. It was realizing I didn't have to anymore. It was seeing that I had built my life around assumptions that were never true to begin with.

Because beliefs feel real—until they don't. They feel absolute—until I question them. They feel like the only way to see the world—until I glimpse another perspective.

I once believed that being kind meant being agreeable. That standing firm in my boundaries was selfish. That putting my own needs first was somehow wrong, somehow lesser than perpetual self-sacrifice.

But when I looked deeper, I saw—those weren't beliefs. They were fears disguised as wisdom. They were protective mechanisms masquerading as principles. They were ways of avoiding the discomfort of standing in my own authority.

And when I challenged them, they crumbled. Not all at once, but gradually, as I tested their edges, as I experimented with living differently, and as I discovered that the catastrophes they predicted never materialized.

Bridging the Gap Between Inner and Outer Worlds

If belief is the foundation, action is the structure built upon it. I cannot say I believe something and then live in contradiction to it without fracturing myself from within.

If I believe in truth, I must speak honestly, even when silence would be more comfortable. If I believe in love, I must give it freely—not just to others, but to myself when I need it most. If I believe in courage, I must be willing to walk into discomfort when growth requires it.

Because belief, without action, is just a story I tell myself. And I do not want a life of untested stories, of theoretical values, of principles that sound good but wither under pressure.

I want to know, when I lay my head down at night—that I did not just think about the life I wanted. I lived it. I embodied it. I chose it in a thousand small moments that seemed insignificant in isolation but together formed the architecture of a life I can stand behind without reservation.

The Moment of Choice

Every day, I am faced with small moments of choice that reveal what I truly believe, regardless of what I claim.

Do I tell the truth, even when it's uncomfortable? Do I set the boundary, even when it disappoints someone I care about? Do I act from integrity, even when no one is watching and compromise would be easier? Do I honor what matters to me, even when the external rewards point in a different direction?

Do I align my external world with what I know to be true in my heart, even when it means dismantling structures I've spent years building?

Because the life I want is not built in grand gestures or dramatic declarations. It is built in these small, ordinary choices that accumulate over time to form the foundation of who I am.

And the more I choose integrity, the easier it becomes. The more I live what I believe, the stronger my foundation grows. The more I align my actions with my values, the lighter I feel, unburdened by the weight of contradiction.

This is the work before the work. Not just shaping my beliefs but shaping my life to match them. Not just knowing what matters but living as if it matters in every choice I make.

The Question I Keep Asking

So today, I pause. I ask myself with unflinching honesty:

Where does my outer world not yet match my inner beliefs?

Where am I still living in contradiction? Where am I saying one thing but doing another? Where am I betraying what matters most to me for what matters least?

And I listen. Not to the loud voices of fear but to the quiet pull of truth. Not to what's easy, but to what's aligned. Not to what others expect but to what I know is right for me.

Because the only way to find peace—the only way to live a life without regret—is to let my actions reflect the deepest knowing of my heart.

To stop living in contradiction. To close the gap. To build a life where what I believe and how I live are one and the same.

And step fully into the life I say I believe in. Not someday, but today. Not when conditions are perfect, but in this imperfect moment, with this imperfect courage, through this imperfect action.

Chapter 57. The Alchemy of Judgment and Curiosity

I have spent a lifetime refining my ability to see what's wrong. I can walk into a room, a conversation, a business, a relationship—and instantly find the flaw. A contradiction. A misalignment. A missing piece. A weakness in the structure.

It's a skill I've honed over decades. Crafting systems. Coaching others. Leading teams with precision. Building businesses that required me to anticipate problems before they emerged. And yet, the sharpness of my vision has often cut inward just as deeply as it has outward.

Because the mind, when trained to find what's wrong, does not turn that skill off when it looks in the mirror.

The Hidden Cost of Judgment

I judge. I judge myself for not moving fast enough, for not achieving more, for moments of weakness I would forgive in anyone else. I judge others for inefficiency, for lack of clarity, for not meeting my impossible standards. I judge time—too fast when I'm in flow, too slow when I'm in pain, always slipping away before I've done enough. I judge the past for what it should have been. I judge the future for what it might not become.

And the most insidious form of judgment? The one I imagine others are placing on me.

Like this morning. The unmade bed. I glanced at it, a simple observation—but instead of just seeing it, I judged it. Not because I personally cared whether it was made, but because I imagined what someone else might think if they saw it. What conclusions might they draw about my discipline, my standards, and my character?

I turned an inanimate object into a verdict. Handed down by a jury that wasn't even present. Created by a story in my mind that had nothing to do with reality.

And then—I laughed at myself. At the absurdity of it.

Because when I finally asked my partner about it, when I stepped out of judgment and into curiosity, the answer was one I never expected—

"Your bed is on vacation today."

Simple. Playful. Free of the weight I had placed on something so insignificant.

What else in my life is on vacation that I keep dragging into the courtroom? What other simple realities am I complicating with unnecessary judgment? What freedom awaits on the other side of this habit?

Judgment and Curiosity Cannot Coexist

I am learning that judgment and curiosity cannot occupy the same space. One must always evict the other.

The moment I become curious, I am no longer judging. And the moment I judge, curiosity has already packed its bags and left the room.

Curiosity breathes. Judgment suffocates. Curiosity expands. Judgment constricts. Curiosity asks. Judgment assumes. Curiosity connects. Judgment separates. Curiosity creates possibility. Judgment eliminates it.

And here's the truth I am sitting with today, the truth that changes everything if I let it:

Every judgment I place on the world is first a judgment I have placed upon myself.

When I find fault in others, it is because I have already found it within me and deemed it unacceptable. When I am impatient with others, it is because I am impatient with myself in ways I may not even recognize. When I question someone's integrity, it is because I am wrestling with my own, projecting outward what I haven't resolved within.

So what happens when I meet those same thoughts, those same observations, with curiosity instead?

Instead of thinking, "Why did they do that?" → I ask, "I wonder what led them to that choice?"
Instead of thinking, "Why can't I get this right?" → I ask, "I wonder what's underneath this pattern?"
Instead of thinking, "They should know better," → I ask, "What might they know that I don't?"
Instead of placing blame → I replace it with wonder.

And suddenly, the world opens up. Suddenly, people aren't obstacles or disappointments—they're mysteries to be understood. Suddenly, my own struggles aren't failures—they're clues pointing toward deeper truths.

The Risk of Letting Go

There is a part of me that believes judgment keeps me safe. That believes criticism is clarity and that standards equal strength.

That if I find the flaw first, I can protect myself from being hurt by it later.

That if I see the weakness in someone else before they see mine, I can maintain the upper hand in any interaction.

That if I judge my own work, my own choices, my own self—before someone else does—I can stay in control of the narrative.

But control is an illusion. And judgment is its most fragile disguise.

Letting go of judgment means stepping into the rawness of curiosity. Letting go of judgment means admitting I don't have all the answers. Letting go of judgment means I may have to face a humbling truth—I was wrong. My assumptions were limited. My perspective was just one among many.

Letting go of judgment means I may no longer define myself by what I am not but by the infinite possibility of what I am and what I might become.

And yet—the risk of holding onto judgment is greater.

Because judgment kills what could have been. It ends conversations before they begin. It closes doors before we check if they were ever locked. It assumes, defines, and constrains. It calcifies potential into rigid certainty.

Curiosity, on the other hand, is alive. It is movement. It is breath. It is the bridge between what I think I know and what is still waiting to be discovered.

The Invitation

So, I make this choice today:

To be curious about my own assumptions. To be curious about the stories I tell myself about others. To be curious about the way I speak to myself—and to listen for the places where judgment still whispers in the background.

To be curious about what happens when I let judgment go.

And to see what rushes in to take its place.

Because judgment is final. Curiosity is infinite.

And today, I choose infinity.

Closing the Loop – Coming Full Circle

I began this chapter with a single image—an unmade bed. A symbol of something I judged. A thing I believed needed fixing, needed correcting, needed to conform to some standard I hadn't even consciously chosen.

But today, my bed is not a verdict. It is not evidence of failure. It is not a flaw in need of correction.

Today, my bed is simply... on vacation.

And maybe, just maybe, so am I. Taking a vacation from the exhausting work of judgment. Resting in the spaciousness of curiosity instead.

Chapter 58. The Discipline of Curiosity

I heard it said that if you let go of your passion and follow your curiosity, your curiosity will probably lead you back to your passion.

That line lingers in me. It follows me through my days. It whispers to me in moments of decision.

Because I know passion—the fire, the hunger, the relentless pursuit that has driven me for decades, I have built empires from it. I have inspired thousands with it. I have burned myself out with it, pushing beyond what was sustainable because the flame burned so bright I couldn't see the cost.

But curiosity?

Curiosity asks something different of me. It asks me to soften where passion demands intensity. To wonder where passion insists on certainty. To step outside of what I think I already know and enter the realm of what might be possible if I let go of my predetermined destination.

And that's where I find the paradox that has been hiding in plain sight:

The opposite of curiosity isn't apathy. It's judgment.

Curiosity as an Antidote to Judgment

Whenever I feel myself slipping into judgment—of another person, of a situation, of myself—I pause.

And I ask:

"What would happen if I turned this into curiosity instead?"

Because when I judge someone—when I see them acting out, being reckless, cruel, defensive—I don't just see their behavior in isolation.

If I look deeper, if I let curiosity lead, I see their childhood. I see the wounds they never learned to name. I see the moments that shaped them. I see the fears that drive them. I see the love they're seeking in all the wrong places.

And I get curious: "What must have happened to them for them to become this?"

Not in a way that excuses. Not in a way that justifies harm. But in a way that keeps my heart open enough to see beyond the surface. To recognize our shared humanity. To remember that behind every behavior, no matter how difficult, is a person trying to meet a need the only way they currently know how.

Because I know where I ended up. And I know what I went through to get here. I know the internal struggle that no one else could see.

Popcorn & Memory: The Mind's Imprint

Popcorn.

It's ridiculous, almost, how something so simple can carry so much emotional weight.

I can't think about popcorn without thinking about my mother.

The giant Christmas tins—three sections divided neatly: Caramel corn, cheddar corn, and plain butter.

She sent them to me every year like clockwork. A tradition that became sacred through repetition.

And every year, I opened them like a child, the scent pulling me back into something deeper—something imprinted, wired into the folds of my memory. Something that connected me to her across distance, across past hurts, across everything that had come between us.

Taste, smell—they don't just exist in the present. They are time machines, flashes of the past transported into now.

And I wonder, with the curiosity that opens rather than closes my heart...

"Was the popcorn her way of saying 'I love you'?"

Because for the first 30 years of my life, love wasn't something she knew how to give directly. She was drowning in alcohol, in pain, in a cycle so deep she couldn't pull herself out.

I didn't have a mother in the way other children did. I didn't have a father who could fill the gap.

And then, at 30, she got sober.

She started sending me popcorn. For 15 years, from my 30th year to my 45th, she found a way back into my life through this simple gift, this wordless expression of care.

And then, she died.

And now, every time I walk into a movie theater, the scent of buttered popcorn hits me—and suddenly, I'm standing in two places at once.

In the present. And in a moment that no longer exists except in my memory.

That's how memory works. That's how the past lingers in the body, in the senses.

And that's why curiosity matters—because without it, we repeat the same loops, interpret through the same filters, and react from the same wounds without ever questioning whether there might be another way to see, feel, or respond.

Discipline vs. Motivation

People talk about motivation as if it's something to chase. As if the key to success is feeling inspired, feeling driven, and feeling passionate every day.

I don't believe that anymore. I've lived long enough to know better.

Motivation comes and goes like the weather. It cannot be relied upon.

Discipline is what remains when motivation has left the building.

Discipline is the bridge between where I am and where I want to go. Discipline is the container, the structure, the riverbanks that allow my life to flow with purpose rather than spilling in every direction.

And I have built my life around discipline—My morning ritual that begins before dawn. My writing practice that doesn't wait for inspiration. My cold plunge that shocks my system awake. My meditation that centers me before the world's demands begin. My physical training that keeps my body strong as the years advance.

I don't rely on motivation to get me to the gym at 5 am, just like I don't rely on motivation to build my business or write when deadlines loom.

I trust discipline. I trust the habits I've cultivated with intention. I trust the structures I've built to carry me through the inevitable valleys where passion wanes, and resistance rises.

But I also know this—sometimes, my discipline is a mask for avoidance.

Sometimes, my routines protect me from sitting with something I don't want to feel. Sometimes, the very practices I claim are about growth become ways to hide from deeper truths that would require me to change in ways that terrify me.

And that's where curiosity comes in again—not just for understanding others, but for understanding myself with honesty that cuts through self-deception.

Letting Go of What I No Longer Need

If I imagine myself as a man in the jungle, swinging from vine to vine to cross a gorge—there always comes a moment when I have to let go.

I can't move forward while gripping the past. I can't grasp the next vine while clutching the last one. Movement requires release.

So I ask myself, with both courage and curiosity:

What am I still holding onto that I no longer need? What vision truly fulfills me now, regardless of what fueled me in the past? What skills have served their purpose, and what new ones must I develop for the chapter ahead?

And maybe the hardest question of all—

Am I finally ready to receive?

Because discipline has been my foundation. Giving has been my identity. Building, coaching, creating—I know how to do all of that. I've mastered it. I've been celebrated for it.

But receiving? Allowing? Trusting that I am enough without the constant proving, the relentless output, the ceaseless striving?

That's my edge. That's the new discipline I need to train. That's where curiosity must lead me now, into territory I've avoided because it feels so unfamiliar, so vulnerable, so contrary to the self-image I've spent decades constructing.

And maybe—just maybe—this is the year I learn how. This is the chapter where I discover that the true test of strength isn't how much I can carry but what I'm willing to set down.

Chapter 59. The Gravity of Motivation and the Fire of Intensity

Motivation is movement. It is not a thought, not an intention, not a plan written in a journal—it is the force that turns inertia into momentum, turns an idea into action, turns a whisper into a roar.

Motivation is the thing that makes me move when stillness would be easier.

And yet, motivation is not constant. Some days, it arrives like wildfire—unstoppable, consuming, blazing through resistance. Other days, it is a flickering ember, barely holding its heat, threatening to extinguish with the slightest breeze of difficulty.

If I wait for motivation to arrive fully formed, I remain at the mercy of its inconsistency. If I depend on feeling motivated before I act, I surrender my power to the whims of emotion.

I refuse to live that way. I refuse to be a passenger in my own life.

Instead, I build it. I shape it. I feed it like a craftsman tends a fire that must not go out.

I wake up every day and ask: What do I want beyond what my ego craves? Why do I want it beyond external validation? And what must I do today to make sure I get it, regardless of how I feel?

This is not philosophy. It is physics.

A body in motion stays in motion. A mind in momentum stays in momentum. A life in creation stays in creation.

So, the real question is not whether motivation will show up on its own. The real question is:

How will I turn up the intensity when the path grows difficult? How will I find the gravity to stay anchored when distractions beckon?

The Fire and the Gravity

I have come to understand that motivation has two forces, both essential:

The Fire—the hunger, the passion, the desire to create, to express, to build something that did not exist before. Fire is what makes me light up when I speak about my work, my creations, my ideas. Fire wakes me up early. Fire fuels my writing, my movement, and my devotion. Fire spreads to others, igniting their own possibilities.

The Gravity—the weight, the grounding force of responsibility, the knowledge that my work matters beyond myself. Gravity keeps me from floating into distraction. It reminds me that my time is finite, that my choices carry consequences, and that my work is not just for me but for those who need what only I can create in the particular way that I create it.

Some days, the fire carries me—unstoppable, effortless, exhilarating. Other days, the gravity holds me accountable—reminding me that I don't have the luxury of waiting until I "feel like it" and that commitment transcends convenience.

If fire is the ignition, gravity is the discipline. Together, they are unstoppable. Apart, they are incomplete.

The Dial is in My Hands

I used to think motivation was something that happened to me. Something external, unpredictable, outside my control.

Now I know—it is something I create. Something I cultivate. Something I command rather than await.

The dial is in my hands, not governed by circumstance but by choice.

Every morning, I decide: Do I turn it up, or do I let it fade? Do I bring intensity to this day, or do I sleepwalk through it?

When resistance creeps in—when excuses start forming like storm clouds—when my mind whispers that I can afford to take it easy today, that no one will know the difference, that the work can wait—that is the exact moment I must turn the dial up.

I ask myself:

What am I avoiding? What fear lurks beneath this hesitation? What story am I telling myself that makes inaction acceptable? What will this cost me—not just today, but in the accumulation of days—if I don't move?

Because I have learned something profound through years of pushing limits: Resistance is the loudest right before a breakthrough.

The very moment I feel myself pulling back—that is the signal to push forward harder. That is the universe testing my commitment to becoming the person I claim I want to be.

The Cost of Not Dialing Up

If I do not actively create my motivation, I am left with passivity. And passivity is the slow erosion of everything I have built. The quiet decay of potential that happens not in dramatic collapse but in the accumulation of small surrenders.

If I do not write today, I weaken the muscle that allows me to say what needs to be said. If I do not move today, my body forgets that it was designed for strength, endurance, and agility. If I do not teach, coach, or create, then the people who need what I have to offer do not receive it.

Every hesitation has a cost. Every resistance I surrender to strengthens the habit of surrender.

And just as inaction ripples outward, so does action.

Chapter 60. The Power of the Pause

Between what happens and what comes next, there is a space.

A breath.

A pause.

A moment where nothing is fixed, where everything is unwritten, where possibility exists before choice collapses it into reality.

It is here—before reaction, before assumption, before momentum sweeps me forward—that I hold the greatest power.

Because my future self is not shaped by what happens to me. It is shaped by how I respond to what happens. By what I choose in the space between stimulus and response.

And in this space, this sacred pause, I have the chance to choose who I am becoming rather than react from who I have been.

The Choice That Shapes Everything

The untrained mind reacts. It flinches, grips, defends, and clings to narratives that keep it safe but small. It sees an event, a word, a glance—and takes it as truth rather than one possible interpretation.

But truth is not in the event. Events simply happen.

Truth is in the response. In the meaning I assign. In the story I tell. In the choice I make.

A sculptor does not fight the marble. A sculptor shapes it, works with its nature, and reveals what lies within.

And so it is with me and the raw material of my life.

A moment arrives—a challenge that threatens my plans, a sharp word that triggers an old wound, an unexpected twist in the story of my day.

The old self lunges, reaching for the familiar—defensiveness, control, withdrawal, whatever pattern has become most automatic.

But in the pause, I hear a different voice. Not the voice of past wounds or conditioned habits—but the voice of the self I am becoming.

The voice that does not react but responds. The voice that is not bound by fear but moves with clarity and intention. The voice that asks not "What does this mean about me?" but "What is needed here?"

The Sculpting of Self

What determines my future is not what happens to me but who I become in response.

Each response is a step forward or a step backward on my path. Each response builds my foundation or erodes it. Each response strengthens the bridge to my potential or leaves it unfinished.

In the pause, I breathe, I center, I choose, I sculpt.

With presence, I refine my thoughts. With wisdom, I shape my words. With clarity, I decide my actions.

This is how my future self is forged. Not in the grand moments that everyone sees but in the quiet ones that only I witness.

Not in what happens, but in how I meet what happens. Not in the cards I'm dealt but in how I play them.

The Space That Holds Everything

Pause.

Feel the breath enter. Feel the breath leave.

The inhale is a door. The exhale is a key.

Here, in this stillness, I become aware of how much is possible. How many paths lie before me. How many selves I might become.

There is no urgency. There is only the next right move.

This is the art of mastery. This is the path of conscious creation.

The moment between stimulus and response—that is where I shape who I am becoming. That is where I write the next chapter of my story.

And so I ask myself, with both curiosity and commitment:

What future self am I stepping into in this very breath? What choice honors not just who I have been but who I am becoming?

Taste 6: Becoming - The Active Process of Transformation and Evolution

There comes a moment in every journey when the search for knowledge, clarity, and a sense of who we are and where we belong is no longer enough. We reach a threshold—a line between understanding and embodiment, between knowing and being. It is here, in this space, that we either step forward into the next iteration of ourselves or remain tethered to an old identity that no longer serves us.

This section is not about learning something new. It is about **becoming** someone new.

Becoming is not passive. It is not something that happens to us. It is something we claim. It is something we do. It is an active, deliberate process of stepping into the highest version of ourselves—not someday, not when the conditions are perfect, but **now**.

The shift from becoming in theory to becoming in practice is where many hesitate. It is easy to collect insights, to sit with revelations, to understand the patterns that shape our lives. It is far harder to embody them. To act as if we already are the person we aspire to be. To move with the certainty that growth is not something we wait for—it is something we create.

At this stage of the journey, the questions change.

We no longer ask, *Who do I want to be?* We ask, *Who am I willing to be right now?*

We no longer ask, *What is holding me back?* We ask, *What excuse am I still believing?*

We no longer ask, *When will I be ready?* We ask, *What am I waiting for?*

Here, we let go of what we thought we needed—the old fears, the old stories, the old definitions of success and safety. Here, we dismantle the resistance, the subtle ways we hold ourselves back. Here, we stop playing small, stop hesitating, stop waiting for permission to be extraordinary.

The edge of transformation is uncomfortable. It demands that we step into the unknown without a guarantee. It requires us to trust that the future self we are becoming already exists—we simply have to catch up.

And so, the invitation is clear: Let this be the moment you stop preparing for your next level and step into it. Let this be the moment you stop circling change and become it. Let this be the moment you stop dreaming about your future and embody it.

Because the future is not something waiting for you. It is something you are creating with every thought, every decision, every step. Now is the time to become.

Capter 61. The Future Me Already Exists

I stare at my reflection in the mirror this morning, not at the lines forming around my eyes or the stubble on my chin, but deeper—past the physical form into the eyes of a man I'm still coming to know.

"Who am I becoming?"

The question catches in my throat. There's a painful honesty required to truly answer it. I've asked it before, circled it like a reluctant swimmer testing water that might be too cold. But today, I dive in.

There's a version of me that already exists—beyond today, beyond my routines, beyond the narratives I've whispered to myself in moments of doubt and darkness. A me who has stepped fully into the greatest expression of what I am capable of. A me who has released everything that no longer belongs. A me who no longer hesitates, no longer clings, no longer negotiates with fear.

That version of me is not a stranger. It's not a distant possibility.

It's *me*.

I just haven't caught up to him yet.

The First Domino

I feel the weight of my coffee mug in my hand, the warmth spreading through my palm. Steam rises, and I remember something that changed everything for me: Identity is the first domino.

It doesn't matter how many habits I refine, how many tweaks I make to my environment, or how many times I try to "force" change—if I don't shift my identity, everything else stays the same.

Because everything about my present self—my values, my beliefs, my actions—follows a single, invisible force: Who I believe I am.

So, if I change that belief... if I topple that first domino... all the others fall in a new direction.

And that's the real question that burns in me now. Who do I *believe* I am?

Not in theory. Not in wishful thinking. But in reality.

Not the person I present in carefully curated moments of strength. But the person I am when no one is looking. When I'm tired. When I'm afraid. When I've failed.

Who am I then?

Not Finding—Creating

This isn't about finding myself.

That's the mistake I made for years—thinking that "one day," I'd just stumble upon the best version of myself, waiting like an unopened letter.

But that's not how this works. That's not how any of this works.

I am not lost. I am not searching. I am *creating*.

The self I want to become does not exist until I step into it.

If I sit here, waiting for some grand sign that says, "Now you are ready"—I will wait forever. The coffee will grow cold. The days will pass. And I will still be waiting.

Instead, I choose. I define. I decide.

My hand trembles slightly as I set down my mug. Because the only way to become is to act. And action means I must leave the safety of contemplation.

The Bridge Between Me and My Future Self

There is a gap between the me of today and the me who has already arrived.

But it's not a gap measured in time.

It's measured in choices.

Every thought I reshape. Every old belief I release. Every moment I step forward when it would be easier to stand still—

That's what closes the distance.

Last night, I sat with my son. He asked me a question about courage. I started to give him the careful answer, the measured response. But then I saw something in his eyes—a hunger for truth, not platitudes.

So I told him about my fear. About the times I've hesitated. About the regrets that still visit me at 3 AM when the house is quiet.

And in that moment of truth-telling, I felt the gap narrow. Just a little. Just enough to know it's possible.

Because my future self isn't waiting for me to "figure it out."

He is waiting for me to catch up.

Chater 62. The Chisel in my Hand

The chisel feels cold against my palm as I stand in front of the marble. I'm no sculptor, but I know what needs to be done.

"What must I let go of to become who I am meant to be?"

This is the real work.

Not adding more. Not piling on new strategies. Not drowning in self-improvement.

The process of becoming isn't about stacking more on top of who I already am. It's about removing everything that no longer fits.

Because who I want to be is already inside me.

I don't need to build him from scratch. I need to chisel him free.

Letting Go is Harder Than Holding On

I want to pretend that letting go is easy.

That once I recognize what no longer serves me, I can simply release it and move forward, light and unburdened.

But the truth?

Letting go is grief. It's grief for the old versions of me that kept me safe. Grief for the stories that defined me—even if they were limiting. Grief for the comfort of the familiar, even when the familiar is no longer serving me.

I feel it in the tightness of my chest when I consider setting down a belief I've carried since childhood. The belief that I must always be strong. That vulnerability is weakness. That asking for help means failing.

I've built empires on that belief. I've pushed through impossible barriers. I've endured when others might have broken.

But I've also stood alone when I needed connection. I've hidden my wounds until they festered. I've denied myself the very help I so freely offer others.

And yet—

Holding on is heavier.

Because every time I cling to what is no longer aligned, I make my own evolution impossible.

The Art of Subtraction

Michelangelo once said that he didn't "create" David. The sculpture was already inside the marble—he just removed everything that was not David.

That's what this process is. I am not creating my future self.

I am uncovering him. I am chiseling away every limiting belief. I am carving off the weight of hesitation. I am stripping away the stories I've told myself that are no longer true.

My hand hovers over the marble. Where do I begin? What is the first piece that must fall away?

Perhaps it's the story that I am only as valuable as what I produce. Perhaps it's the fear that if I stop moving, even for a moment, everything will crumble. Perhaps it's the voice that whispers I must always be extraordinary, that ordinary moments are somehow a failure.

And every time I let go, every time I release, I get closer to him—the version of me that is already waiting.

What Am I Avoiding?

If identity is the first domino, then fear is the hand holding it in place.

So I ask myself, my voice barely a whisper in the quiet of my own heart:

What am I avoiding?

What truth am I resisting?

What belief am I gripping so tightly that it's keeping me from my own evolution?

The answers aren't buried deep.

They're right here. I just have to have the courage to look.

I'm avoiding the possibility that I might still be worthy even when I'm not achieving. I'm resisting the truth that love doesn't have to be earned. I'm clinging to the belief that my worth is measured by my output, not my presence.

The Future Self Speaks

I close my eyes.

I see him. My future self—steady, unshaken. The man who has already figured it out.

And I listen.

What does he tell me?

"You already know who you are becoming. Stop hesitating."

"Let go of what's holding you back. It won't serve you where you're going."

"Commit fully. Step forward. Be relentless in your becoming."

And so I do. I pick up the chisel again. I make the first cut. Something falls away.

I breathe easier.

The Risk of Not Becoming

There is risk in transformation. Risk in stepping forward. Risk in shedding the old self and standing bare in the unknown.

But there is a far greater risk in staying the same.

The risk of waking up ten years from now, still wondering *what if?*

The risk of knowing I had more inside me... and never doing something about it.

The risk of dying with my potential still inside me.

That is a risk I refuse to take.

The Decision

Today, I choose.

To not hesitate when I already know the next step. To act instead of waiting for more clarity. To own my future self, instead of treating it like a distant possibility.

Because the only way to become is to decide. And today, with my hand still on the chisel and marble dust at my feet, I decide.

Chapter 63. The Space Between Identities - Navigating Transitions

There is a space between who I have been and who I am becoming. A threshold, neither here nor there. It exists between the inhale and the exhale, between knowing and unknowing, between the past that shaped me and the future that calls.

I have been here before. Many times.

The unraveling of an old self does not happen all at once. It comes in layers, in the slow peeling back of familiar ways of being, in the quiet realization that what once felt like home now feels like a constraint.

I know this space. I know it's silence. I know the unease it stirs—the way my body tightens, my mind negotiates, my heart hesitates.

The space between identities is not empty. It is a passage. And it is where reinvention begins.

The Grip of the Old Self

I walk through my day carrying two selves—the one I've been and the one I'm becoming. Sometimes, they are at war.

Before every transformation, there is a moment when I tell myself I cannot let go.

I have clung to identities long past their expiration. I have told myself stories about who I am—who I must be—until they became too familiar to question. The roles I played, the systems I mastered, and the approval I collected like currency.

Just last week, I caught myself doing it again. Someone asked me a simple question about my work, and I defaulted to the old narrative—the practiced, polished version that has served me well. It wasn't untrue. But it wasn't the whole truth either. It was the comfortable truth. The safe truth.

Letting go was never graceful. It was clawing my way out of an old skin, shedding it in pieces—sometimes reluctantly, sometimes with relief.

And yet, the illusion of permanence is intoxicating. It whispers that if I hold tightly enough, nothing will change.

But everything changes.

The only question is whether I move with it or resist.

I feel resistance in my body before I acknowledge it in my mind. The subtle contraction. The tension. The false comfort of the familiar. I tell myself the old self still fits. But it doesn't. It never does once I have outgrown it.

The Freefall of Not Yet Knowing

Between one identity and the next, there is freefall.

A moment when I have let go of the old but have not yet grasped the new.

This is where fear thrives.

What if I am making a mistake? What if I am losing something essential? What if I never land?

The mind searches for something solid, something familiar. But there is no certainty in transformation. There is only the next breath, the next step, the next unknown.

I've felt this vertigo before. When I left the safety of a career that no longer fit. When I stepped away from relationships that were comfortable but no longer served my growth. When I abandoned beliefs that once defined me but had become too small.

And I remind myself: I have been here before.

Every time, something has caught me.

A new insight. A new direction. A new way of being that felt more like home than anything I had known before.

The fear is not a warning. It is a threshold.

It is my body recognizing that I am stepping into the unknown.

And the unknown is where all transformation lives.

The Discipline of Reinvention

Reinvention is not a moment of inspiration.

It is an act of discipline.

It is not waiting for clarity. It is moving without it.

There are days when I want certainty and want to know exactly what comes next. But certainty is a prison. It keeps me tethered to what I have already done, locked into what I already know.

This morning, I felt the pull to stay in the familiar. To return to the comfort of what I know, I do well. The projects I can execute with my eyes closed. The conversations I can navigate in my sleep.

But I chose differently. I set aside the work that comes easily and instead embraced the work that makes my hands shake. The work where I don't yet have all the answers. The work that demands I become more than I have been.

Reinvention demands something else. It requires me to step into the next version of myself before I feel ready.

It requires movement in the dark. It requires me to build the bridge as I walk across it.

What do I need to let go of? What part of me is resisting? What am I still holding onto that no longer serves me?

I sit with these questions. I do not rush the answers.

I let them rise in their own time.

The Threshold of Becoming

I close my eyes and see myself months from now, a year from now.

The future self, already living in the identity I am only beginning to touch.

He does not hesitate. He does not cling to what is passing. He trusts the process of becoming.

So I ask myself:

What does he know that I do not yet see? What would he tell me if I could hear his voice? What does he need me to do today to step into his reality?

I listen.

And I begin.

The Space Between Identities is Sacred

I have stood at this threshold before, and I will stand here again.

Each time, the terrain is unfamiliar. Each time, the process is the same.

There is a letting go. There is a freefall. There is a landing.

But the landing is never a return to what was. It is always an arrival into something new.

The space between identities is not an absence.

It is a creation.

It is a sacred pause. A moment of reassembly. A quiet reckoning with what was and what will be.

I am not lost.

I am in transition.

And that, too, is part of becoming.

Chapter 64. The Hesitation Before Becoming

The moment before transformation is always the hardest.

There is a version of me I have yet to meet. And he is waiting.

He already exists—fully formed in the realm of potential—beyond the limits of my past, beyond the habits of my present. He has already solved the problems I am wrestling with. He has already crossed the finish lines I am still straining toward.

He stands just ahead, looking back at me. Not with impatience. Not with judgment. But with an invitation.

"Come," he says. "Be brave enough to step into me."

And I hesitate.

Not because I don't want to. But because stepping into my future self means leaving behind the comfort of my old self.

And that's the part I don't always want to face.

The Resistance That Holds Me Here

For years, I've imagined growth as momentum—a steady progression forward, a natural unfolding. But real transformation?

It's not a smooth ascent. It's a threshold.

And every time I stand on the edge of that threshold, I feel it:

The resistance.

The hesitation.

The internal pull to stay where I am.

Because stepping forward doesn't just mean gaining something new—it means losing something old.

And even when the old self no longer serves me, I still reach for it.

It happened again just yesterday. I was on a call—an opportunity to speak a deeper truth, to show up with more authenticity than I usually allow myself. And right there, I felt it. That familiar tightening in my chest. That voice that says, "Not yet. Not here. Not with these people."

The habits that gave me an identity.

The beliefs that kept me safe.

The way I've structured my days, my work, my thoughts—all built around who I have been, not who I am becoming.

To step into the future means letting go of the version of me I've worked so hard to build.

And that is terrifying.

The Armor I No Longer Need

I have spent years—decades—building my way to this moment. Yet I can still feel the weight of old patterns, old stories, old hesitations clinging to me like layers of armor.

Armor I no longer need. Armor I am afraid to remove.

Because what happens when I take it off? Will I still be strong without it? Will I still be me?

I've worn the armor of perfectionism, believing that if I could just do everything flawlessly, I would finally be worthy of love and belonging. I've worn the armor of busyness, filling every moment with productivity so I never have to face the questions that arise in stillness. I've worn the armor of expertise, hiding behind what I know so I don't have to be vulnerable in what I don't.

This is the hidden cost of transformation. It is not just about stepping forward—it is about the things I must leave behind.

The excuses.

The comfort of self-doubt.

The quiet reassurance of staying small because small is familiar.

And yet— Holding onto this armor is far more exhausting than taking it off.

The Two Roads

I see two paths before me.

One is the road of resistance.

It is the path where I cling to what I know, even when it no longer serves me. It is the path where I hesitate, overthink, and replay old doubts. It is the path where I wait for permission that will never come.

The other is the road of bravery.

It is the path where I move forward, even when my voice shakes. It is the path where I decide as if I am already the person I am becoming. It is the path where I stop waiting and start walking.

And right now, I stand at the fork between them.

My hand reaches out, touching both possibilities. Which way do I turn? Which story do I choose to live?

The Last Excuse Before the Leap

I tell myself I need more time.

"I'll step forward when I feel ready."

"I just need a little more clarity."

"Maybe tomorrow."

But deep down, I already know—

There is no "ready." There is no perfect moment. There is no version of my past that will ever justify my future.

There is only this moment.

And in this moment, I choose.

Not yet to move. Not yet to take action. But to admit—to finally admit—

That my hesitation has nothing to do with lack of clarity.

And everything to do with fear.

And that is where transformation begins.

Chapter 65. Becoming the Future Me

What if I simply acted as if I were already him?

There is a version of me that no longer hesitates. He does not overthink. He does not replay old doubts. He moves.

And today, I step into him.

The Power of Orientation

There is an old saying: "If you don't know where you're going, any road will take you there."

But I do know where I am going.

I know the goals that call to me.

I know the problems I was meant to solve.

I know that inside me, there is a version of myself who already lives in the future I crave.

So why am I still facing backward?

I have trained my mind to analyze, to reflect, and to seek meaning in what has already happened.

But today, I shift my orientation.

I stop looking back. I stop asking *Why?* and start asking *What's next?* I stop waiting for permission to step forward as the man I already know I am.

This is not about self-improvement. This is about self-acceptance.

I am not striving to become someone else. I am allowing myself to become more of who I truly am.

The Shift—The Instant Everything Changes

I close my eyes and picture him. Not some abstract, distant version of me. The real me.

The one who has already:

Built what I want to build. Solved what I want to solve. Lived into the depth of relationships, creativity, and purpose I desire.

And I ask:

How does he move?

How does he make decisions?

What does he do differently?

And then I take a deep breath—

And do that.

Not tomorrow. Not later. Now.

I step into my day with a different posture. I speak with a different tone. Not an act, not a performance—but the authentic expression of the self I am becoming.

In a meeting, I find myself listening differently. Not planning my response, but truly present with what is being said. Not trying to prove my value, but connecting from a place of service.

Someone asks a question I would normally deflect with humor or expertise. Instead, I pause. I consider. I speak a truth I would usually hide.

And I feel it. The subtle shift. The alignment. The sense of stepping into a version of myself that has always been waiting.

The Insight That Changes Everything

I see it now.

The only thing separating me from my future self is my willingness to act like him before I feel ready.

There is no magic moment when it suddenly becomes easy.

There is no permission slip that says, "Now you may step forward."

There is no version of my past that will ever be enough to justify my future.

There is only this moment.

And in this moment, I choose.

To act bravely. To step forward. To move as if I am already him.

Because the truth is, he has been waiting for me all along.

And today, I finally start walking toward him.

Chapter 66. The Art of Transformation - Releasing and Rebuilding

The old self must be shed before the new self can be sculpted.

Transformation is not a single moment. It is a series of thresholds—doorways between who I have been and who I am becoming.

Each threshold requires a choice: To cling to the old or to step into the unknown.

I have stood at these thresholds many times. And each time, I have felt the same resistance.

The moment just before change— When the familiar tightens its grip. When the old self whispers, "Stay." When fear makes a case for why it's safer to remain the same.

But I know something now.

That whisper? That resistance? That hesitation?

It is not a sign to stop. It is the signal that I am on the edge of something real.

The Weight of the Old Self

For years, I defined myself by what I do— By my roles, my routines, my expectations of who I was supposed to be.

But what happens when I step outside those definitions?

There comes a moment in every transformation when the old self tightens its grip— A reflex. A last attempt to hold onto the known before stepping into the unknown.

I feel this moment in my body before I acknowledge it in my mind. The tightness in my chest. The resistance in my breath. The false comfort of the familiar.

The part of me that wants to transform collides with the part of me that is terrified of what lies beyond.

I remember the first time I truly felt this collision. I was standing on a stage, about to share a story I had never told publicly. A story of failure. Of vulnerability. Of the places where I had fallen short of my own expectations.

In that moment, everything in me wanted to retreat. To tell the polished version. The safe version. The version where I remained the hero, unscathed and wise.

But something in me knew better.

The body remembers what the mind tries to forget: That I have been here before. That I have already survived so many reinventions. That the fear does not mean stop— It means step forward anyway.

So, I spoke the truth. My voice shook. My hands trembled. But I spoke it.

And in that speaking, I stepped into a new version of myself.

Fear as a Doorway

Fear is not the enemy. It is an invitation.

It is the body's way of saying: "You are at the edge of something significant."

But transformation does not happen in the mind alone. It happens in the body. In the breath. In the willingness to be intensely present with whatever arises.

I close my eyes. I let awareness settle into my body. I notice the old fear, the old self-definition pulling me back into its orbit.

I feel its grip. I do not fight it. I breathe into it.

And something shifts.

The fear does not disappear. It dissolves. Into awareness. Into clarity. Into movement.

The old self is not ripped away. It is released. One breath at a time.

Training the Architect of My Future Self

I sit here this morning, pen in hand, staring at the empty page.

But it isn't empty.

It is filled with possibility— Waiting for me to give it form.

This is what I train for. This conversation with myself. This act of sculpting the future from the raw material of my:

Thoughts

Emotions

Associations

Memories

This is my T.E.A.M.

And I am the architect. I am the sculptor.

Because the quality of my future is not shaped by time— It is shaped by how well I train my mind today.

The Power of Releasing and Rebuilding

What I let go of creates space for what I build next.

If I do not train my thoughts, they will run wild. If I do not train my emotions, they will rule me. If I do not consciously choose my associations, I will remain bound to old patterns. If I do not examine my memories, they will dictate my future.

I release the old self. And I train the new one.

I ask myself: "What is the self-concept I am willing to let go of?" "What belief about myself no longer serves me?" "What story do I refuse to carry into my future?"

And then, I choose a new frame. A new thought. A new belief. A new way of seeing.

This is not just mindset work. This is self-construction.

I've spent too long believing the lie that doubt is humility. That playing small is service. That staying safe is wisdom.

Today, I release those stories. I don't need them where I'm going.

Mastering the Mind—The Art of T.E.A.M. Training

I used to believe wisdom was something earned over time. That it arrived slowly, accumulating with age and experience.

But I see it differently now.

Wisdom is not a product of time. It is a product of clarity.

It emerges when I slow down enough to:

See my thoughts for what they are—not truths, just neural patterns.

Feel my emotions fully—not suppress them, but not obey them blindly either.

Choose my associations consciously—surrounding myself with those who call me forward.

Reshape my memories—learning from them rather than being trapped by them.

I am not waiting for wisdom to arrive. I am creating it.

Each choice. Each moment of clarity. Each shift in thinking.

A Shift in Energy, A Shift in Reality

Lately, I have been imagining my mind as a movie projector.

The light source is my energy, my focus. The film running through it is my thoughts, emotions, associations, and memories. The image projected onto the screen of my life is nothing more than a reflection of those inner frames.

If I don't like what I see, I don't need to fight the projection.

I need to change the film. I need to adjust the source of light.

And this is where training my T.E.A.M. becomes everything.

I practice shifting the soundtrack— Lowering the volume on the relentless noise of everyday thinking And tuning in to the soft harp of inner wisdom.

I pause. I breathe. I remind myself:

Clarity is always here. I just have to stop shaking the snow globe long enough to see through the storm.

What I Imagine Is Possible

What do I imagine is possible when I master this training?

I imagine…

A mind that is spacious, not cluttered, and creative, not chaotic.

A presence that is unshaken by circumstances—because I know I am the source, not the effect.

A body that moves with intention fueled by choices made in alignment with my highest self.

A life where the future is not something I fear but something I sculpt with joy, precision, and trust.

I imagine waking up each morning knowing that I have the tools, the discipline, and the awareness to shape this day into something beautiful.

And I imagine looking back, years from now, at the man I have become with deep gratitude for the man I am today.

The man who sat down, picked up the pen and decided:

I train my mind. I train my emotions. I train my associations. I train my memories.

And in doing so, I create the future self I desire.

This is my work. This is my practice. This is my life.

And I wouldn't trade it for anything.

The Art of Transformation

Letting go is an act of courage. Rebuilding is an act of mastery.

Together, they are the art of transformation.

And I am living it.

Chapter 67. The Edge of Comfort - Living in Constant Expansion

There is no arrival—only deeper thresholds to cross.

There was a time when I believed transformation had an endpoint.

I thought there was a moment of arrival— A threshold I would cross where I would finally become who I was meant to be.

That I would gather enough wisdom, cultivate enough discipline, and align my life so precisely that I would stand in some perfected version of myself— Unshaken. Fully realized. Complete.

But that was an illusion.

Every time I thought I had arrived— At a level of mastery, at a deep understanding, at a point of stability— Life had a way of revealing more.

A deeper layer. A new edge. A place within me still waiting to unfold.

The idea that I could arrive was never real. And in clinging to that illusion, I was resisting the very nature of growth itself.

Mastery or Mere Endurance?

There is a difference between tolerating growth and thriving in it.

Tolerance is white-knuckling discomfort, waiting for equilibrium. But what if equilibrium itself is an illusion?

What if real mastery isn't in getting back to center— but in expanding what center means?

I have seen this pattern in myself:

In Business, When I embraced AI, I didn't just adopt a tool—I reshaped an industry's approach to storytelling. But have I truly gone far enough? Or am I still playing safely inside the edges of my own understanding?

In Relationships, I pride myself on deep, meaningful connections. But do I allow those connections to evolve as I do? Or do I unconsciously hold expectations that keep people in old roles—just as others might expect me to stay the same?

In Identity, I have never been just one thing—coach, builder, creator, teacher. But I also know I have outgrown versions of myself before fully stepping into the new. Am I in one of those transition spaces now? And if so, am I resisting the next emergence?

Just last week, someone introduced me at an event using a description of work I did years ago. I felt a strange blend of pride and discomfort. Pride in what I had built. Discomfort in being defined by what I am no longer becoming.

I smiled and nodded, but inside, I wondered: Who am I now? What am I becoming next?

The Real Practice

I have trained my mind to recognize patterns. But have I also trained it to let go of them when they no longer serve me?

The real practice— The thing that stretches my neural pathways, my relationships, and my capacity to create— Is not in mastering the next thing.

It is in allowing the unknown to shape me before I try to shape it.

It is in the pause between mastery and reinvention— Where I am most vulnerable yet most alive.

The Trap of Thinking I'm Done

I have seen this in myself.

That subtle, creeping feeling that I have done enough work. That I have healed enough wounds. That I have expanded enough for one lifetime.

It is resistance in disguise.

Because every time I have thought I was done, I have soon found myself restless.

A part of me begins to shrink— Not in an obvious way, But in a quiet way— Where I stop questioning, stretching, and engaging the uncomfortable edges of my own evolution.

Growth is not about reaching a summit and planting a flag. It is about continually finding new mountains to climb.

And when I stop looking for the next mountain, I start looking for distractions.

I felt it last month when I completed a long-term project. The initial relief. The celebration. The well-deserved rest. And then, the subtle emptiness that crept in. Not because the achievement wasn't significant but because the journey had ended.

I caught myself filling that space with noise—with social media, with busywork, with anything to avoid the discomfort of the question: What's next?

The Edge Between Expansion and Contraction

At every point of transformation, There is a choice:

To expand or to contract.

I have lived both.

I have been at a crossroads where I felt the pull toward something new, something unknown— And I have chosen to step forward.

I have also been at a crossroads where I turned away— Where I stayed within the familiar boundaries of what I already knew.

Looking back, I can see the difference between those choices.

The moments of expansion led to a more alive version of me. The moments of contraction led to a slow, imperceptible dulling of my spirit.

Expansion feels risky. Contraction feels safe.

But safety is often an illusion.

Because what I have learned is that contraction does not protect me from discomfort— it only prolongs it.

Every time I resist growth, I am simply delaying the inevitable.

Five years ago, I stood at such a crossroads. An opportunity presented itself—one that would require me to step beyond what I knew, to risk failure publicly, to put my name on something without certainty of success.

I hesitated. I made excuses. I found logical reasons to stay where I was.

And for a year after, I carried a heaviness I couldn't name. A knowing that I had chosen contraction over expansion. Safety over possibility.

It was a slow, quiet pain. The pain of potential unlived.

Until finally, I could bear it no longer. And I stepped forward—into a different opportunity, but with the same courage that had been asked of me before.

The relief was immediate. Not because the path was easy but because I was finally aligned with my own evolution.

The Wisdom of the Future Self

I often use a practice where I imagine my future self— Three years ahead. Five years ahead.

I sit on the edge of my bed in the early morning light, eyes closed and my breath steady. I feel the weight of the sheets beneath me and the warmth of the sun through the window.

And I ask him:

"What do you know that I do not yet see?"

The answer is always the same.

Every fear I have today will one day seem small.

Everything I am holding onto is not as necessary as I think it is.

My greatest expansion will come the moment I stop trying to protect myself from it.

And then he asks me:

"What action can you take today that will lead to the transformation you seek?"

The answer is never about waiting. It is never about gathering more information, seeking more reassurance, or holding out for the perfect moment.

The answer is always about stepping forward—before I feel ready.

The Nature of Mastery

If transformation is ongoing, Then so is mastery.

Mastery is not about reaching a level where I no longer need to practice. It is about the deepening of practice, over and over again.

I have learned that there are no shortcuts.

If I want to be more present, I must practice presence.

If I want to be more courageous, I must practice courage.

If I want to be more disciplined, I must practice discipline.

Every day. Not just once. Not just until I arrive.

Because there is no arrival. There is only the commitment to keep showing up.

I think of the days when I don't want to sit down and write. When the resistance is loud. When I would rather do anything else.

Those are the days when practice matters most. When I show up, not because it's easy, but because it's who I am becoming.

The Art of Letting Go

With every transformation, There is something to release.

An old story. A limiting belief. A way of being that once served me but no longer fits.

Letting go is not always easy.

It is the moment of stepping away from the known— From the comfort of an identity I have built— And trusting that what comes next will be enough.

I remember the day I realized I needed to let go of a friendship that had once been central to my life. Not because of conflict or betrayal but because we had grown in different directions. Because holding on was keeping both of us from the next evolution.

The conversation was painful. The release was necessary. The space it created allowed new growth for both of us.

But every time I have let go— Every single time— Something greater has taken its place.

The life I am living now is built on the ashes of the lives I have outgrown.

And if I want to continue expanding, I must be willing to keep burning down what no longer serves me.

The Discipline of Becoming

This is the real work:

To wake up every day and choose growth, even when it is uncomfortable.

To step beyond what I think I am capable of, again and again.

To trust that there is no arrival—only the becoming.

I do not know who I will be in five years. But I know this:

If I keep asking the right questions,

If I keep leaning into the edges of my own evolution,

If I keep choosing expansion over contraction—

Then, the man I become will be someone I could not even imagine today.

And that is the beauty of it.

The illusion of arrival dissolves the moment I accept that I will always be in motion.

So, who do I choose to be today?

The answer is simple.

The next version of myself.

Chapter 68. The Weight of Truth

Truth is heavy. That's why so few people choose to carry it.

Who would I be if truth was my highest priority?

Not the carefully curated version. Not the well-rehearsed vulnerability that makes for a compelling story but never touches the marrow.

The real truth. The one I keep just beneath the surface. The one I hesitate to say out loud.

I close my eyes. I inhale deeply. I let the question settle.

Something shifts.

There is a stillness beneath the question— But also a pressure.

Like standing at the edge of something vast, Knowing I can't turn back.

Because truth, when fully embraced, changes everything.

The Truth About My Loneliness

I tell myself I enjoy my solitude. And I do.

But that's not the whole truth.

The deeper truth is: Sometimes, the silence is too much.

Sometimes, I long for the kind of companionship that makes words unnecessary. I miss being known— Not just by the people who admire me but by someone who sees beyond the work, beyond the wisdom, and beyond the roles I've built my life around.

I have convinced myself that relationships are complications I don't need. That I'm better off without the entanglements of love, without the weight of expectations.

Last night, I finished a long day of creating, teaching, and connecting with hundreds. I returned to an empty home, made dinner for one, and sat on my balcony watching the city lights. The contrast was stark—from the energy of many to the stillness of none.

At that moment, I felt it acutely. Not just being alone but being unseen in the fullness of who I am.

But here's the real truth: I still crave it.

I still want to be chosen—not because I am needed, But simply because I am.

The Truth About My Need to Be Needed

I have spent my life in service— Teaching. Coaching. Creating.

I tell myself it's my calling, my passion, my purpose.

And it is.

But it's also something else.

It's my safety. My significance. My way of ensuring I matter.

Because if I stopped today— If I walked away from it all—

What remains of me?

Who am I without the expectations, Without the people looking to me for guidance?

There was a period last year when illness forced me to step back. To cancel commitments. To be unavailable. It was physically challenging, yes, but the deeper pain was existential.

If I wasn't creating, teaching, serving—who was I? If I couldn't offer value, did I still have worth?

I tell myself I've built a life of freedom.

But if I'm truly free— Why does the idea of being unnecessary unsettle me?

The Truth About Control

I talk about embracing uncertainty, about living on the edge of possibility.

But if truth is my highest priority, Then I have to admit—

I keep a firm grip on the reins.

I structure my world carefully. I create safety in systems, in frameworks, in knowing what's next.

Just this morning, I felt the anxiety rise when a meeting was canceled unexpectedly. Not because the meeting was crucial but because it disrupted the order I had created. The plan I had made. The control I thought I had.

Have I truly surrendered to the unknown— Or have I just mastered the art of navigating it on my terms?

There has always been a quiet battle within me— Between control and surrender.

I know the power of letting go, But I also know the comfort of holding on.

And if I am being honest, I'm not sure which side is winning.

The Cost of Truth

If truth was my highest priority, I would have to be willing to face its full weight.

Truth does not negotiate. Truth does not make exceptions. Truth does not let me hide behind the parts of myself I prefer.

It strips away the excess. It leaves me bare, unguarded, and—if I let it—free.

Truth requires me to let go of the version of myself that is always in control. It asks me to stand as I am without embellishment. It asks me to release the need:

To be right.

To be admired.

To be understood.

And that is terrifying.

Because if I am not the things I've built— If I am not the achievements, the insights, the influence— Then who am I?

I sit with this question. I feel its weight. And I don't look away.

Chapter 69. The Lightness of Being

Truth is heavy—until we let it set us free.

If I made truth my highest priority, I would:

Say what I mean without shaping it for impact.

Stop hiding behind my work and experience life beyond creation.

Let people see me— Not just the strong, certain version, but the man who is still searching, still longing, still learning.

Allow love, even if it disrupts the solitude I've built so carefully.

Make peace with the parts of me that are unfinished, uncertain, and unguarded.

The truth is, I don't need to have all the answers. I don't need to be the one who always knows the way forward. I don't need to fill every space with something I've created.

What if I let it all be? What if I allowed myself to simply exist— Not as a leader, a teacher, or an entrepreneur—

But as a man, still unfolding?

I tried it yesterday. A small experiment in being rather than doing.

I sat in a café without my notebook, without my laptop, without an agenda. Just a cup of coffee and the simple act of being present. No performance. No productivity. No purpose beyond the moment itself.

A woman at the next table asked what I was working on. "Nothing," I said. "I'm just... here."

The unfamiliarity of those words in my mouth. The slight discomfort. And then, the unexpected relief.

The Moment Everything Changes

Truth doesn't just reveal itself. It undoes me.

The moment I stop controlling it, It carries me.

Like a river— Like wind over an open field— Like breath.

Truth is not static. It is not a thing I possess. It is a state of being.

And in this moment, I feel it— Not as a weight, But as lightness.

It happened during a conversation with a friend. I started with the practiced version of my current challenges—the one that acknowledged difficulty but wrapped it neatly in wisdom and growth.

But something made me pause. Made me put down the narrative I had crafted.

"The truth is," I said, "I'm scared. I don't know if I'm making the right choice. I don't know if I have what it takes for this next chapter."

The moment the words left my mouth, I felt it—the release. The lightness. The beautiful absence of the weight I had been carrying.

Not because my friend had solutions but because I was no longer pretending to have them all myself.

The Gift of Letting Go

What happens when I stop choosing the versions of truth that feel safe? What happens when I stop resisting the things I already know deep inside?

My loneliness was never the problem— It was my belief that it had to remain that way.

My need to be needed was never the problem— It was my fear that without it, I would be nothing.

My desire for control was never the problem— It was my unwillingness to trust that life unfolds without my grip on it.

And the moment I let go, I see it—

I was never meant to carry these things. Not in the way I have been.

Last week, I reached out to someone I've kept at a careful distance. Not with an agenda or a project in mind but simply to connect. To be seen. To be known beyond what I create.

It felt foreign. Vulnerable. A little terrifying.

But in that small act of reaching, something shifted. A door opened—not just between me and this person, but within me.

A door to the possibility that I don't have to orchestrate every connection. That I can let people in without knowing exactly where it will lead.

Who Would I Be Without the Weight?

Lighter. Freer. More alive.

Not because I have figured it all out but because I have stopped holding onto the illusion that I ever would.

I do not need to create a perfect narrative. I do not need to structure my life in a way that makes sense to others. I do not need to be the thing I've always been.

What if I allowed myself to simply be... Whatever I am meant to be next?

I stand in front of the mirror this morning, and for a moment, I see myself without the labels. Without the roles. Without the achievements and the failures.

Just a man. Breathing. Being. Becoming.

And in that reflection, I see something I've been missing—the lightness of a life not burdened by the need to be anything other than what it is.

The Question That Remains

So, who would I be if truth were my highest priority?

Maybe— I would be a man who is finally willing to stop answering that question and start living into it.

Fully. Fiercely. Without reservation.

And maybe—just maybe— That would be enough.

Chapter 70. The Discipline of Stepping Into the Unknown

If I wait until I am ready, I will wait forever. If I act before I feel ready, I will become the man who is.

There is a line in the sand— Invisible, yet undeniable.

On one side: self-sabotage— The whisper of hesitation. The slow erosion of intention. The space where dreams decay in the waiting room of inaction.

On the other: self-discipline— The quiet, steady force that turns intention into reality. The bridge between who I am and who I am becoming.

And here I stand, looking at that line, Knowing that every meaningful transformation in my life begins here.

The Art of Keeping Promises to Myself

Self-sabotage is not an accident.

It is a precision tool wielded by the part of me that fears: Change. Responsibility. The weight of my own potential.

It does not come in the form of destruction, But in the quiet, slow erosion of intention.

It starts as a whisper: "You'll start tomorrow." "One more distraction won't hurt." "You've already failed, so why keep going?"

I know this voice. I heard it yesterday when I sat down to write. When I promised myself, I would create without distraction for three hours.

Thirty minutes in, the whisper came. "Check your messages. Just for a moment. You've been so focused; you deserve a quick break."

I listened. I broke my promise to myself.

And in that small betrayal, I felt the weight of all the others. The commitments not kept. The intentions abandoned. The quiet erosion of my own trust in myself.

But discipline is a voice, too.

A voice that says: Do it anyway.

Discipline is not punishment. It is self-respect.

Because every time I break a promise to myself, I diminish my own trust.

And every time I keep a promise, I grow stronger.

So I ask myself:

What have I been saying I want, yet acting in ways that ensure I will never have it?

What small betrayals of my own word am I allowing to accumulate?

What would my life look like if I only spoke words I was willing to prove with action?

Because self-discipline is not restriction. It is expansion. It is the key that unlocks the future self I say I want.

The Space Between Wanting and Becoming

What happens between the moment I say I want something— And the moment I get it?

That space is discipline.

It is the bridge between:

Desire and reality.

"I should" and "I did."

Who I think I am and who I prove myself to be.

That space is my life.

I've lived in that space between wanting and becoming. Sometimes, crossing swiftly, with purpose and clarity. Sometimes wandering, lost in the gap between intention and action.

Five years ago, I said I wanted to write a book. For four years, I talked about writing a book. I planned to write a book. I thought about writing a book.

But I didn't write a book.

Until one day, I realized the space between wanting and becoming was filled with everything but the actual work. The actual discipline. The actual showing up.

So, I created a simple rule: Write 500 words every morning before anything else. No exceptions. No excuses.

It wasn't glamorous. It wasn't always inspired. But it was discipline.

And the book now sits on my shelf—not because of grand inspiration or extraordinary talent, but because I finally understood:

Because I will never arrive at any destination worth reaching Without the journey of discipline.

And the more I step into discipline, the more I see: Self-sabotage is an illusion.

It is not real. It is only the ghost of hesitation.

And ghosts only have power when I believe in them.

I choose to believe in action.

The Edge of Everything I Know

There is a line I keep coming back to— An invisible boundary between who I have been and who I could become.

It is the line between certainty and possibility, Between the familiar and the unknown.

It is the edge of my comfort zone.

And every day, I stand at that edge, deciding— Do I step forward, or do I shrink back?

I know what's behind me. The rhythms, the habits, and the routines that have created this version of me.

Some of them are solid and built with intention. Others? They are merely familiar—not necessarily useful, not necessarily empowering, But predictable.

And predictability feels safe.

But what I want isn't here.

What I want exists just beyond that line.

I felt it yesterday when an opportunity arose—one that would require me to be more visible, more vulnerable, more exposed than I've been before. My instinct was to step back, to find reasons why "now isn't the right time."

But I recognized that feeling. The tightening in my chest. The sudden flood of practical concerns. The subtle reframing of courage as recklessness.

These are not warnings. They are signposts. They are my body and mind, recognizing the edge of everything I know.

What Lives Outside the Line?

I was born with only two fears: The fear of falling. The fear of loud noises.

Every other fear— The fear of failure, the fear of rejection, the fear of losing what I know— I learned.

And if I learned them, That means I can unlearn them.

It means those fears are not absolute. They are not laws of nature. They are not unchangeable.

They are just my T.E.A.M. running old scripts— Thoughts, emotions, associations, and memories looping in the background.

And if I can hear those scripts playing, I can change them.

But only through experience.

No amount of thinking will overwrite them.

No amount of planning will dissolve them.

Only action has the power to rewrite fear.

So, I look at the edge of my comfort zone and ask myself:

What is waiting for me on the other side? What version of me already lives beyond it? What am I missing by staying where it's safe?

Because the truth is— Everything I truly want lives outside this line.

The Gamble of Yes

Saying yes to new experiences is a gamble.

Yes, it is uncertain. Yes, it is unpredictable. Yes, it opens the door to failure, discomfort, and rejection.

And yet, yes is the only way forward.

I can either:

Stay where I am—safe but unchallenged, secure but stagnant.

Or gamble on myself.

I can trust that my future self already knows what to do.

I remember the biggest "yes" of my career. The moment when I was offered an opportunity that seemed beyond my capabilities, beyond my readiness, beyond what I thought I deserved.

Every rational voice said, "Wait. Prepare more. Get ready."

But something deeper said, "Now. Not later. Now."

I said yes. With shaking hands and a racing heart, I said yes.

And that, yes, changed everything. Not because the opportunity was perfect but because saying yes changed me. It forced me to grow into the space I had claimed before I felt ready.

I imagine a future where I have said yes more often than I have said no.

Where I have lived more than I have hesitated.

Where I have stepped into opportunities not because I felt ready but because I knew I never would.

What difference does it make?

It makes all the difference.

Because life is not shaped by the things I refuse to do. It is shaped by the risks I take.

And the greatest risk?

Never stepping forward at all.

Making the Leap

So today, I take a breath and step forward.

I step into the space where I have never been. I step into the version of me who already lives there. I step into the life that is waiting for me.

Because on the other side of fear is freedom. On the other side of hesitation is growth. On the other side of my comfort zone is everything I have been waiting for.

And I am done waiting.

I have reached the edge of everything I know. And now, I step beyond it.

Chapter 71. Resolving the Inner Disturbance

There comes a moment in every journey when I realize— I am not just moving forward. I am moving inward.

The obstacles before me are not in the world. They are in me.

They live in the spaces between my thoughts. In the stories I have lived so long, I have mistaken them for truth.

But truth does not tremble under scrutiny. Truth does not require blind loyalty. Only falsehoods demand to be clung to.

So I ask myself: What happens when I loosen my grip? What happens when I stop protecting the very walls that keep me from soaring?

The Beautiful Work of Resolution

A friend once told me:

"I had to love myself enough to create the systems to make money consistently. Then, I had to love myself enough to step into leadership. Then, I had to love myself enough to be present with my family. Then, I had to love myself enough to stop fearing I would lose everything.

And every time I resolved one issue... another one appeared.

And now, I see— That's the indication I'm actually growing."

I breathe into this.

I see my own reflection in her words.

Growth is not the absence of struggle. It is the relationship I develop with it. It is the willingness to step into the fire of self-examination, knowing it will burn away the illusions that keep me small.

I've been in that fire recently. Facing a pattern in my work where I create, release, and then immediately focus on what's lacking. Where I never fully celebrate achievements because I'm already seeing their flaws.

For years, I thought this was drive. Ambition. The mark of someone who refuses to settle.

But sitting in the fire of honest self-examination, I see it differently now.

It's not drive. It's disturbance. It's the inability to be at peace with what is because some part of me still believes worth comes from what's next, not what's now.

False Truths: The Foundations of My Issues

John Sharp calls them false truths— Beliefs I formed as a child, Stories crafted from limited experience, Stories I now mistake for reality.

I see them in my own life.

The father who was absent, who I once believed had no interest in me— until I saw him through wiser eyes.

The authority I once rebelled against, Believing it could not be trusted— Until I realized I had projected my father onto every leader, Every mentor, Every voice of guidance.

How many false truths are still shaping the way I see the world? How many stories am I still living as if they were unchangeable?

What happens when I rewrite them?

Last month, I found myself in conflict with a collaborator. My reaction was immediate and intense—defensiveness, withdrawal, a sense of being misunderstood.

But in a moment of clarity, I saw it: This wasn't about the current situation at all. This was about a false truth I had carried for decades—that criticism means rejection, that disagreement means abandonment.

In that recognition, something shifted. I could respond to what was actually happening, not to the ghost of an old wound.

The Joy of Being Hidden, The Disaster of Never Being Found

There is a comfort in staying hidden. A familiarity in the struggle.

Even when I suffer, it is suffering I know.

I've perfected the art of revealing just enough to seem authentic while keeping the deepest parts carefully concealed. I've mastered the craft of vulnerability that doesn't actually risk anything.

But the moment I name it— the moment I say I see you and I no longer believe you— I begin to rise.

I am not meant to live in the shadows of old wounds. I am not meant to repeat the same cycles just because they are familiar.

I am meant to resolve. I am meant to transcend. I am meant to outgrow.

So, I ask myself now— what have I been carrying that is no longer mine to hold?

Patterns, Language, and the Power of Awareness

Recurring issues are not random. They are patterns. They are habits, engrained in thought and action.

Step one is awareness. Step two is choosing new words.

I pause. I listen.

I hear the language I use when I speak about myself. I hear the absolutes, the limitations, the self-imposed ceilings.

"I always get overwhelmed when I take on too much."

"I never find the right balance between work and rest."

"I can't create my best work under pressure."

"I can only lead effectively when I have complete clarity."

These words are spells. They shape my reality.

I write them down. I see them staring back at me.

And I ask— What is missing?

The Rewrite: Calling Forth My Aspirational Self

Now, I choose differently.

I always... find the resources I need when I commit fully to what matters.

I never... lose my capacity for growth, even when the path is unclear.

I can't... be defined by old limitations when I am actively creating new possibilities.

I can... trust the wisdom that emerges when I stay present with challenges instead of avoiding them.

I see the shift. I feel it in my body.

This is what growth looks like.

Not dramatic overnight transformations, but quiet, intentional choices— One thought at a time. One belief at a time. One sentence at a time.

The Hero's Journey of Resolution

Joseph Campbell mapped it out long before I recognized the path I was walking.

The twelve stages of transformation are not just mythical stories— They are my stories.

Limited awareness of the problem – I don't know what's wrong, but something isn't working.

Increased awareness of the need to change – The discomfort grows too loud to ignore.

Resistance to change – The fear of losing what is familiar.

Overcoming fear – The moment I step forward, despite uncertainty.

Commitment to change – The decision to do the work.

Experiments with new conditions – Testing, failing, adjusting, growing.

Preparing for major change – The deepening of conviction.

Big change – A shift in identity, in story, in self.

Acceptance of the new story – This is who I am now.

New challenges – Life will test me, but I will not return to old ways.

Last-minute dangers – The final trials before mastery.

Mastery – The new way of being becomes my default.

I breathe into this.

I see where I am in my own hero's journey. I recognize the work still ahead. I recognize the work already done.

And I trust— This process will not fail me.

The Risk of Not Resolving

What happens if I refuse this work?

If I ignore the whispers? If I hold onto the stories? If I protect the wounds instead of healing them?

I stay the same. I keep repeating the cycle. I keep circling the same jet stream, never rising to the next.

I see it in my relationships—the same misunderstandings, the same triggers, the same walls that keep authentic connection at bay.

I see it in my work—the same fears of inadequacy, the same patterns of overcommitment and exhaustion, the same resistance to asking for help.

I see it in my quiet moments—the same restlessness, the same inability to simply be, the same need for constant validation and achievement.

And what is the risk of resolving?

That I will have to let go? That I will have to face myself fully? That I will have to admit I was wrong about some things?

Yes.

But the eagle does not fear the sky. And neither do I.

Handing the Pen to My Future Self

I sit in stillness. I breathe. I listen.

I let my future self speak.

I always... move toward growth, even when it requires letting go of what once defined me.

I never... lose the capacity to begin again, no matter how many times I falter.

I can't... be limited by who I have been when I am actively choosing who I am becoming.

I can... trust the unfolding of my own evolution, even when the path is not clear.

The words come. Clearer. Lighter. Truer.

I see the path ahead. And I take the next step.

What's Occurring Now?

What insight is rising?

What is possible when I fully accept that I am here to:

Resolve. Evolve. Step forward into my future self—

One truth at a time.

Taste 7: Cultivate Vision - The Threshold of What Comes Next

There comes a moment in every journey when the past is no longer a question. The path behind me—the trials, the turning points, the lessons, the losses—has shaped me with a sculptor's precision. I no longer wonder how I arrived here. I know with bone-deep certainty.

But ahead? Ahead is something else entirely. Not a fixed destination, not another mountain to conquer, but an opening. A vast expanse where certainty no longer leads, where control no longer defines, where only vision—true, unshackled vision—can illuminate the way forward.

This is the threshold.

Not a transition, but a crossing. Not an adjustment, but a transformation. Not an iteration but an arrival.

Not into something new, but into something deeper.

This is not the moment for more goals, more proving, more relentless motion. This is the moment to decide what is essential. To strip away the weight of obligations that no longer serve. To surrender the scaffolding that built me so I can step fully into the foundation of what remains.

This is where the fire refines me. Not to harden me but to make me softer and truer.

This is where clarity calls me. Not to push me forward but to pull me into alignment with what has always been waiting.

This is where the decision is made. Not in theory, not in hesitation, not in the comfortable in-between—but in action. In motion. In the step that changes everything.

The road ahead will not reveal itself before I move. That is the nature of thresholds. The moment I trust—The moment I commit—The moment I stop waiting for certainty and instead choose presence—

That is when the path will appear.

This final taste is an invitation. Not to dream but to decide. Not to wonder but to walk forward.

And the only question that remains is this:

Will I answer the call?

Chapter 72. Questions for My Future Self

There is a version of me waiting in the distance, watching. He is not impatient, but he is expectant. He does not measure time in days or years—he measures in choices. He is not a possibility. He is a certainty. The inevitable result of what I do now.

And so, I sit with my questions. Not idle curiosities but instruments of becoming. These are the questions that carve the path beneath my feet.

What will I do today to strengthen my desire for the future I long for?

Desire is not passive. It does not appear like weather. It is fed, sculpted, and forged. I do not wait for motivation. I summon it. I wake up and meet it. I create conditions where it can thrive. And so I ask—what will I put in front of me today that strengthens my hunger for what's possible?

What thoughts will I trust?

My mind is a landscape of shifting weather—storms, clear skies, gusts of past fears and future anxieties. But beneath it all, there is a still place. A deeper knowing. If a thought does not bring me peace, it is not mine to keep. So, I will not chase every gust of wind. I will listen for the stillness. I will trust the knowing beneath the noise.

What does my future self see through the window of time?

He sees me becoming. He sees me unshackled from old patterns, choosing presence over distraction, growth over stagnation, wisdom over certainty. He sees a man who no longer needs to be right—only real. A heart unguarded. A mind open. A presence undeniable.

What feeling am I willing to change?

Some emotions have become furniture in my mind—heavy, familiar, long past their usefulness. But I do not have to carry what is no longer mine. What if I stopped clinging to the weight of what was? What if I set it down? What if I let my past be a story instead of a sentence?

What does my mind sound like when I have clarity?

Like still water. Like breath before words. Like the space between heartbeats where nothing is missing. The mind is always speaking, but it is the quiet mind that speaks truth. So, I will stop filling the silence with noise.

What will I do today to elevate the quality of my energy?

Energy is the source of everything. My life is a projection of the quality of my energy. If I do not like what's playing on the screen, I must change the reel. More stillness. More depth. More of what is in harmony with the man I am becoming.

What adjustments will sharpen my concentration?

The unfocused mind scatters its power. The trained mind directs it. Attention is an offering—what I give it to becomes my reality. So, I will choose where my focus belongs. I will not chase distractions masquerading as urgency. I will concentrate like a sculptor chiseling away the unnecessary.

And so, I return to my future self—the man who stands just beyond this moment, waiting. He does not doubt me. He does not rush me. He only watches, knowing I will arrive in my own time.

And I will.

Step by step. Breath by breath. Thought by thought.

And when I meet him, he will smile and say, I knew you'd make it. And I will smile back because I will know—I had been walking toward him all along.

Chapter 73. What Would I Attempt If I Knew I Would Not Fail?

For as long as I can remember, I have measured myself by what I create. By what I bring into the world. By how much of myself I can pour into something that endures beyond me.

Creation has always been my currency, my language, my way of proving that I exist. And yet, beneath the surface, there has always been a tension—between what I long to create and what I allow myself to create. Between what I dream of doing and what I actually give myself permission to pursue.

So I ask: What would I attempt if I knew I could not fail?

I Would Let Go of the Need to Prove

I would write without agenda. Not for business. Not to build a brand. Not to educate, inspire, or position myself as an expert.

I would write purely because there is something inside me that needs to be said. Not for performance. Not for validation. Just for the sheer truth of it.

I would create things that do not need to succeed. I would make art that does not need to sell. I would pour myself into things that exist simply because they are beautiful, because they matter to me, and because they make me feel alive.

I would stop trying to be so useful. And that—more than anything else—feels radical.

The Myth of Productivity as Purpose

For decades, I have tied my worth to output. I have measured my value by what I produce, how much I contribute, and how many people I serve.

I have built things that matter. I have made an impact. I have helped people.

But do I need to spend the rest of my life proving that I can?

What if I have outgrown this? What if I no longer need to prove my value through output? What if, at this stage in my life, the real work isn't in producing more—but in allowing myself to be more?

If I knew I could not fail, I would allow myself to play. To step outside the frameworks of business and strategy and create for no reason at all.

I would dance—not just in structured settings, not just in familiar rhythms, but wildly, freely, in ways that make no sense. I would move without planning, without performing, without control.

I would take myself out of the known. Disappear for a while. Walk for days in silence just to hear what my soul has been trying to tell me beneath all the noise.

I would stop explaining myself. Stop defending my choices. Stop shaping my expression to be palatable, acceptable, and easily understood.

I would let myself be seen—unfinished, unpolished, unfiltered.

Maybe failure isn't the thing I fear. Maybe what I fear is who I am when I'm no longer striving. When I'm no longer trying to be impressive, productive, and respected.

I have spent a lifetime mastering the art of creating things that matter. But what if I don't need to matter in the way I once did?

What if my next act isn't about legacy at all? What if it's about stepping into something far more vulnerable—a life that is fully, beautifully, unreservedly mine?

So what would I attempt if I knew I could not fail?

I would risk irrelevance. I would risk being misunderstood. I would risk being seen—raw, unpolished, unapologetically true.

I would create not because the world needs it but because I do.

Chapter 74. The Decision That Shapes the Next Three Years

For so long, my life has been measured in milestones—the books written, the businesses built, the events hosted, the people helped. A lifetime of achievement, of forward momentum—always asking, What's next?

But when I strip away the structures and the strategies and when I stop measuring my worth in terms of output, what remains?

The Next Three Years Are Not About Expansion—They're About Depth

I no longer need to build more. I no longer need to prove my capacity to create, teach, or lead.

The question I am asking myself now is: What happens when I stop looking ahead and instead fully inhabit what is already here?

For the next three years, I imagine something radical. I imagine staying—not chasing, not reaching, not expanding, but sinking in. Deeply.

I imagine allowing myself to be still enough to hear the quieter voice beneath the hum of productivity. I imagine choosing presence over performance. I imagine creating without an audience, writing without an agenda, moving my body not to improve it, but to feel it fully. I imagine no longer measuring my days by how much I accomplish but instead by how much I experience.

What If Nothing Needed to Be Justified?

For decades, everything I created had a purpose—a business, a legacy, an impact. Everything I built was justifiable—to serve others, to leave something behind, to matter.

But what if the next three years were not about service? What if they were not about legacy? What if they were about allowing myself to be exactly as I am—without the need to prove, perform, or produce?

I have lived in the public-facing world for so long. What if I stepped away from it? Not in retreat, but in re-immersion—into my own life. Into the people and places that nourish me. Into the simple, sacred rhythm of being.

I imagine a slower pace. A more fluid, less structured existence. A deeper trust that who I am without a plan is enough.

Daring to Walk Away from the Known

It would be easy to keep doing what I have always done. The systems are built. The structures are in place. The machine runs itself.

But I have learned something: What is easy is not always what is alive.

In the next three years, I imagine myself walking away from the predictable paths—not because they are wrong, but because I am ready for something truer.

Maybe it means selling my house and moving somewhere warmer. Maybe it means exploring relationships differently—more intimacy, more vulnerability, more surrender. Maybe it means letting go of control in a way I never have before.

For the first time in my life, I am not asking, What do I need to build? I am asking, What do I need to unbuild?

The Decisions That Shape a Life

A life is not made in one sweeping gesture. It is carved in the quiet moments—the ones where we choose courage over comfort, clarity over confusion, commitment over hesitation.

And today, I have arrived at one of those moments.

The question is simple: What decision does my future self need me to make today?

Not tomorrow. Not next week. Not someday.

Today.

Because the life I dream of five years from now is not built in five years. It is built in a single day, repeated over and over again.

Breaking the Loop

If I do nothing different, tomorrow will look a lot like today. And the day after that, and the day after that.

Momentum works in both directions.

I can move forward by default—drifting in the current of my past patterns, bound by stories I never challenged, trapped in beliefs that were never truly mine.

Or I can move forward by design—disrupting the autopilot, choosing something new, writing a different story.

But that requires something of me:

A decision.

A commitment to a future I haven't yet lived. A willingness to act without proof, without certainty, without guarantees.

And that—that is what my future self is asking of me today.

The Decision That Feels Like a Risk

I feel the pull of comfort. The temptation of what is familiar.

But if my future self could speak, he would say:

"Stay the same, and you will feel safe. But safe is not the same as fulfilled."

"Do what you've always done, and you will feel certain. But certainty is not the same as growth."

"Wait for the perfect moment, and you will feel patient. But patience is not the same as progress."

There is a cost to staying the same. A hidden risk in not choosing. A quiet erosion of dreams that only reveals itself years too late.

So the question is not if I should change. The question is when.

And the answer, always, is now.

What Needs to Happen Next?

I know the decision. I have felt it rise in me. It has been waiting for me all along.

It is not a decision to be considered. It is a decision to be acted upon.

Because decisions are not made in the mind. They are made in motion.

And so—

I move. I step forward. I begin.

Not because I am certain. Not because I am fearless.

But because I trust the voice of the one who has already lived the life I want.

And that voice, my future self, is telling me:

"Go."

The Question That Remains

I have chosen. I have acted.

And now, I ask—

What does this one decision set in motion? What is the first ripple of the life that now unfolds?

I do not know yet.

But I will.

Three years from today, I will look back at this moment—at this single choice—and I will know, without a doubt—

This was the day everything changed.

Chapter 75. The Courage to Transform: The Call and the Answer

Transformation isn't just a shift in behavior—it's a shift in being. It's an unraveling of the familiar, a shedding of old skins, a surrendering of identities that once served me but now hold me back. It isn't neat or linear. It's disruptive, uncomfortable, often involuntary.

But what if I choose it before it chooses me?

There is a part of me standing at the edge—sensing that I can't stay the same, yet resisting the leap. I have transformed many times before. I have burned versions of myself to the ground and risen from the ashes with new clarity, new purpose, new direction. The coach became a creator. The traveler became a lighthouse. The performer became a guide.

Every transformation was painful, but none of them broke me.

They broke me open.

The Illusion of Completion

There's a story I've told myself—maybe unconsciously—that I have arrived. That I have built something enduring, something complete. That my structures are solid, my impact secure, and my purpose defined.

But the part of me that wants to transform knows completion is a trap.

What if the structures I've built are now my confinement? What if, in this moment, the very things I once longed for—the business, the influence, the frameworks—are now the walls between me and my next evolution?

I tell others to embrace pattern disruption, question assumptions, and let go of what no longer serves them. But do I?

What would happen if I dismantled the scaffolding that has held me up for decades?

The Self That Resists

I know there is a part of me that resists transformation. It clings to certainty, to familiarity, to the safety of what's known. It whispers:

"You've done enough. Haven't you worked hard enough? Haven't you built enough? Haven't you given enough?"

But transformation doesn't happen when I feel ready. It happens when I can no longer deny the truth that I have outgrown where I am.

And that's what I feel now. A tightness. A knowing. A restlessness.

The Pattern I Can No Longer Ignore

I've always been a seeker, constantly evolving, constantly becoming. But sometimes, the most courageous act isn't forward motion—it's standing still and letting myself be fully met.

I see the pattern:

When I don't face something, it finds a way to act itself out.

Unspoken grief seeps into my restlessness.

Unprocessed fear hides in my constant motion.

Unhealed wounds show up in the stories I tell about others.

What I don't integrate, I repeat.

What Am I Afraid to Lose?

Every transformation requires a sacrifice. It asks me to release something. To say, this is no longer mine to carry.

So what am I afraid of losing?

The identity of the creator. If I step into a new version of myself, will I lose the creative force that has fueled everything I've built?

The community I've built. Will people still recognize me if I evolve beyond what they expect?

The sense of being needed. If I stop showing up in the same way, who am I to others? Who am I to myself?

These are the questions transformation forces me to ask.

My Courageous Self Speaks

"You need to surrender the illusion that you'll reach a point where you've 'figured it all out.'

Stop waiting for the perfect vantage point where everything makes sense. You will never have all the answers, and you don't need them. You only need presence. Radical, raw, unapologetic presence.

It's easy to stay sharp in business. It's easy to maintain momentum in creation. But in the quiet spaces, where nothing needs to be built, nothing needs to be achieved—

Do I still feel at home in myself?

The Lessons I Must Carry Forward

This is what I'm being called toward:

To break life-draining patterns, not just recognize them.

To stop making suffering my proof of transformation—I don't need pain to validate my growth.

To build on the past instead of hiding in it.

To stop waiting for clarity and start trusting my next step.

To open my heart fully, even if it terrifies me.

And this one:

To let myself be loved.

Not for what I offer. Not for what I create. Not for how well I guide others. Just for who I am, stripped of my titles, my achievements, my brilliance.

Can I let myself be held the way I've held others?

The Choice

Every day, I make a choice:

To turn toward my deepest self or to turn away.

To open or to close.

To integrate or to fragment.

And here's the truth I have to accept:

If I don't choose courage, I choose repetition.

If I don't break the pattern, I will live it again and again.

If I don't fully own my presence, I will look back one day and wonder where I went.

And I refuse to live a life where I disappear from myself.

So I ask again:

What does my courageous self want me to learn next?

It wants me to wake up. It wants me to drop the armor. It wants me to stop performing transformation and fully step into it.

And it wants me to stop waiting for permission to live the life that's already calling me forward.

No more hesitation.

No more delay.

Now.

Chapter 76. Cost of Half Commitments

I've spent years standing in the gray space between commitment and obligation, pretending they were the same thing. Pretending that just because I had agreed to something, or started something, or told myself I should do something—that I was in it.

But I wasn't.

Not fully. Not in the way that actually mattered.

And I know the weight of that.

I've been the guy who says yes with his words but no with his actions. I've stayed in things too long—holding on out of duty, out of fear, out of some misguided sense of loyalty that wasn't really about loyalty at all—it was about avoiding the discomfort of letting go.

I've watched my own hesitation create messes.

Times when I let obligation pull me forward but never found the energy to fully lean in.

Business ventures that felt more like burdens than creations.

Relationships where I lingered past the moment they were meant to end.

Promises I made to myself, only to break them quietly, slowly, one compromise at a time.

I think about my years as an endurance athlete—the long races, the brutal training sessions, the way I learned to override my own body's resistance.

When I trained for the civilian version of Navy SEAL Hell Week, I turned my commitment into a vow:

No matter what, I finish. Or I die.

That's how I did it. That's how I became the oldest person to complete Kokoro.

Because I decided.

Fully. Completely. No halfway.

So why is it easier to commit to suffering than to commit to joy?

Why can I vow to finish a race but hesitate when it comes to letting go of what no longer serves me?

The Cost of Staying in the Middle

I look at the things in my life right now where I'm just walking the line—where I show up out of obligation, but my heart isn't really there.

And I wonder:

What's the cost of staying in the middle?

Because I know what happens when I don't choose:

It creates suffering.

It creates resentment.

It creates a slow erosion of energy, a quiet but persistent drain that takes more from me than just walking away ever would.

So today, I name it.

The places where I'm in, but not really in. The obligations I've mistaken for commitments. The things I've said yes to but never fully embraced.

And I ask myself:

Do I Recommit, or Do I Release?

Because those are the only two choices that leave me with my integrity intact.

Halfway has never been my way. Not really. And I'm done pretending that it works.

So here's my vow:

If I stay, I go all in.

If I let go, I let go completely.

Nothing in between. No more pretending. No more living in the gray. The next step is mine to take. And I take it.

Chapter 77. The Fire That Softens Me

Conflict arrives like an unexpected guest—uninvited but inevitable. It is both a mirror and a storm, a force that shakes loose the illusions I've held about myself, about others, about the way things should be.

I used to think avoiding conflict was the path of wisdom. That silence was resolution. That retreat was a form of self-preservation.

But the truth is this: Avoidance is just another name for fear. And fear has never led me anywhere worth going.

The Refining Fire of Experience

For years, I have lived inside a cycle:

Learn. Integrate. Teach.

But I have come to understand something deeper—before I share, before I teach, before I invite others into my world to experience the lessons I've uncovered, I must first be cooked by them.

I must let the fire of experience break me apart and put me back together, reshaped, refined.

I do not rush this process. I do not hand out wisdom that is still raw, still bleeding, still open.

If I am still flinching from the wound, then it is not yet time.

But when the wound has closed, when the scar remains but no longer aches, then—and only then—do I know I am ready.

This is how I live:

I grow. I learn. I experience. I integrate. I sit with it. I settle, putter, ponder. I walk it out. I work it out.

I let it get into my bones, into my marrow.

And only when it has become part of me—only when it no longer carries the charge of pain but the clarity of understanding—do I teach, do I share, do I give. Then, and only then, do I step forward as a guide.

The Skill of Staying Inside the Fire

And conflict? It is one of the greatest teachers I have ever known.

So I ask myself:

What skill do I need to develop to become more effective in conflict?

To stay when I want to run.

To breathe when I want to react.

To soften when I want to defend.

To listen when my mind is busy forming its next argument.

To hold space for both my truth and theirs—without the need to erase one in service of the other.

Conflict is the fire that softens me.

It does not harden me. It does not make me brittle.

It teaches me that true strength is not force.

True strength is the ability to stand inside the fire, to let it refine me without making me rigid, to let it shape me into something truer.

So I do not rush to resolve. I do not fight to be right. I do not escape to avoid discomfort.

Instead, I allow. I listen. I breathe. I learn.

I let the fire do its work.

And when the lesson has settled into my bones—when the wisdom no longer carries the weight of pain but the lightness of understanding—then, and only then, do I share.

Taste 8: Mastery & Wisdom

An Invitation to the Next Evolution

There comes a point in the journey when mastery is no longer about getting better—it is about seeing differently. It is no longer about proving, refining, or achieving but about trusting, surrendering, and embodying.

Wisdom is what mastery becomes when it stops being about control and starts being about integration. It is not something to reach for; it is something to live.

These next six chapters are not about adding more knowledge, more structure, or more effort. They are about removing what is unnecessary, loosening the grip, and stepping fully into a new way of being.

Here, we explore the sacred space between mastery and surrender, where skill meets flow, where certainty dissolves into deeper knowing, and where growth is no longer measured in accumulation but in alignment.

The Tightrope Between Mastery and Surrender examines the exquisite tension between control and trust—how true mastery requires both disciplined practice and complete release.

The Meta Principle: Owning My Category of One explores what it means to stand fully in my uniqueness, not as something to prove to the world, but as something to inhabit completely.

The Quiet Mastery of Becoming reveals how the path to mastery isn't found in grand declarations but in the whispered devotion to daily discipline.

The Embodied Path: Breath, Food, and Movement as Devotion shifts mastery from the conceptual to the physical, grounding wisdom in the body's natural intelligence and rhythms.

Learning to Become unveils how true learning isn't about accumulation but transformation—the patient unfolding of what has always waited within.

The Long Game of Becoming reminds me that there is no finish line to this work—only a lifelong practice of deepening into presence.

Each chapter is an invitation. To move from grasping to allowing. To shift from seeking to embodying. To recognize that mastery is not a destination but a way of walking through the world.

The path ahead is not one of striving—it is one of surrender. The only question is: Am I willing to trust it?

Chapter 78. The Tightrope Between Mastery and Surrender

The Threshold Between Mastery and Surrender

I wake up with a strange sensation— A tingling in my left hand. A congestion pressing against my lungs. The sharp edge of garlic still lingering in my breath.

My body is speaking to me, though I am not yet fluent in its language. The noise inside my mind drowns out the wisdom that pulses beneath the surface of awareness.

So I sit with it. I breathe into the discomfort, into the weight of whatever is moving through me. And as I do, the eternal questions rise like morning fog:

Who am I? Why am I here? What am I moving through?

For so long, I believed mastery was about knowing. About refining, sharpening, and controlling. I spent decades accumulating knowledge, building intricate structures to hold everything I had gathered.

But now, watching the first light break across the horizon, I wonder— Is the path forward really about more mastery? Or is it about surrender?

The Illusion of Knowledge

Knowledge feeds the intellect. Wisdom feeds the soul. Knowledge helps me make a living. Wisdom helps me make a life. Knowledge is what I possess. Wisdom is what possesses me.

I have spent my life pursuing knowledge—mastering systems, refining frameworks, and building something that would outlast me. But knowledge alone is a half-truth, a partial seeing.

The tightrope walker understands this profound duality. They do not rush across the wire. They do not cling to safety. They do not freeze in fear.

They move with a rhythm that transcends both effort and abandon.

Leaning forward into knowledge. Leaning back into wisdom. Shifting weight. Adjusting. Feeling. Trusting. Never too far in one direction. Never abandoning one world for the other.

The secret is not in choosing mastery or surrender—it is in the sacred balance between them.

The Great Unlearning

Mastery, as I once understood it, was about building—about refining, about control. But true mastery is the art of undoing—the willingness to release the stories, assumptions, and certainties that no longer serve me.

I used to think learning was about acquiring more—more strategies, more frameworks, more skills. But wisdom is subtraction. Wisdom is unlearning.

It is releasing the noise to hear the truth. It is stripping away the unnecessary to reveal the essential. It is standing in the stillness long enough for what is real to rise.

And the real question that confronts me now is— Can I sit in that stillness long enough to listen? Can I bear the discomfort of not knowing? Can I trust the silence more than the noise?

Mastery is Bringing Awareness to the Wobble

I have spent years unraveling the wounds of my childhood. The echoes of feeling unseen, unsafe, too much, not enough.

But mastery is not surrendering to those defaults.

Mastery is bringing awareness to the wobble. Awareness to the grief. Awareness to the power I hold to move forward.

Because when I stop resisting my own wobble—when I bring loving attention to my unsteadiness instead of fighting it—I see the truth:

The path is revealing itself. One step at a time.

Every wobble contains wisdom if I am willing to feel it fully. Every moment of instability is an invitation to find a deeper balance.

The Call to Cross the Threshold

Like every hero's journey, the path begins in the ordinary world. The life I know. The routines that have held me. The identity I've crafted.

But mastery is not the same as wisdom. And the real question hanging in the air is:

What's next?

Am I willing to heed the call? To meet the guide who will challenge my assumptions? To step into the trials that will demand more from me than I have given before?

Because the reward is not instant gratification. It is not external validation.

It is earned experience.

And when the journey is complete, I will return home— Not as the same man, but as the one who has learned how to stand fully inside himself.

The Step That Changes Everything

There is a breathless moment before the step. Before the first foot touches the wire. Before the heart leaps and the mind hesitates.

In that moment, everything hangs in balance—all possibility, all fear, all potential.

But the truth is— I am already on the tightrope. I have always been on the tightrope.

And now, the only thing left to do— Is take the next step.

Not knowing if I will fall. Not knowing if I will fly. Simply trusting the wire, the space, and the quiet knowing inside me.

Chapter 79. The Meta Principle: Owning My Category of One

Owning My Category of One

There is no one else like me. Not in real estate. Not in business. Not in teaching. Not in leadership. Not in creativity. Not in life.

I know this. I've known it for decades. And yet, there's a part of me that still hesitates to own it fully—to stand without apology in the full spectrum of who I am.

I teach others to recognize their unique constellation of gifts, to stop trying to be better versions of someone else, and instead become more of who they already are. I help people see their essence, articulate it, and build around it. I make them undeniable.

But what about me?

What does it truly mean to be a category of one—to step beyond comparison, beyond frameworks, beyond the comfort of external validation?

What does it mean to stand alone, not as an act of ego, but as an act of profound self-recognition?

The Fear of Standing Alone

I've spent a lifetime cultivating a combination of skills that no one else has:

The ability to see and hear people at a level they've never been seen or heard before.

The instinct to read between the words, finding the deeper truth behind what someone is saying.

The relentless, almost obsessive drive to distill insight until it's undeniable.

The gift of turning language into architecture, words into transformation, ideas into movements.

The discipline to build, execute, and deliver consistently—no matter what.

If I were sitting across from myself, coaching myself, I'd say:

"Joe, you are the best at what you do—not because you've outworked others, but because there is no one else in your category. You are irreplaceable. Not better. Not bigger. Just the only one who can do exactly what you do, the way you do it."

And yet, I still feel hesitation.

Not because I doubt my abilities. But because being a category of one is terrifying.

When you're truly singular, there is no roadmap. No peer group to mirror back your worth. No comparisons to ease your uncertainty.

You stand alone in the knowing that what you do, how you think, what you create—is entirely your own.

And that's where the fear creeps in, quiet but persistent.

What if I lose it? What if I stop creating? What if I walk away from everything I've built and realize the best of my work is behind me?

I don't want to be someone who polishes his greatest hits, staying inside a machine that no longer inspires him just because he built it. I don't want to be someone who knows he's the best at something—but secretly wonders if that something is still worth doing.

So here's the part I don't usually say out loud:

I have nothing left to prove to anyone. Not in business. Not in wealth. Not in skill. Not in influence. Not even to myself.

The only thing left to prove is whether I have the courage to let go of proving.

Going Meta—Seeing the Frame That Contains Me

There is always a bigger story than the one I'm living inside. Always a larger pattern. Always a wider frame.

And the move that has saved me—again and again—is what I call going meta.

It's the moment I step back and realize:

The thing I thought was the whole picture is actually just a small piece of something bigger.

The success I was chasing is actually contained inside an even deeper longing.

The problem I've been obsessing over isn't even the real problem—it's just a symptom of something more fundamental.

Going meta is not about detachment. It's not about overanalyzing. It's not about escape.

It's about waking up to the fact that even my most deeply held assumptions—about myself, my work, my future—are just another frame.

And I am capable of stepping beyond it.

The Frame I Couldn't See

I've done this before. In business. In relationships. In my own identity.

I built a company that became larger than me. Then I stepped back and realized the company was inside me.

I built a coaching methodology that was bulletproof. Then I stepped back and saw that the real work wasn't in the method—it was in the presence behind it.

I built a life of achievement. And then, one day, I zoomed out and saw that it was still missing something I couldn't name.

Because here's the hard truth: You can achieve your way into a prison just as easily as you can fail your way into one.

And this is where I find myself now.

Standing at the edge of everything I've built, with the strange sensation that there is still something more. Something I can't see because I'm standing too close to the canvas.

What Happens If I Zoom Out Too Far?

What happens when I step back—not just from one business, one project, one goal—but from the entire scaffolding of my identity?

What happens when I let myself see that even my ambition, my drive, and my ability to create—are all just smaller parts of something even bigger?

What happens when I finally admit that no amount of building will ever be enough to contain my full becoming?

And here's the part I don't want to admit: I'm scared to zoom out too far.

Because what if I discover that the life I've built—the one so many people admire, the one that has given me financial security, reputation, and deep impact—isn't the final form of what I was supposed to do?

What if there's still more? What if I'm not done? What if I have to step beyond the empire I created and trust that something new is calling me?

What if my greatest act of mastery is to surrender what I've mastered?

What Happens If I Zoom In Too Far?

And here's the other part: I'm scared to zoom in too far.

Because when I slow down, when I stop doing long enough to really feel...

I have to sit with the awkwardness of not knowing. I have to sit with the grief of what's ending. I have to sit with the fear that I might not be as needed, as relevant, and as powerful outside of the structures I've built.

But maybe that's exactly what's required.

Maybe I need to let myself feel the full weight of the transition. Maybe living an awakened life isn't about achieving more—it's about surrendering to something larger than achievement.

Maybe the real miracle isn't what I've built. It's what I'm becoming.

Becoming is Terrifying

And that, right there, is what I have been resisting.

Because becoming is terrifying.

It requires me to walk away from certainty and into the unknown.

It requires me to let go of my grip on who I thought I was supposed to be and open myself to who I actually am.

It requires me to trust that even if I don't have the whole map, the next step will reveal itself when I'm ready.

At first, going meta feels like zooming out to see the bigger picture.

But eventually, it leads me right back to the most intimate, raw, vulnerable truth:

I am not done. I am still unfolding. And the next phase of my life will require me to surrender, not strive.

So the question I ask myself now is this:

Am I willing to let go of the old scaffolding to allow the next version of my life to emerge?

Or will I cling to what I know, afraid to trust the space between?

I know the answer. Now I just have to live it.

Chapter 80. The Quiet Mastery of Becoming

The Stillness Before the Shift

There is a moment, just before dawn when the world holds its breath. A hush before the sun stretches its golden arms across the sky. A stillness before everything shifts.

I am in that moment now.

On the edge of something unseen yet deeply known. The breath before the inhale. The step before the leap. The pause before the first note of a song that will change everything.

I have walked this path for a while now—this intimate conversation with my future self. I have unraveled pieces of who I was and gently laid them aside, making space for the self I am becoming, moment by moment.

Not through grand declarations. Not through force or urgency. But through the whispered devotion to discipline.

The Devotion of Discipline

I used to believe discipline was restriction. That it was a set of rules meant to contain me, to strip the joy from the spontaneous, to bind me to a rigid structure I did not want to inhabit.

But now I see:

Discipline is devotion. Discipline is love. Discipline is choosing—again and again—to return to what matters most.

It is not about control. It is about care.

When I tend to something daily, I am telling it—you matter to me. Whether it's my breath, my body, my creative work, my relationships. Everything flourishes under steady attention.

The tightrope walker doesn't practice to control the wire. The tightrope walker practices to know themselves so deeply that when they step onto the wire, they become one with it.

Discipline is not about forcing myself to do things. It is about choosing presence over distraction, commitment over avoidance, and depth over stagnation.

It is showing up on the days when inspiration fails me. It is breathing deeply when anxiety constricts me. It is moving slowly when urgency tempts me. It is saying no to what distracts me from what matters most.

This is the quiet mastery of becoming—not the loud achievements that everyone can see, but the silent devotions that no one sees but me.

The Grace of Witnessing

Osho once said, "Balance is not something we force. It comes of its own accord, with beauty and grace."

And he was right.

When sadness comes, I do not grasp at it or push it away. When joy arrives, I do not cling to it in fear of its departure. When uncertainty whispers, I do not rush to silence it.

I witness. I trust. I allow.

Because I know: all things pass—except the one who is watching.

It is not about fixing or controlling. It is about becoming aware. Becoming the witness to my own unfolding.

And the more I witness, the more I see:

My breath shapes my thoughts. My food shapes my emotions. My movement shapes my energy. My stillness shapes my wisdom. My sleep shapes my dreams.

Everything is connected.

When I change one element, I change the whole. When I attend to the smallest details of my life with presence, the larger patterns shift.

This is the power of witnessing—not changing what I see, but being changed by what I see.

The Risk of Stagnation

Excuses will always be there for me. Opportunity will not.

There is no such thing as standing still. I am either growing or decaying. Expanding or contracting. Evolving or staying small.

And stagnation is just slow decay.

I am not a boat meant to stay in the harbor. I am meant to sail, to drift beyond the known, to meet the wind and let it take me places I cannot yet see.

Yes, untethering is uncomfortable. But I am not here for comfort. I am here for depth.

The tightrope walker knows that to stay in one position too long is to lose balance. Movement—even the smallest, most subtle adjustments—is what keeps us from falling.

So I move. Daily. Intentionally. With presence. Not because I have to. But because movement is life.

One Step. Close In.

David Whyte, in the poetry of his wisdom, whispers: "Start close in. Take the first step. The one you don't want to take."

The first step is always the hardest. But it is also the most powerful.

So today, I take it.

One deep breath that expands not just my lungs but my awareness. One moment of stillness that quiets not just my body but my mind. One meal that nourishes not just my cells but my energy. One night of rest that replenishes not just my fatigue but my creativity. One movement that reminds me not just that I have a body but that I am a body.

Not all at once. Not all perfectly. Just one.

Because all I have is today. And today, I choose to become.

Today, I place one foot on the wire. Today, I trust the space beneath me. Today, I let go of the rail and step into the unknown.

The Invitation to the Reader

Now, close your eyes. Breathe.

Feel the wire beneath your feet. Feel the space around you. Feel the next step calling you.

What is your one step today?

Chapter 81. The Embodied Path - Breath, Food, and Movement as Devotion

The Foundation of Everything

Breath. Sleep. Food. Stillness. Movement.

These are not separate from my mind, my emotions, and my ability to create. They are the foundation of everything.

I used to think personal growth happened in the mind—through books, insights, revelations, and breakthroughs.

But now I know: Transformation begins in the body.

If I am tired, I will make poor decisions. If I am eating in a way that clouds my energy, I will struggle to find clarity. If my breath is shallow, my mind will be restless. If I do not move, my emotions will stagnate.

The way I live inside my body is the way I live inside my life.

This is not philosophy. This is physiology.

Breath as the First Discipline

Before I change my thinking, before I shift my habits, and before I take on any grand transformation, I start with my breath.

Because the way I breathe tells me everything.

Am I rushing? My breath will be short and shallow. Am I holding tension? My breath will be tight and constricted. Am I present? My breath will be slow, deep, and open.

The breath is the only system in the body that is both automatic and conscious. It is the bridge between what happens to me and how I choose to respond.

If I change my breath, I change my mind.

Practice: The 4-7-8 Breath Inhale for 4 counts, expanding the belly. Hold for 7 counts, letting the oxygen saturate your cells. Exhale for 8 counts, emptying completely. Repeat 4 times.

This isn't just a breathing exercise. It's a reset for the nervous system. A way to shift from stress to calm in under a minute.

When I'm on the tightrope and feel myself wobbling, this is the practice that brings me back to center.

Food as Energy, Not Reward

Food is more than fuel. Food is communication.

If I eat what makes me sluggish, I am telling my body: You do not matter. If I eat in a rush, I am telling myself: There is no time for presence. If I eat in a way that nourishes me, I am saying: I respect my energy.

I no longer eat for comfort. I no longer eat for entertainment. I eat to feel alive.

I eat in a way that gives me clarity. I eat in a way that supports my future self.

Because what I eat shapes the next three hours of my life.

Practice: The First Bite Ritual

Before each meal, I take a moment of silence. I look at my food, acknowledging all that brought it to me. I take the first bite with full attention, noticing texture, flavor, and sensation. I place my utensil down between bites.

This simple practice transforms eating from mindless consumption to mindful nourishment. It's not about perfection. It's about presence.

Sleep as Sacred Restoration

I spent years treating sleep as optional. As if rest was something I had to "earn."

Now, I see: Sleep is non-negotiable.

A bad night's sleep will distort my thoughts. A rested mind can hold more complexity, more nuance, and more presence.

I do not "hack" my sleep. I do not sacrifice it for more work. I protect it like my most valuable resource.

Because the way I rest tonight is the way I will meet the world tomorrow.

Practice: The Evening Descent

Two hours before bed, I begin to lower the lights. One hour before bed, I put away all screens. Thirty minutes before bed, I write down what's on my mind. Ten minutes before bed, I focus only on my breath.

This isn't just a routine. It's a ritual that tells my body: It's safe to let go. It's time to restore.

Movement as Medicine

I do not move to "burn calories." I do not move to "stay in shape." I move to feel alive.

I stretch to create space in my mind. I walk to clear stagnant energy. I lift to remind myself of my strength. I dance to break patterns of rigidity.

Movement is not just about fitness. Movement is about freedom.

If I do not move, I become stagnant—in body, in thoughts, in life.

Practice: The Daily Unlocking

Upon waking, I place my feet on the floor and feel my connection to the earth. I slowly roll my spine, vertebra by vertebra, letting each segment wake up. I gently move each joint—ankles, knees, hips, shoulders, wrists—in circles. I shake out any tension, letting my body lead, not my mind.

This practice takes less than five minutes. But it changes how I move through the day. It reminds me that I am not separate from my body—I am my body.

Stillness as Integration

For years, I filled every moment with stimulation. Podcasts. Audiobooks. Conversations.

Now, I make space for silence. Because if I never sit in stillness, I will never hear my own wisdom.

Presence is not something I achieve. It is something I return to. Again and again and again.

Practice: The 5-Minute Sanctuary

I set a timer for five minutes. I sit in a position that allows my spine to be both relaxed and alert. I close my eyes and focus on the sensation of my breath in my nostrils. When my mind wanders (and it will), I gently bring it back to the breath.

This isn't meditation to achieve enlightenment. This is a sanctuary from the noise. A daily reminder that beneath all the doing, there is being.

The Invitation to the Reader

This is the embodied path. Not just philosophy. Not just insight. But breath, food, movement, rest, and stillness—lived.

So, I ask you:

What part of your body is asking for attention today? And will you listen?

What breath pattern would bring you back to center? What food would nourish not just your hunger but your clarity? What movement would release what you're holding? What rest would restore what's depleted? What stillness would allow you to hear what's true?

Your body knows. It's always known. The question is—are you listening?

Chapter 82. Learning to Become

There was a time when I believed learning was something I did to achieve a goal. Something external. Something I had to gather and stack like bricks—building a tower high enough to prove my worth.

I was wrong.

Learning is not accumulation. Learning is transformation. Learning is the slow unfolding of what has always been waiting inside me. It is the patient chiseling away of what is not true, until only essence remains.

For years, I pursued knowledge with urgency—as if the right book, the right teacher, and the right insight would unlock the final answer.

But learning is not a key to some final door. Learning is the path itself. And I am both the traveler and the destination.

What Have I Yet to Learn?

I have learned how to move forward. But have I learned how to be still?

I have learned how to seek answers. But have I learned how to trust the silence?

I have learned how to build. But have I learned how to let go?

Life whispers to me daily—the lessons I still resist, the truths I already know but refuse to embody, the ways I repeat my own cycles, mistaking motion for growth.

If all of life is learning, then every moment is a lesson.

Not just the books and the training. Not just the practice and the pursuit. But the quiet pauses in between.

The way I breathe when I'm alone. The way I soften when I surrender. The way I listen—to myself, to others, to the space between words.

The tightrope walker's greatest teacher isn't the instructor shouting from below. It's the wire itself. The space around it. The silence within it.

The Art of Falling

I used to believe learning was about mastery. Now, I believe learning is about falling.

Not falling behind. Not falling short. But falling into something deeper. Something truer.

Like a tightrope walker trusting the pull of gravity, I have learned that balance is not a place—it is a practice.

And if I never allow myself to fall, I will never know what true balance feels like.

So I fall. I let myself stumble. I let myself be a beginner.

Because the one who fears falling is the one who never truly jumps.

The one who must be perfect never learns. The one who must be right never grows. The one who must be safe never transforms.

I have fallen many times. I have failed publicly. I have made mistakes that cost me—relationships, opportunities, and growth.

But each fall has taught me something my success never could. Each fall has brought me closer to who I am beneath the armor of achievement.

Becoming the Lesson

What if my greatest teacher is not in a book but in my breath? What if the wisdom I seek is not in some distant future but in the way I sit with myself today?

I no longer wish to simply know things. I want to become them.

I want to inhale knowledge until it sinks into my bones, until it becomes part of the way I move, the way I see, the way I love.

I don't want to learn patience. I want to be patient. I don't want to learn presence. I want to embody presence. I don't want to learn love. I want to become love.

This is the lesson I am learning now. To stop reaching and instead receive. To stop forcing and instead allow.

To let learning be less about acquisition and more about integration.

The Future Self as the Teacher

My future self is already wise. Already full. Already living the lessons I am only now beginning to grasp.

So I ask my future self:

What do you see that I cannot yet understand? What have you learned that I am still resisting? What truths have I yet to surrender to?

And my future self answers—

"You are not here to win learning. You are here to live learning.

There is no finish line. No final test. No certificate of completion.

Only the daily, deliberate practice of becoming.

The moment you think you've mastered something is the moment you stop learning it. The moment you think you know is the moment you close yourself to discovery. The moment you think you've arrived is the moment your journey stalls."

What's Possible When I Trust This?

If I trust that all of life is learning, then—

There is no failure—only feedback. There is no wasted time—only experience. There are no wrong turns—only different lessons.

If I trust that I can learn anything, then—

I am never stuck. Never trapped. Never at the mercy of circumstance.

If I trust that learning is the point, then—

I can let go of perfection. Let go of proving. Let go of comparison.

And instead, I can simply—breathe, absorb, and trust the unfolding.

I can live with the beginner's mind even after years of practice. I can approach what I know as if I'm discovering it for the first time. I can hold my expertise lightly, making space for what I have yet to understand.

The Question That Remains

So I ask myself—

Not what do I need to learn today? But what am I already learning? Not what do I need to master? But what do I need to surrender to? Not what is missing? But what is already here, waiting to be seen?

The answer is always the same:

Everything I need is already within me. Every lesson I seek is already unfolding. Every truth I long for is already revealing itself.

If only I have the courage to listen.

The Final Insight

My future self smiles. Because it knows—I already have everything I need.

All that's left is to live it.

So, I take a breath. I close my eyes. And I step into the lesson of today.

Ready. Open. Learning.

Now, pause. Breathe. Feel your own unfolding.

What are you already learning? What do you need to surrender to? What is already here, waiting to be seen?

The wire is beneath your feet. The lesson is all around you. The becoming is already happening.

Can you feel it?

Chapter 83. The Long Game of Becoming

I used to chase self-improvement like it was a finish line—as if the right books, the right habits, and the perfect routine would one day unlock a version of me that was disciplined, clear, and unstoppable. Like there was a final version waiting at the end of all this effort. Done. Complete. Fully optimized.

But that isn't how it works. I know that now.

The real work isn't in becoming someone else. It's in becoming more myself.

Peeling back the layers. Seeing what's there. Unlearning, as much as learning.

And the deeper I go, the more I realize:

I will never be finished. Not because I'm broken. Not because there's something to fix. But because growth is the natural state of being alive.

I don't need to be fixed. I need to be witnessed.

Seeing Myself Clearly

I've spent years cultivating self-awareness, and still, I miss things. There are blind spots I only notice when I crash into them. Old patterns I thought I had outgrown creep back in when I'm not paying attention.

But the work isn't to be perfect. The work is to notice faster.

To shorten the gap between action and reflection.

And there are moments—clear, undeniable moments—where I do see myself.

When I catch the split second between trigger and reaction. When I pause, instead of falling into the same loop. When I recognize the moment before I become the person I don't want to be.

Those moments feel like air. Like space. Like freedom.

And then, inevitably, I forget.

I slip back into unconsciousness, and the pattern repeats. But each time, I come back a little faster.

This is the cycle. See. Forget. Remember. Repeat.

And I've stopped making that mean I'm failing.

I've stopped expecting the process to be linear. I've stopped waiting to arrive. I've stopped believing there's a version of me that won't wobble on the wire.

Because the tightrope walker doesn't eliminate wobble—they become attuned to it. They feel it before anyone else can see it. They adjust before the imbalance takes over.

That's what I'm practicing now. Not perfection, but attunement.

The Edges of Who I Am

I used to think self-improvement was about accumulating more. More knowledge. More discipline. More skills.

But now, I see—It's just as much about stripping things away.

Letting go of outdated identities. Releasing stories I've told myself for years that no longer serve me. Removing the armor, I no longer need to wear.

I see my resistance more clearly now.

The way I hold onto things—beliefs, habits, roles—not because they are true, but because they are familiar.

There is comfort in the known, even when the known is limiting.

What would it feel like to step fully into the unknown?

Taste 9: Beyond the Self - Moving Into What Lasts

There comes a moment in every journey when the work is no longer about what we build but what remains. A moment when we realize that the chase for more—more success, more influence, more achievement—was never the real pursuit.

What we are truly after is meaning. Not just impact, but imprint. Not just influence but legacy.

And legacy is not what we leave behind—it is what we live now.

The Shift That Changes Everything

The questions begin to change:

What can I accomplish? → **What am I truly here to give?**
How much can I build? → **What will still matter when I'm gone?**
How do I succeed? → **How do I create something that outlives me?**

This is the moment where ego gives way to purpose, where ambition matures into devotion, wand here success expands into something sacred.

It is no longer about effort but alignment. No longer about accumulating but offering. No longer about leading followers but creating leaders.

This is the shift from personal achievement to collective elevation. From being seen to becoming a force. From making an impact to shaping what lasts.

What These Chapters Hold

This section is a threshold—an invitation into a rare kind of success:

The kind that does not just create but endures.
The kind that does not just leave a mark but leaves the world different.

Here, we will redefine:

Contribution—not as relentless effort, but as something sourced from deep truth.
Leadership—not as authority, but as the responsibility to call forth the greatness in others.
Legacy—not as something to be remembered for, but as a way of being right now.

Because the real measure of a life well lived is not found in what we keep but in what we give away—freely, boldly, completely.

This is the work that lasts. And this is the moment we step fully into it.

Are You Ready to Cross the Threshold?

The next chapters are not just words. They are an invitation to step beyond the self—

To build in a way that outlives us,
To lead in a way that multiplies our impact,
To live in a way that becomes the legacy itself.

This is the next frontier. Not the pursuit of success but the pursuit of what is timeless.

And the only question left is—Are you ready to step into what lasts?

Chapter 84. The Nesting Dolls of Relationship Evolution

Every relationship in my life has been a living thing. Not static. Not fixed. But breathing, shifting, and stretching into new shapes over time.

What was once fierce love became quiet reverence. What was once teacher became peer. What was once need became knowing.

Growth does not discard. It does not sever. It does not erase.

It contains.

Like Russian nesting dolls—one version of me inside another, inside another. Each stage of who I have been still exists inside me. Not separate, but stacked. Not forgotten, but carried. Every relationship, every lesson, every moment of transformation still whispering through the structure of who I am today.

Nothing is lost. The past is not behind me. It is within me.

I have come to understand that relationships do not disappear when they change; they simply take on a new form. A mentor becomes a friend. A friend becomes a distant memory, but their imprint remains. A love that once burned intensely cools into quiet respect.

Some relationships remain static because they are meant to. Others shift and evolve, requiring us to let go of the idea that things must stay the same to remain meaningful.

So I ask myself:

What relationship in my life is evolving in a way I haven't fully acknowledged?

What story about a relationship have I been holding onto that may no longer be true?

What happens when I embrace the idea that nothing is lost, only transformed?

This is where relationships become something more—living reflections of the selves we have been and the selves we are becoming. When I honor their evolution, I honor my own.

Chapter 85. The Disruptor's Way - Breaking Patterns to Grow

I have disrupted myself over and over again. Not because I was forced to. Not because I had no other choice. But because something inside me demanded it.

Some people fear change. I have always felt at home inside it. Not because it is easy—but because stagnation is worse.

I have spent a lifetime building, unbuilding, and rebuilding myself. Testing the edges of what I am. Refusing to settle into anything too comfortable for too long. Because I know—if I do not disrupt myself, life will do it for me.

Some patterns are easy to name. Others are woven so deeply into the body that we mistake them for truth.

I was a child who learned that love was unpredictable. That tenderness was rare. That being too much could get you exiled.

I was a boy who became a man who could shape himself to fit any room. Who could scan a space and know what was needed before a single word was spoken. Who could disappear inside the expectations of others without even realizing he was doing it.

And I carried that survival skill into every space I entered. It made me successful. It made me magnetic. It made me impossible to get.

Because for all my skill in connection, there was always an exit strategy. A way to leave before I was left. A way to hold control so that nothing unpredictable could break me.

But here is the truth: What keeps us safe also keeps us small. What once protected us eventually becomes a cage. And we do not break free by waiting.

We break free by disrupting the cycle.

At 54, I did the hardest thing I had ever done. I entered Kokoro—the Navy SEAL Hell Week for civilians. Fifty hours. No sleep. No mercy.

And for the first time in my life—I learned what it meant to be on a team.

For decades, I had survived alone. I had built success alone. I had built safety alone.

I had believed that strength meant handling everything myself.

But in Kokoro, there was no surviving alone. The only way to make it through was together.

And I did. I became the oldest person to ever complete Kokoro. And it shattered something inside me.

It shattered the belief that I had to do it all myself. It shattered the illusion that independence was the highest virtue. It showed me that the deepest strength was not in standing alone—but in trusting myself inside the collective.

So now I ask myself—and I ask you—

What pattern in your life is ready to be disrupted?

What belief about yourself has outlived its purpose?

What is the cost of staying the same versus stepping into something new?

Disruption is not destruction. It is reinvention. It is the conscious decision to break free from what no longer serves us so we can step into what does.

This is the taste of transformation. The question is—are you willing to take the next bite?

Chapter 86. The Five Stages of Business Growth

The Path to Significance

A business, like a life, unfolds in stages. Each one requires a different version of me. Each one reveals a deeper truth about what I am here to create.

1. Survival: The First Test

The early days are a battle against gravity—a relentless balancing act of risk and resilience, of making just enough to see another day. Survival is raw. It is humbling. It strips away illusion and reveals what I am truly made of. It asks, *Do you have the heart for this? Will you fight for your vision when no one else sees it yet?* If I answer yes, I take my first step toward something greater.

2. Stability: The Foundation

Once the storms of survival have passed, there is a shift—From scrambling to standing, From chaos to structure, From reacting to rooting in.

Stability is where systems emerge, and foundations are laid. The frantic energy of early hustle softens into a steady, reliable rhythm. But stability is not the destination—it is the launchpad.

It asks, *Are you ready to expand beyond yourself?* If I answer yes, I begin to breathe deeper into possibility.

3. Success: The Illusion & The Awakening

For many, this is where the journey ends. The world applauds. The numbers climb. The recognition arrives. But success alone is a hollow throne if it is not built on something meaningful.

It asks, *What now? Will you keep playing for yourself, or will you play for something greater?* If I answer yes to something greater, I step forward into significance.

4. Significance: Where Legacy Begins

This is where business transforms into something sacred. Where I am no longer just accumulating wealth but redistributing wisdom. Where my focus shifts from what I can gain to what I can give.

A significant business is not built on profit alone but on principle. It is measured not just in revenue but in the lives touched, the change sparked, and the communities uplifted. It asks, *Will you lead with purpose? Will you create something that outlives you?* If I answer yes, I enter the final stage of mastery.

5. Sacred: The Business Becomes a Movement

This is the rarest space. The highest calling. A business that is no longer just a business but a vessel for something holy.

This is where the work becomes devotion. Where I am not just an entrepreneur but a guardian of impact and a custodian of change. A sacred business is not about empire. It is about legacy.

It is the teacher whose lessons shape generations. The leader whose vision rewires an industry. The movement that shifts the consciousness of a community.

This is business as an offering. A gift to the world. A living testament that work can be divine.

Chapter 87. From Success to Sacred - Transforming Work Into Purpose

The Shift From Achievement to Devotion

There comes a moment when success is no longer enough. When the chase, the numbers, the accolades—all of it—feels hollow without something deeper anchoring it.

It's the moment I realize that business is not just about transactions—it's about transformation. It's not just about income—it's about impact. This is the threshold where the journey shifts.

Beyond Success: The Call to Something Greater

I have reached the stage where my work is no longer just about building wealth but about building meaning. Where my business is not just a career but a calling. Where every decision, every conversation, and every act of creation carries the weight of something bigger than myself.

This is not about scaling for profit. It's about scaling for purpose.

What Changes When Work Becomes Sacred?

I no longer work just for efficiency. I work for transformation.
I no longer seek transactions. I seek impact.
I no longer build for more. I build for meaning.

A sacred business does not ask, *How much can I earn?* It asks, *How much can I give?* It does not measure success in dollars but in depth.

The Moment of Decision

I can feel the shift happening inside me. I cannot return to old measures of success. I cannot pretend that this is just about scaling, optimizing, or maximizing. I am standing at the threshold of something different.

And I have to ask myself: Am I willing to step into it? To release the old goals and step into a new way of being? To trust that my work is meant to be more than just what I can build?

Because this is no longer about business. This is about devotion. To a purpose larger than myself. To a mission that will outlive me. To a calling that cannot be ignored.

The Only Question That Remains

Am I willing to let success evolve into something sacred?

The answer is already inside me. And now, I have to live it.

Chapter 88. Leadership as a Cause - Building More Than a Business

From Running a Company to Leading a Movement

Every day, I make decisions. Some small. Some significant. Some shape the path ahead; others merely keep me moving.

But I know, deep down, that not all decisions are equal. Some reinforce comfort and familiarity, while others push me toward something greater—toward the work I was truly meant to do.

The difference? One is a company. The other is a cause.

A company exists to function—to sustain, to optimize, to expand. A cause exists to ignite, to transform, to matter.

And today, I stand at the threshold of a question I can no longer avoid:

Am I building a company, or am I leading a cause?

The Decision That Changes Everything

I have spent decades building, creating, refining, and mastering. I've built systems, courses, businesses, and communities. I've taught, led, inspired, and served.

And I have done it all well.

But the question that lingers—the question I cannot escape—is:

Is that enough?

Not enough for the world. Not enough for my clients. Not enough in terms of success.

Enough for me.

Have I been building something great while still hiding from something greater?

Because when I picture myself as a cause, I am no longer measuring success by transactions, revenue, or engagement metrics—I am measuring it by impact, transformation, and the wake I leave behind.

And when I see that, I know the truth: I can no longer live small. I can no longer create within the boundaries of 'just enough.' I can no longer pretend that playing it safe is playing it smart.

Because my cause is bigger than me.

The Difference Between a Company and a Cause

A company serves a market. A cause serves a mission.
A company seeks efficiency. A cause seeks transformation.
A company builds an audience. A cause builds a movement.
A company solves problems. A cause changes lives.

And this is what I know: I am here to build a cause.

Not because I need to, but because I can't not.

I have reached the point in my life where I have the wisdom, the resources, the experience, and the perspective to create something that outlives me.

Something that does not just serve clients but awakens something in them. Something that does not just generate value but creates meaning. Something that does not just solve problems but solves the right ones.

The Requirement of Leadership

Leadership is not a title. It is not a position. It is not granted or bestowed.

Leadership is a responsibility. A commitment. A calling.

And today, I must ask myself: What is required of me to grow my impact as a leader today?

Not what is convenient. Not what is comfortable. Not what is optional.

What is required?

The Four Requirements of True Leadership

1. Clarity: A Leader Must Know Where They Are Going

A leader without clarity is like a wandering beacon—shining light but offering no direction. I must be precise. I must be unwavering in my direction. I must embody the purpose I serve.

Because if I am unclear, those who follow me will be even more so.

So today, I recommit to clarity. I will refine my vision. I will communicate it relentlessly. I will ensure that those around me understand not just what we do but why we do it.

2. Service: A Leader Exists to Serve, Not to Be Served

Robert Greenleaf said, "A leader is first experienced as a servant to others."

To lead is to serve. To serve is to listen.

And so, today, I ask myself—Am I truly serving those I lead? Or am I expecting them to serve me?

A servant-leader does not seek power. A servant-leader seeks impact.

I will listen more than I speak. I will seek to understand before I seek to be understood. I will measure my leadership not by my own achievements but by the growth of those I guide.

This is the path of true leadership. Anything less is a facade.

3. Courage: A Leader Must Take Risks

To lead is to stand at the edge of uncertainty and walk forward anyway. It is to embrace risk, take action in the face of fear, and make decisions without guarantees.

And so, I ask—What is the risk of stepping fully into my leadership? What will I lose? What will I gain?

And what is the greater risk—stepping forward or staying the same?

Because there is no neutral ground in leadership. A leader who does not grow shrinks. A leader who does not take risks becomes irrelevant.

So today, I choose courage.

4. Integrity: A Leader Must Be the Message They Deliver

A leader does not lead by command. A leader leads by example.

And so today, I ask—Do my actions align with my values? Am I walking my talk? Am I embodying the standards I set for others?

If I demand growth, I must grow. If I demand discipline, I must be disciplined. If I demand excellence, I must live with excellence.

The One Question That Changes Everything

When I imagine my work as a cause, I no longer ask, "What should I do?" I ask, "What must be done?"

Not what is practical. Not what is profitable. Not what is expected.

But what is undeniably right.

The Moment of Truth

If I truly commit to my cause—
If I stop waiting,
If I stop hesitating,
If I stop making small moves—

Then everything changes.

Because when I move with the force of my purpose behind me, the world has no choice but to move with me.

The right people will find me. The right opportunities will emerge. The right momentum will build.

Because a cause calls forth something greater—Not just in me, but in everyone it touches.

And that is what I am here to do.

So, I Step Forward

Not as a company. Not as a brand. Not as a product.

As a cause.

And in doing so, I leave behind everything that is too small, too safe, too comfortable.

Because I know now, without question, I was never meant to build just a company. I was meant to build a movement.

Chapter 89. Purpose in Life Asking of Me

I wake up each morning knowing that my life is not an accident. I am here for a reason—even if that reason is not always clear in the moment.

There is something pulling me forward, guiding me, demanding of me.

And yet, there are times I resist.

I want to ask, What's next? But I already know the answer.

My purpose is not to wait on some grand revelation. It is not something I need to find—it is something I need to step into.

So I ask again, from the depths of my being:

What Is My Purpose in Life Asking of Me Right Now?

It is asking me to stop overcomplicating my contribution. It is asking me to stop hiding behind mastery and start embodying presence. It is asking me to stop waiting for certainty and start trusting what I already know.

It is asking me to love fully—without conditions, without strategy, without needing to know where it leads. It is asking me to surrender—not in defeat, but in the kind of surrender that expands rather than contracts. It is asking me to serve from a place of joy, not obligation.

To create because I am called to create, not because I feel the need to prove my worth.

It is asking me to let go of the belief that I have to carry it all alone. That I have to do more, be more, and give more before I am allowed to rest in the knowing that I am enough.

The Stories I Must Release

There is a story I tell myself—one that has shaped me, served me, and also kept me trapped.

It says that my worth is in my ability to produce. That my contribution is only as valuable as its impact. That I am loved for what I create, not simply for who I am.

And yet, I know—deep in my bones—that my purpose is not about accumulation, achievement, or recognition.

It is about offering myself fully to this moment.

The people in my life were not placed here by accident. Every soul I encounter is a reflection, a lesson, a chance to give and receive in ways I have yet to understand.

I know that every single event—whether joyous or painful—has been placed here for me.

Not to test me. Not to punish me. Not to see how much I can endure.

But to wake me up.

To strip away every illusion. To remove every excuse. To remind me that I have everything I need right now and to live fully into my purpose.

What I Cannot Avoid Any Longer

I know what happens when I resist what life is asking of me. I distract myself with projects, goals, and movement. I busy myself with the work of serving others while quietly neglecting my own soul.

But avoidance is an illusion—the purpose always remains. The work of my life will not let me go simply because I try to look away.

So I must ask:

What am I avoiding? Where am I hesitating? What truth am I refusing to accept?

Because my purpose does not require more effort. It requires more surrender.

It asks me to see every challenge as a calling. It asks me to turn toward what is uncomfortable because that is where my transformation lives. It asks me to stop seeking validation and start trusting my own inner knowing.

It asks me to wake up today—not someday. To stop waiting for the "perfect conditions" to begin. To stop pretending I don't already know what I need to do.

The Risk of Ignoring the Call

If I ignore what my purpose is asking of me, I know what will happen.

The ache in my chest will not go away. The quiet dissatisfaction will linger beneath every success. The longing for something more, deeper and truer will persist.

But the moment I say yes—fully, unapologetically—everything shifts.

The path becomes clear. The weight lifts. The resistance dissolves.

Not because I have figured it all out—but because I have finally stopped pretending I need to.

The One Question That Matters

When my time comes—when I am looking back rather than forward—what will matter most?

Will I regret that I didn't accomplish more? Or will I regret that I held back my love?

Will I wish I had built one more thing? Or will I wish I had been more present, more open, more willing to let life move through me?

My purpose in life is not asking me to wait.

It is asking me to step fully into what is already mine. To trust what I already know. To give what I was born to give—without hesitation, without fear, without apology.

It is asking me to live fully and completely right now.

No More Waiting.

No More Resisting.

No More Hesitation.

Now. Now. Now.

Chapter 90. Transcend and Include - Evolving Without Abandoning My Foundations

For years, I believed transformation required leaving things behind—shedding skins, burning bridges, and cutting ties with anything that no longer fit. I thought growth was a clean break, a sharp line between what was and what would be.

But now I see—that was survival, not evolution.

Real transformation is not about abandoning what came before. It is about transcending and including.

It is the realization that the past is not something to discard—but something to integrate.

That the version of me that built everything I have today—the structures, the relationships, the mastery—was never meant to be left behind.

It was meant to evolve.

The Version of Me That Got Me Here

For four decades, I have built empires of connection—By Referral Only, BroVance, Inner Circle, Magic Words Dojo, and Turn Your Business Card Into a Book.

Each one is a manifestation of my deepest instinct: to create, to guide, to serve.

But now, I have to ask myself—

Did I let my creations become my identity? Did I mistake what I built for who I am?

I built frameworks that helped thousands of people find their voice, their purpose, and their calling.

But in all of that, did I pause long enough to redefine my own?

Because I feel it now. The pull toward something bigger.

And not bigger in the way I once thought—not more scale, more reach, more numbers.

Bigger in depth. Bigger in authenticity. Bigger in allowing myself to become more of who I already am.

But stepping into that means something has to shift.

I can no longer be the keeper of frameworks, the orchestrator of transformation, the one who always has the answer.

That version of me must still exist—but it can no longer be in control.

Who Do I Bring With Me?

And then there are my relationships—the people who have walked this journey with me.

The clients who first came for business coaching but who are now contemplating their own reinvention.

The colleagues who were once competitors but are now co-creators in something greater.

The mentees who once sought my wisdom but who I now learn from in ways I never expected.

I do not outgrow people. I outgrow roles.

And when I allow my relationships to expand with me, they remain vital.

But I must also ask—

Which relationships have remained static? Where have I stayed out of habit, obligation, or an outdated identity?

Some relationships are meant to evolve.

Not because they are broken but because they were never meant to stay in one shape.

The question is not, Do I leave them behind? The question is, Can they evolve with me?

The Tension Between Evolution and Belonging

And then, the deepest truth of all—

My greatest fear is not growth. My greatest fear is growing out of belonging.

That if I step too far outside the structures I built, I will become unrecognizable to those who have been with me for years.

That if I fully become who I feel called to be, I will be alone.

But belonging that is conditional on staying the same—is not belonging.

The people who are meant to walk this next phase with me will recognize me even as I evolve.

They will not cling to what I was—they will celebrate what I am becoming.

And those who can't?

They were part of my past, not my future.

What I Am Ready to Transcend and What I Am Ready to Include

I am ready to transcend the need to be the authority—the one who has it all figured out.

I am ready to transcend the belief that my past creations define my future.

I am ready to transcend transactional relationships that don't expand into something more human, more alive, more real.

But—

I will include my wisdom. My ability to see people deeply, to speak the words they didn't know they needed to hear.

I will include my craft. My ability to write, to create, to connect, to express what others cannot yet articulate.

I will include my faith—that something larger than me is guiding this next chapter.

And I will include the people who are willing to evolve alongside me.

The Question That Calls Me Forward

What relationship in my life is ready to transcend its original boundaries while including the foundation that made it meaningful in the first place?

And—

Am I brave enough to let that evolution happen?

Chapter 91. The Art of Elegant Change - Finding My Riverbanks

There was a time when I believed success required rigid control. That if I could just structure my days, my relationships, and my work with enough precision, I could create something unshakable.

A fortress of discipline. A system so airtight that everything inside it would run flawlessly.

And for years, it worked. Until it didn't.

Until the very structures that once supported me began to feel like cages.

Until the systems I built no longer felt like freedom but obligation.

Until I realized—transformation isn't about control. It's about flow.

A river doesn't force itself forward. It moves because it is held and guided.

It doesn't resist change. It carves new paths as needed.

And yet—without riverbanks, without something holding space for its flow, it would disperse into nothingness.

That's what I'm searching for now. Not rigid systems. Not freefalling chaos. The balance between the two.

What Structures Support My Flow?

I've been reflecting on the difference between artificial constraints and organic structures.

Artificial constraints feel like rules imposed from the outside—things I do because I think I should, because the industry says so, or because a past version of me believed they were necessary.

Make X calls per day. Attend networking events I hate. Follow strategies that feel lifeless.

But organic structures? They arise naturally from who I am.

A morning rhythm that nourishes me before I create. Intentional conversations that deepen relationships instead of surface networking. Boundaries that honor my energy, allowing my best work to emerge.

When I move within organic structure, I am held but not confined. The river has its banks, but it is free to shape them over time.

This is what I want now—Structure that holds but does not restrict.

How This Changes My Relationships

I've noticed that relationships built on artificial constraints don't last.

The partnership based on habit rather than growth eventually fades. The friendship maintained by guilt rather than connection eventually exhausts. The client relationship sustained by performance rather than authenticity eventually breaks.

But when a relationship is guided by organic structure, it flows.

The values remain, even if the context changes. The rhythm of communication continues, even if the purpose evolves. The trust deepens, even if the form shifts.

I've seen this happen in my own life.

Some relationships transitioned effortlessly as I evolved—because they were never about what I did but about who we were to each other.

Others? They remained frozen in a version of me that no longer exists. And those are the ones I must let go.

What Riverbanks Do I Need Now?

I am no longer interested in forcing myself to fit outdated structures.

I need values that guide, not rules that constrict.

I need relationships that expand, not ones that stagnate.

I need rhythms that sustain me, not ones that drain me.

This is the art of elegant change—

To evolve without abandoning.

To carry forward what serves me and release what no longer does.

To allow my relationships to grow with me or set them free with love.

To trust that the path ahead is already forming—I only need to flow toward it.

The Question That Holds Me

What organic structures—values, rhythms, boundaries, or intentions—will guide my next evolution without confining it?

And—Am I willing to trust the flow?

Chapter 92. The Weight of What I Give

I used to think contribution was about effort—about doing more, offering more, proving more. I measured my impact in outputs, in effort expended, in how much I could create, deliver, and leave behind.

But I see it differently now.

The most important contribution I can make is not in what I produce—but in who I am while I give it.

The Gravity of Presence

There is a weight to what we offer the world. Not in its size but in its substance.

Two people can say the same words—and one will sink like a stone into deep water while the other scatters like dust in the wind.

The difference? Presence. Integrity. Alignment.

The weight of a thing comes not from its volume but from its truth.

So I ask myself—Not, what more can I give? But how can I give more of what is real?

The Illusion of More

If I give from depletion, I am not really giving.

If I give from obligation, I am not truly serving.

If I give to prove my worth, I am not actually contributing.

I used to believe impact was about producing at scale. Now, I understand—the depth of a thing matters more than its reach.

More content is not the answer.

More strategies are not the answer.

More noise is not the answer.

The answer is more presence. More truth. More clarity.

The answer is the slow burn of deep work—the kind that simmers beneath the surface before revealing itself, fully formed.

The answer is in patience—to let what wants to be given ripen before forcing it into the world.

The answer is in restraint—to trust that what must be said will arrive at the right time, in the right way, to the right people.

The Depth of True Giving

So now, I ask myself—What is my most important contribution?

It is not found in my words but in the space I hold.

Not in what I say but in how I say it.

Not in what I do but in how I am while doing it.

To be steady in my presence.

To give from fullness, not from empty.

To offer what is needed, not just what is easy.

To make sure that what I give is something I would want to receive.

That is the work.

The Gift That Lasts

When I give this way—from depth, not depletion—something shifts.

People do not just hear what I say. They feel it. They absorb it. It moves them—because it was real when it left my hands.

That is the difference between giving and giving something that lasts.

So, I return to the question: What is the most important contribution I can make?

It is not to be everything to everyone.

It is not to give endlessly without boundaries.

It is not to measure my worth by how much I offer.

It is to offer what is real.

It is to let my presence be my gift.

It is to give only what I have first given to myself—truth, stillness, love, depth.

And when I do that—my work is not just heard.

It is felt.

And that changes everything.

Chapter 93. What Do I Want the People Who Matter to Me to Say About Me When I'm Gone?

I imagine the voices of those who knew me well. Not in polished eulogies. Not in grand narratives. But in the quiet, unguarded moments—when they sit together, remembering.

I don't want them to speak of accomplishments or accolades. I want them to speak of presence. Of how I showed up. Of the way they felt when they were around me.

A Man Who Lived at the Edges

I want them to say—"Joe wasn't afraid of the unknown. He lived inside of it."

That I stood at the edges of things—my own identity, my own limitations, my own longings—without rushing to define them, without needing certainty to feel safe.

That I lived inside my questions, not just my answers. That I was never in a hurry to simplify what was meant to be complex. That I had a deep reverence for mystery—not as something to be solved, but as something to be inhabited.

A Man Who Chose Aliveness Over Comfort

I want them to say—"Joe never let himself settle into patterns that dulled his spirit."

That I was willing to start over—again and again. Not out of restlessness but because I refused to let life become predictable.

That I never let past success keep me from stepping into new terrain. That I was willing to be a beginner, to feel foolish, to look unpolished—because I understood that real mastery requires a willingness to unmake yourself over and over.

That I never let age dictate what was possible. That I danced when I could have sat still. That I lifted when I could have rested. That I embraced life as something meant to be felt fully, not merely extended.

A Man Who Was Willing to Be Seen

I want them to say—"Joe didn't hide behind his intellect, his work, or his achievements. He let people see him—really see him."

That I stood in front of the people I loved and said, "I don't have this figured out. I am hurting. I am afraid."

That I could hold others in their pain without trying to fix them. And be held in my own without shame.

That I was soft where it mattered, strong where it counted, and that I had the wisdom to know the difference.

A Man Who Did Not Die With His Music Still Inside Him

I want them to say—"Joe poured everything he had to give into the world—not for recognition, but because he had too much inside him to keep it locked away."

That I wrote, not to be read, but because I had to write. That I taught, not to be followed, but to ignite something in others. That I gave, not out of obligation, but because giving was my language of love.

That my creativity was relentless. That my curiosity was tireless. That my fear never dictated the edges of my life.

A Man Who Found His Way to Love

Above all, I want them to say—"Joe lived in devotion. To his people. To his craft. To his calling. To his soul."

That, for all my years of learning, all my searching, all my personal work—what I really discovered was how to love.

That I let myself be loved in return. That I let it in.

That my relationships weren't just deep in thought but deep in presence, tenderness, shared laughter, and shared silence.

That when I was with someone, they felt like the only person in the world.

The Final Truth

I don't want them to say I was perfect. I don't want them to say I had it all figured out.

I want them to say—"Joe made me feel something real."

And when they think of me—I want them to smile.

Taste 10: The Depth of Connection

There is a moment—just before a real conversation begins—when something in us hesitates. A pause where we decide, often without realizing it, how much of ourselves we're willing to share. How much we're willing to risk. How much we're willing to let another person see.

This section is about what happens when we lean in anyway.

It's about presence—not just being physically there, but offering ourselves fully, without distraction or defense. It's about love—not as a fleeting emotion, but as a daily practice, an intentional way of being. It's about appreciation—not just saying thank you but truly witnessing the people in our lives. It's about asking for help—not as a sign of weakness, but as an act of trust. It's about seeing others—not just their words, but their unspoken fears, their quiet longings, their deepest truths.

I've spent my life in conversations—coaching, negotiating, mentoring, leading. I know how to listen, how to ask the right questions, and how to help others feel understood. But real connection isn't about mastering communication. It's about something much harder:

Letting go of control. Letting ourselves be seen. Allowing connection to change us.

The deepest relationships are not built through strategy, skill, or technique. They are built in the moments where we drop the script, remove the armor, and step fully into the space between us—not as a role, but as a person.

That is where transformation happens. This section explores those moments—the ones where we risk stepping beyond our carefully constructed identities and into something real. The spaces where:

Appreciation is not an afterthought but a way of moving through the world. Safety is not something we construct but something we embody and offer. Love is not something we chase but something we allow ourselves to become.

There is no formula here. No step-by-step process. Only an invitation.

To see what happens when we choose to stay in the moment instead of pulling away. To see what shifts when we ask instead of assuming we have to do it alone. To see what opens when we trust that connection is not about what we say but about who we are willing to be with each other. This is where depth begins.

Chapter 94. The Art of Presence

Presence is not about showing up. It's about *how* I show up. It's about *who* I am when I do.

For years, I believed presence was about focus—listening intently, responding thoughtfully, making eye contact, and nodding at the right times. I treated it like a skill, something to refine and perfect.

But real presence isn't performative. It isn't something I do. It's something I become.

Presence is not the act of paying attention. It's the art of being available.

It is the absence of everything that is not here. The distractions. The agendas. The mental rehearsals of what I'll say next. The urge to fix, to solve, to explain.

Presence is not a skill. It is a surrendering.

The Illusion of Presence

I have been absent in the company of people I love, even with my body in the room. I have been lost in thought while someone was speaking. I have been checking my phone, checking my watch, checking out. I have heard words but missed meaning because I wasn't truly there when they were spoken.

Presence is the quietest form of love. It is not saying, *I hear you*. It is becoming the space where hearing happens.

Presence asks nothing but this: Be here. Fully. Not just as a listener. Not just as a problem solver. Not just as a thinker. As a human being, wholly attuned to this moment, nothing else.

Returning to the Moment

The art of presence is not about never drifting. It is about noticing when I have left—and returning.

Returning when my mind is racing.

Returning when my attention fractures.

Returning when my defenses rise.

Letting go of the illusion that my presence is measured by my words. Because presence is not about making people feel seen. It is about making them feel safe enough to show themselves.

Chapter 95. Practicing Presence in Relationships

If presence is an art, then relationships are its canvas. To be present with another person is to become the space where they can exhale.

I want to be the kind of person others can exhale around. The kind of person who listens not to respond but to witness. The kind of person whose presence is felt—not because I am filling the space, but because I am holding it.

The Skill of Staying

The most important skill I can develop is the ability to stay.

Staying when the conversation gets uncomfortable.

Staying when my mind wants to race ahead to a solution.

Staying when my ego wants to defend, to justify, to push back.

The people I love don't need my solutions. They don't need my interruptions. They don't need my polished words.

They need me. Here.

I think back to when Olivia was 16. She came to me with an upset, her emotions tangled in knots she couldn't yet unravel with words. I saw her struggling to express what she needed from me.

"Olivia," I said, "I've never had a 16-year-old daughter before. I'm learning as we go. Would you please teach me how to be the dad you need me to be?"

Those words cracked something open in both of us. They gave her room to find her own language, to show me how to love her in the way she needed. And they gave me permission to not know.

Presence is not knowing. It is not rushing to fill the silence. It is waiting long enough for the truth to rise.

Noticing When I Have Left

True presence is not about perfect stillness. It is about recognizing when I have drifted—and finding my way back.

When I am lost in my own thoughts.

When I am preoccupied with fixing rather than listening.

When I am thinking about what to say next instead of simply being.

I return. I place my attention back on this moment. I become the space where connection can happen again.

Becoming the Space Where Others Can Exhale

This is the deepest form of presence. To become the pause in a world that never stops. To become the stillness that llows another to breathe. To become the moment someone realizes—they are not alone.

Because presence, at its core, is an invitation. An invitation to feel safe. An invitation to be known. An invitation to simply be.

Chapter 96. Love as a Way of Being

There are days when love flows effortlessly through me—when it shapes every word I speak, moves through my hands, and fills every space I enter. And then there are days when love feels distant, like a language I once knew but have somehow forgotten how to speak.

But love is not something to be found. It is something to be returned to.

It is in the way I arrange my life—the books on my shelves, the fire in my fireplace, the wind chimes singing their quiet song outside my window.

It is in the way I notice—the squirrels leaping from branch to branch, the morning light filtering through the trees, the way my body feels when it is warm and cocooned in stillness.

Love is not a thing to be measured. Love is the space in which everything meaningful happens.

Love Is Not a Transaction

For years, I believed love had conditions. That it had to be earned, chased, and proven. That it was something outside of me—something I had to get.

But real love is not transactional. It does not keep score. It is not given in portions measured out just enough to feel safe.

Love is a way of being.

It is in the way I listen when someone speaks without rushing ahead to my response.
It is in the way I sit with someone in their pain without trying to fix it.
It is in the way I care for my body, no out of obligation but out of reverence.
It is in the way I forgive myself for all the times I have been unkind to my own heart.
Love is not an emotion. It is not a destination. Love is a discipline. Love is a practice.

The Courage to Love

But love is not always easy.

Love requires me to let go of my need to control. Love requires me to face the parts of myself I would rather avoid. Love requires me to risk being seen—truly seen—without the armor of perfection.

There is a reason love is called courage.

Because love asks me to step forward, even when I am afraid.
Because love asks me to trust, even when I have been hurt.
Because love asks me to keep my heart open, even when it would be easier to close.

I have spent a lifetime learning that love is not something I have to chase.

I am not waiting to arrive at love. I am not waiting for someone else to give me love. I am love.

The Shift from Doing to Being

And so today, I do not ask myself what I love. I ask myself how I love.

Do I love in the way I move through the world?
Do I love in the way I listen?
Do I love in the way I create?

Do I love in the way I forgive?
Do I love in the way I breathe?

And most of all—do I love in the way I love myself?

Because I have learned this: I can only love others as deeply as I love myself. And I cannot give love if I do not first become love.

Chapter 97. The Practice of Living With Love

Love is not just an idea. It is a practice. It is the daily discipline of love, the small, quiet moments that, when strung together, become a life built on love.

Love is not a feeling that arrives when conditions are perfect. Love is a choice. A moment-to-moment decision.

To notice. To give. To soften.

Love in the Micro-Moments

The way I look into someone's eyes when they speak. The laughter that catches me off guard. The silence that does not need to be filled. The comfort of knowing I am not alone.

These are the moments love is made of. Not grand gestures, not sweeping declarations—but the quiet, steady presence of care.

A Life Built on Love

I once thought my life would be defined by my accomplishments—the books I wrote, the businesses I built, the goals I crushed.

But those things, as meaningful as they are, are not the foundation of my life.

Love is.

Love is in the way I greet the morning.
Love is in the way I choose to respond instead of react.
Love is in the way I show up, even when I don't feel like it.

Love is in the way I stay.

Giving Love Freely

When I create my life with love, I do not wait for perfect conditions to open my heart. I do not ration it, holding back in fear of loss.

I give freely because love is not something I run out of. Love is something I become.

And the more I give, the more I receive.

The Practice of Forgiveness

One of the greatest practices of love is forgiveness.

Forgiveness for the times I have been impatient. Forgiveness for the times I have closed my heart in fear. Forgiveness for the ways I have been unkind to myself and others.

Love is not about never failing. Love is about always returning.

The Question That Guides Me

Every day, I ask myself:

How can I live with more love today?
How can I create more space for love in my presence?
How can I let love shape the way I move, the way I listen, the way I create?

Because love is not something I wait for. Love is not something I search for. Love is not something I prove.

Love is something I practice.

And maybe, just maybe, that is the greatest thing I will ever create.

Chapter 98. The Art of Appreciation

I have come to believe that appreciation is not a gesture. Not a passing thank you. Not a polite nod before moving on to the next thing.

Appreciation is a way of being.

It is a lens through which I choose to see the world. A practice. A discipline. A sacred offering.

Because life moves fast. It is easy to assume people know they are valued. Easy to let a moment slip away—unspoken, unnoticed, unappreciated.

But I do not want to live like that.

I want the people who move through my world to feel something in my presence. I want them to leave an interaction with me, knowing, without a doubt, that they matter. That their existence is not just tolerated but treasured. That they are seen.

Appreciation Begins With Presence

When someone speaks to me, I do not just hear them. I receive them.

I soften my eyes. I release the tension in my face. I let my body communicate what words cannot—*I am here with you.*

I put my phone down. I slow my mind down. I do not rush to respond, to fix, to prove I am listening.

Because presence is not just about paying attention. It is about making them feel like the most important person in the world in that moment—because they are.

I do not just see a person. I see a story.

A lifetime of moments that brought them here. To this very conversation. To this very breath.

And something shifts.

The air between us changes. The moment becomes real.

Appreciation Is Spoken Aloud

But not just in passing. Not just in a casual, *thanks for that.*

Appreciation should be felt.

I tell the barista, "I appreciate how you take your time to make each cup of coffee with care. It makes a difference."

I tell my friend, "I appreciate how safe you make me feel when I share my truth. I never take that for granted."

I tell my daughter, "I appreciate the way you let me see the world through your eyes. It's a gift to me."

I do not assume they know. I say it. I name it. I offer it.

Because what good is gratitude if it remains locked inside me?

Appreciation Is Action

A handwritten note. A voice message filled with warmth. A follow-up that says, *I remember you. I still care.*

A small act of kindness that carries weight. Holding a door open and looking someone in the eyes. Leaving an extra-large tip with a note that says, *You are doing a great job. Keep going.*

Choosing to see the invisible work, the unnoticed effort, the moments that usually pass by unacknowledged.

Appreciation Is Seeing People Bigger Than They See Themselves

When I look at someone, I do not just see who they are today. I see who they are becoming.

I see their potential, their radiance, and the way their presence shapes the world around them.

And I tell them.

Because I know what it's like to doubt my own light. I know what it's like to need someone to reflect it back to me.

What Is Appreciation, Really?

It is love.

It is the way I extend my heart into the world. It is the way I remind people they are worthy. It is the way I give what I hope to receive.

It is the way I choose to live.

The Commitment to Appreciation

So today, and every day, I commit to practicing appreciation.

Not just in thought but in action. Not just when it's easy but when it's inconvenient. Not just for strangers but for the ones closest to me—the ones I sometimes forget to thank.

Because life is not measured by the things I accomplish. It is measured by the love I leave behind.

And maybe, just maybe, the greatest legacy I will ever leave is making sure that the people who cross my path know, without a doubt—

That they mattered. That they were appreciated. That they were loved. That they were seen.

Chapter 99. The Courage to Open - Asking, Receiving, and Creating Safety in Connection

The Illusion of Strength

For so much of my life, I believed that strength meant standing alone. That needing less made me more. That asking for help was an admission of weakness, a surrender of control.

It took me years to unravel this illusion. Years to understand that asking is not a sign of failure—it is a bridge.

A bridge to connection. A bridge to truth. A bridge to becoming more than I could ever be on my own.

And yet, even now, I hesitate. Even now, there are places in my life where I stand at the edge of that bridge, afraid to step forward.

Afraid of what it will reveal. Afraid of what it might cost.

The Resistance to Asking

Where does this resistance come from?

Maybe it was in childhood when I learned that independence was praised and needing too much made me a burden.

Maybe it was years of forging my own path, proving my worth through sheer grit and will.

Maybe it was all the times I did ask and was met with rejection, indifference, or silence.

Somewhere along the way, I internalized a story: *If you want something done, do it yourself.*

But is that truth? Or just a belief I've carried for too long?

Because when I look at my life—really look—I see that I have never done anything truly meaningful alone.

What If Asking Was Strength?

What if asking was not an admission of weakness but a declaration of trust?

What if it was a way of saying: *I believe in you. I believe in our connection. I believe we are stronger together than apart.*

What if asking was an act of courage? An invitation. A doorway. A chance for someone else to step forward, to offer their wisdom, to feel the deep fulfillment of being needed.

The Illusion of Safety

There was a time when I equated safety with control.

If I had enough money, I would be safe.
If I kept my body strong, I would be safe.
If I anticipated every possible outcome, I would be safe.

But life humbles you. It reminds you, again and again, that safety is not a fortress built from certainty.

No matter how tightly I grip, there will always be something just beyond my reach.

I learned this the hard way—the sudden fractures, the unexpected goodbyes, the late-night calls that change everything.

The moments when life's fault lines shift beneath my feet, reminding me: I never had control to begin with.

The Safety That Comes From Presence

I am learning that safety is not the absence of risk but the presence of awareness.

It is the breath I take before I react. It is the stillness I cultivate within. It is the way I listen—not just to words, but to energy, to intuition, to what is left unsaid.

When I am present, I am safe. When I am aware, I see beyond myself.

And maybe that is the secret—safety is not an individual pursuit.

It is woven into the spaces between us, into the care we offer each other, into the silent gestures that say: *I see you. I am here.*

Where Do I Need Help Right Now?

I close my eyes and let the question settle:

What do I imagine is something occurring in my life right now that I could ask for help on?

Help with trusting again, with allowing myself to be vulnerable in relationships.

Help with slowing down, with embracing stillness instead of always chasing the next mountain.

Help with letting go, with loosening my grip on what I cannot control.

Help with expansion, with bringing my work into the world in a way that doesn't drain me but fills me.

Help with forgiveness—not just of others, but of myself.

I breathe into that. I feel the weight of it.

And then I ask— *Who could I turn to? Who has walked this path before me? Who could hold space for me the way I have held space for so many?*

The Risk and the Reward

There is risk in asking.

The risk of rejection.
The risk of disappointment.
The risk of not receiving what I hope for.

But there is also risk in not asking.

The risk of isolation.
The risk of carrying burdens I was never meant to carry alone.
The risk of staying stuck when I was meant to grow.

If I never ask, I rob someone of the chance to give. If I never ask, I deny myself the opportunity to receive. If I never ask, I close a door before I even see if it was meant to open.

The Sacred Responsibility of Awareness

I once read that when monks walk through a forest, they step with reverence, conscious of every leaf, every branch, every unseen creature beneath their feet.

They do not move through the world carelessly.

I want to walk like that today.

Not just through the physical world but through the world of human hearts.

To move with awareness. To speak with kindness. To notice the invisible burdens others are carrying.

Because when I move with care, I create safety. And when I create safety, I create love.

So I Will Ask. And I Will Open.

I will ask with an open heart. I will ask without attachment to the answer. I will ask, not from desperation, but from knowing—knowing that I am worthy of support, of guidance, of love.

I will ask, not because I am weak, but because I am strong enough to know that I do not have to do this alone.

And neither do you.

So I ask you now:

What do you imagine is something occurring in your life right now that you could ask for help on?

And more importantly—*who will you ask?*

Chapter 100. The Orange Principle - Negotiating Interests, Not Positions

I have spent a lifetime mastering the art of seeing beyond the surface. In business, in negotiation, and in human behavior—I instinctively recognize that what people claim they want is often just the wrapper around what they truly need.

I've taught this principle for years: don't negotiate positions; negotiate interests.

The classic example—two people fighting over an orange. The logical solution? Cut it in half. But when you ask why each person wants it, you discover something deeper: one only wants the juice, while the other needs the rind. If they had focused on their interests instead of their positions, they both could have gotten exactly what they needed.

I have built entire businesses, relationships, and communities on this principle. I don't just listen to what people say they want—I listen for what they don't say. I tune into their deeper motivations—security, legacy, identity, lifestyle aspirations.

This is why my relationships last beyond individual deals, beyond industries, and beyond specific ventures.

And yet...

When I shift my gaze inward, when I take this same framework and apply it to my most personal relationships, the realization lands hard:

Do I allow myself to be seen in the same way that I see others?

The Truth Beneath the Surface

I know how to navigate interests beneath positions in business.

I naturally look beyond surface demands to understand people's deeper needs. I know how to ask the right questions and how to guide someone toward their own truth. I know how to create a space where they feel fully understood.

But in my closest, most intimate relationships—do I trust that someone else is willing to go that deep with me? Do I even allow them the chance?

The truth I may not want to hear, but need to, is this:

I deflect. I protect. I withhold.

I have spent years developing the skill to help others feel understood and to create spaces where they can be fully received. I ask the right questions, guide them to their deeper truths, and hold them in their contradictions without judgment.

But when the tables turn—when someone tries to do that for me—something inside me resists.

I move. I shift. I intellectualize.

I have trained myself to be the guide, the observer, the orchestrator. I am comfortable being the one who holds space for others.

What happens when I am the one who needs to be held? When I am the one who needs to be understood—not as a teacher, not as a leader, but simply as a human being?

The Real Negotiation

So I sit with this:

What if the most profound shift in my relationships isn't about mastering another layer of insight but about allowing someone to truly see mine?

What if I let go of negotiating, analyzing, and anticipating—just for a moment—and simply let someone meet me where I am without needing to control or frame the interaction?

I know how to help others reach what they need.

The real question is: Do I trust that I, too, can be met in that same way?

And if I did...

What might that change?

Chapter 101. The Work of Being

The biggest obstacle between my ideal and my reality isn't time. It isn't resources. It isn't skill.

It's me.

It's the subtle resistance to just being—
To having fun for the sake of fun,
To creating for the sake of creation,
To living for the sake of this moment, right here, right now.

Because the truth is, I know how to build. I know how to structure, teach, coach, and create systems that hold people through transformation. I've done it over and over again.

But there's a different kind of work—the work of simply letting go into the moment. That's what I'm looking at today.

What Really Matters?

When I strip it all back, what really matters?

That I am kind. That I am kind to the people who cross my path. That I am kind to myself. That I nurture the parts of me that still need tending.

That I respect and honor my body, my mind, my spirit. That I love my relationship with God, with nature, and with all that is.

That I make some kind of impact—not for ego, not for legacy, but because I can. Because I have grandkids growing up in a world that moves fast, and if I can be a source of wisdom, of steadiness, of something real, then I want to be that for them.

Maybe I'll run down to see them soon. Maybe this week. No plan, no overthinking—just go.

What Do I Risk?

This is where my mind always lands. The risk equation.

What do I risk if I do it? What do I risk if I don't do it?

And the truth is, the biggest risk I take is staying relevant. Not in the way most people mean it—not chasing trends, not grasping for significance.

But staying relevant inside my own evolution. Staying connected to what's real, to what still excites me, to what is alive in me.

Right now, AI is alive in me. Teaching is alive in me. I'm putting myself out there, creating things that didn't exist before, letting this technology work with me, not against me.

I could stand in front of a room of people and pour out insights faster than they could absorb them. And I love that. I love that I can still bring it.

And then there's PrivateWork—this beautiful, intricate algorithm of self-coaching that I built.

Hundreds of hours. Hundreds of recorded sessions. Self talking to self.

A massive library of me, working through the layers, the selves within selves. I don't know if people even realize what I built with it.

I read all of Hal Stone's work on self-awareness. I lived inside those frameworks, those selves, those dialogues. I didn't just study it—I created something entirely new from it.

A structure where anyone—myself included—could step into a conversation with themselves and actually hear what was true.

Not in some vague, journaling way, but in a systematic, structured, guided way.

It's all there.

The questions. The reflections. The pathways to seeing what I was avoiding, what I was resisting, what I was blind to.

The Irony of It All

And maybe that's the biggest lesson of today.

I built PrivateWork because I knew that no one else could ever know me as well as I could know myself.

And yet, the irony?

I still resist simply being with myself. I still find ways to stay in the structure, the system, the teaching, the building—rather than just sitting in the moment and having fun for the sake of fun.

So maybe this is what today is about.

Not what I built. Not what I created. Not what I teach.

But the reminder that all of it, every bit of it, comes down to this:

A man, in a room, alone, asking himself—

Can I just let this moment be enough? Can I let myself be enough?

Without building something from it. Without structuring it into a lesson. Without turning it into a process.

Can I just be here?

Because the truth is, I don't need to stay relevant.

I need to stay present.

And if I do that, relevance takes care of itself.

Taste 11: The Path Forward

I stare at my reflection this morning and see the journey written in my eyes. Not a stranger, but someone who has shed many skins I once thought were me.

The work is never finished. It deepens, it expands, it refines. Every insight, every breakthrough, every moment of clarity has not been an ending but a beginning—a preparation for what comes next.

This section is not about seeking another transformation. It is about living from the transformation that has already occurred. It is about integration—allowing everything we have uncovered, everything we have released, and everything we have stepped into to become not just something we know but something we embody.

This is where awareness becomes wisdom. Where the lessons don't just shape our thoughts but shape the way we move through the world.

So, I ask myself questions that matter:

Who am I now? Not the person I was when I began this journey, but the person I have become through it.

What is ready to be released? What beliefs, identities, and patterns have served their purpose and no longer belong?

What is calling me forward? What next version of myself is already forming, waiting for me to step into it fully?

This is where I stop looking back for proof and start standing in my future with certainty. This is where I stop searching for the path and recognize—I am the path.

The final stretch is not about accumulating more. It is about letting go of what no longer serves. Less resistance. Less hesitation. Less attachment to what was. More presence. More alignment. More courage to be exactly who I have become.

The path forward is not something to figure out. It is something to step into. And that step begins now, with these words, with this breath, with the courage to be authentic.

Chapter 102. Meeting Others in their Becoming

I used to think I met people where they were. But the deeper truth is, I meet them where their soul has evolved to.

And they meet me there, too.

That's the unspoken agreement between two people whose paths intertwine—not to fix each other, not to carry each other, but to bear witness to one another's unfolding. To walk beside each other, not pulling, not pushing, just moving in rhythm with the becoming.

And yet, how often do I cling to people who are not meant to walk with me any further? How often do I hold onto connections that no longer reflect who I am—out of nostalgia, out of obligation, out of fear that if I let go, I'll be alone?

But integration isn't just an internal process. It happens in connection.

The people who show up in my life, the ones who linger, the ones who disappear—each of them is a mirror. Some reflect back the parts of me I've integrated. Others show me what is still waiting to be healed. Some stay because we are still walking the same path. Some leave because our paths have diverged. Either way, they are teachers.

That's why I see Lysa Castro every Monday at 2:30. Not just for movement. Not just for dance.

Because she holds my story. Because she bears witness. Because she reflects back the pieces of me that I might otherwise leave behind.

We all need someone like that. Someone who remembers us when we forget ourselves. Someone who holds our truth when we slip into an old belief, an old story, an old wound.

For years, I believed healing was something I had to do alone. But I was wrong.

Healing happens in the presence of others—in the safety of being seen without needing to perform, in the warmth of being held without needing to be fixed, in the quiet moments where someone else looks at you and says, I see you.

Because the deepest integration is relational.

The question I ask myself now is not just: Who am I becoming?

But also, Who do I surround myself with? Who lingers? Who meets me in the depth of where I am? Who reflects back my light, my truth, my growth? Who is willing to sit with me in the discomfort without trying to rush me through it? Who is still walking beside me, not because they have to, but because they choose to?

Because integration isn't just about me. It's about who I choose to walk with.

Chapter 103. The Embodied Path of Integration

What would I be if I were no longer struggling?

That question lands deep within me. I've built much of my identity around overcoming.

Struggle has been my proving ground, my forge, and the way I have defined myself. It has made me resilient, resourceful, and relentless. But if I strip it away—if I remove the need to overcome something—then what's left?

Zuza Engler once asked me: What is the feeling you don't want to feel?

I sat with that question longer than I wanted to. And I saw it:

The little boy in the crib. The soiled diaper. The safety pin pressed into his skin. The mother, overwhelmed, unavailable, and unable to meet his needs.

And the boy—me—closing his eyes.

Because the reflection he longed for wasn't there. Because the love he was giving had nowhere to land. Because the grief of seeing was too much to bear.

So, I shut down.

And now? Absent a big, challenging project, I default to my trauma.

That's why I move. That's why I dance. That's why I return to somatic work.

Because integration isn't just about processing. It's about embodiment. It's about moving through.

I have spent decades thinking my way through healing. But the body remembers what the mind forgets. If healing only happens in the intellect, then I stay trapped in loops of insight without transformation.

I learned this in a different way when I finally put down cigars.

I had smoked for years—good cigars, Cuban cigars—daily, sometimes twice a day, and on those odd days, three a day. Then I'd go a couple of days without them, always in this tug-of-war with myself. Each fine cigar was a ritual, a momentary escape, a buffer between me and something deeper I wasn't ready to face. I told myself it was about appreciation, about the craftsmanship, the flavors—but beneath that story was another truth.

I was always struggling with it. The inner conflict between the momentary pleasure and the knowing that this wasn't serving me. The way I'd promise myself "just one today" and end up with two. The morning cough I'd pretend not to notice. The dependency I didn't want to acknowledge.

And then, one day, I woke up unable to breathe.

And I knew—it was time.

Not because I forced myself to quit, not because I used willpower, but because something in me had shifted. Because I finally met the part of myself that needed to be held. The little boy who had been using smoke to cover the wounds. And when I held him, when I acknowledged what the cigars were really doing for me, the need began to dissolve.

That's integration.

Not just understanding but embodiment. Not just knowledge but wisdom.

So I ask myself:

What am I still clinging to as a buffer between me and my own truth? What parts of me are still waiting to be integrated? What would I have to let go of if I truly allowed myself to be whole?

Because integration is integrity.

It is patience—the strength to grow in the soil. It is perseverance—seven times down, eight times up. It is humility—the root of all true greatness. It is wisdom—the sunlight of the soul. It is forgiveness—the turning of faith. It is leadership—living with purpose.

And at the deepest level, integration is the realization that no one is coming.

Not to save me. Not to rescue me. Not to fix what was broken.

Because the wisdom, the love, the healing—it's me.

It's the adult king inside me finally stepping forward, taking the throne, standing in full ownership of his being.

Holding myself. Trusting myself. Needing myself. Paying attention to myself.

Because if I do that—if I fully integrate—then I am no longer searching. No longer waiting. No longer looking for something outside of me to fill the gaps.

I am whole. Scarred, imperfect, still learning—but whole.

And from that place, I can guide others. Not because I need to. But because I am.

Chapter 104. The Only Time I Look Back

I wonder how much of my life has been spent looking back at the wrong things. Not the victories, not the quiet moments of resilience, but the gaps. The almosts. The places where I measured myself against a future I hadn't reached yet and called it failure.

It's a peculiar thing—the way the mind works against itself. How it keeps stretching the horizon further, like chasing the edge of the ocean with every step deeper into the tide.

But today, I try something different.

I close my eyes and place myself in a moment 25 years ago. The version of me standing there couldn't have seen this life. Couldn't have known what was coming.

I trace my life backward—not to regret, not to measure against some impossible standard, but to honor the path I have walked. The mountains I have climbed, the storms I have endured, the love I have given, the lessons I have gathered in the pockets of my soul like smooth river stones.

And when I turn my gaze forward again, something shifts.

If my future self could reach back through time and whisper to me now, I think he would say: "Look at what you've already done. That is the proof. That is the evidence. Stop worrying about the distance left to travel. Stop fixating on the peak. Instead, turn around and see how high you've already climbed. Feel the ground beneath your feet and know that it is enough. You are enough."

I take a breath and let it settle inside me.

The future has always been a moving target. The past, an endless echo of moments that cannot be touched. But here—right here—is where I get to decide:

I will use my past as fuel, not a weight. I will measure my progress, not my lack. I will step forward, not because I feel ready, but because I have already proven I can.

And the only time I will look back—is to see how far I've come.

Chapter 105. The One Change That's Been Waiting for Me

I can feel it pressing against the edges of my life—this change, this shift, this quiet unraveling of something old and the slow emergence of something new.

It isn't sudden. It isn't dramatic. It isn't the kind of revelation that strikes like lightning. It's been circling for a while now, lingering in the periphery, waiting for me to turn toward it.

And yet, I haven't.

Not because I don't want to. Not because I can't see it.

But because stepping into it means stepping out of something else.

And if there's one thing I know about myself, it's that letting go has never been easy. Even when I know—deep in my bones—that something is finished, there's a part of me that lingers. A part that grips the familiar just a little longer, hoping for a gentler ending, a softer release.

But change rarely grants that kind of mercy.

The Weight of Real Change

I think about all the times I've stood here before—on the precipice, toes curled over the edge of something real, something necessary—only to turn back at the last moment.

Not because I didn't want it.

But because I wasn't sure I trusted myself to carry it through.

Change has a weight to it.

Even the good kind.

Especially the good kind.

Because real change—the kind that actually matters—isn't about gathering more, adding more, building more. It's about subtraction.

It's about stripping away what no longer belongs.

And maybe that's the hardest part.

We like to think that transformation is about becoming. But sometimes, it's about unbecoming. It's about releasing identities, habits, and attachments—the things we've outgrown but still hold onto because they feel like home, even when they no longer fit.

So why do I hesitate?

Because subtraction feels like loss.

Because I have spent a lifetime filling space, and now, space is asking to be emptied.

The Trickster Called 'Soon'

I tell myself, soon.

Soon, I'll make the shift. Soon, I'll stop carrying what's too heavy. Soon, I'll stop making excuses for why I'm not ready.

But soon is a mirage.

It recedes the closer I get.

And I know better.

I know that life doesn't wait. That someday is a place where nothing ever happens. That real change doesn't arrive like a perfectly timed invitation.

What If This Is the Day?

What if, instead of waiting for the perfect conditions, I just decide?

What if I stop making change an event and start making it a practice?

A quiet, steady unfolding. A slow, deliberate opening to what's next. A choice made not once but over and over again—until it is no longer a decision but a way of being.

I don't need to have it all figured out. I don't need to know how the whole story unfolds. I don't need guarantees, or proof, or a safety net.

I just need to take the next step.

To loosen my grip on what no longer serves me. To move forward, even if I don't feel entirely ready.

Because maybe readiness isn't a feeling.

Maybe it's a decision.

And maybe the only real question left is this:

What happens when I stop waiting?

Chapter 106. The Eagle's Flight - Trusting the Wind of Change

I imagine an eagle. Wings stretched wide, muscles taut with purpose, eyes sharp with knowing. It does not flap frantically. It does not resist the wind. It rides the currents—surrendered, yet in complete command.

Now, I imagine the eagle looking up— Seeing a higher jet stream, sensing the call to ascend. The space between where it is and where it desires to soar is vast.

But the eagle does not panic. It does not doubt. It does not force.

It simply knows that the ascent will happen. Not by struggle. Not by willpower. But by aligning— With the right moment. With the right wind. With the right inner shift.

The Shift Begins Within

All great transformations begin inside before they are ever seen outside.

The shift in my world will come only when I shift within myself. I don't need to force it. I don't need to chase it. I only need to allow it.

I imagine myself as the eagle. I feel the weight of the old jet stream, the one I have outgrown. I feel the space between where I am and where I know I am meant to be. And I remind myself—I am not stuck. I am simply in the space between.

This is where faith lives. This is where transformation breathes. This is where I prepare to rise.

Loving the Currents, Loving the Thoughts

I do not grow by rejecting my past. I do not evolve by waging war with my mind. I change when I accept, when I love, when I embrace all that I am.

Every thought, every belief, every pattern has served me in some way. Even the ones that held me back. Even the ones that kept me circling in familiar currents.

They were once necessary. They were once the best I knew how to do.

And now?

Now, I can love them into release. Now, I can whisper gratitude to them and let them go.

Because the moment I stop resisting, I open myself to the next wind that will lift me higher.

Chapter 107. The Chase and the Stillness

What am I chasing today?

If I strip it all down—the projects, the goals, the numbers, the impact—what's underneath it?

I've been a chaser my whole life. Chasing excellence, chasing achievement, chasing the next great thing. And I've won a lot of those chases. Built businesses. Created movements. Helped thousands of people. I've stood at many "finish lines" and felt the weight of victory.

But here's the truth.

Somewhere along the way, I started to wonder:

What if I'm running toward something that I could have walked toward? What if I'm chasing things that were meant to arrive naturally? What if the best things don't require pursuit but presence?

That's where I find myself today. At the intersection of pursuit and presence.

The Two Versions of Me

There are two sides of me.

There's the Achiever, the relentless builder. The one who sets a goal and goes after it with precision. This part of me is calculated, disciplined, and sharp. It's the side that made me successful, the part that built a business and a name. It's the part that gets things done.

And then there's the Seeker, the part of me that wants more than just accomplishment. This is the part that values depth over speed. Meaning over metrics. Fulfillment over finish lines.

For most of my life, the Achiever has been in the driver's seat. But the Seeker is getting louder. And today, instead of just chasing, I'm asking...

Is what I'm chasing still the right thing? Or is it just what I've always chased?

The False Urgency of Chasing

I used to believe that if I wasn't chasing something, I was falling behind. That stillness was stagnation. That slowing down meant losing ground.

But I've learned something.

Chasing is often just disguised restlessness. A way to avoid the discomfort of being still. A way to prove—to ourselves or others—that we're doing enough, being enough, achieving enough.

And if we're not careful, we chase not because we truly desire something... but because we're afraid of who we are without the chase.

So today, I'm flipping the question:

What if I stop chasing, just for a moment? What if I let my desires come to me instead of sprinting after them?

Not in a passive, "sit back and hope" kind of way. But in a way that trusts that what's meant for me won't require exhaustion to obtain.

Because the best things—the things that truly matter—often come not when we chase harder but when we align better.

Balancing Pursuit with Presence

I'm not here to say ambition is wrong. I still have goals. I still have dreams that light me up. I still wake up ready to build, create, and impact.

But today, I'm choosing to pursue without panic. To chase without losing myself.

To move toward my goals while staying deeply present to the life that's happening around me.

Because what's the point of reaching the destination if I missed the entire journey getting there?

So, What Am I Chasing Today?

Today, I'm chasing alignment instead of exhaustion. Depth instead of distractions. Meaning instead of just momentum.

And I'm asking myself— Is my chase serving me, or am I serving the chase?

Because chasing only makes sense if the thing I'm running toward is actually worth it.

So today, I pause. I breathe. I realign.

And then, I move forward— Not in a frantic sprint, but in a powerful stride, knowing that the best things in life don't have to be chased. They simply have to be claimed.

This is my chase today. What's yours?

Chapter 108. The Power of Who - Surrendering the Need to Know

There's a weight I've carried for as long as I can remember—the unspoken belief that I have to figure it all out myself. That if something is to be done, it's up to me. That every challenge, every problem, every unanswered question rests solely on my shoulders.

But what if that's never been true? What if the real mastery isn't in the struggle but in the surrender? Not in knowing how, but in knowing who?

For most of my life, I have been obsessed with how.

How do I solve this? How do I make this happen? How do I build this?

And how has served me well. It has taught me resilience, self-reliance, and persistence. But how has also exhausted me. It has kept me in cycles of effort, locked inside my own limitations, forcing me to rely only on what I already know—when the real answers have always been beyond me.

So today, I stop asking how. Today, I ask who.

Who sees what I cannot? Who holds the key I do not have? Who can walk beside me, bringing their wisdom, their vision, and their heart to what I am creating?

The Illusion of Self-Sufficiency

For years, I prided myself on being the one who figured it out. I didn't want to need anyone.

Maybe it was old wounds—the times I asked for help and was met with absence. Maybe it was a belief that needing help meant weakness. Maybe it was the fear of trusting, of opening myself up, only to be let down.

But the truth is undeniable: Self-sufficiency is an illusion.

Nothing great has ever been built alone. Not the most powerful businesses, not the most transformative ideas, not the most beautiful works of art.

If I want to create something bigger than myself, If I want to expand beyond what I already know, If I want to step into a vision that stretches beyond my own current abilities, I have to stop asking how and start embracing who.

The Power of 'Who'

The moment I surrender to who, the how takes care of itself.

I have seen this truth in my own life.

When I tried to write every word, edit every page, and manage every detail of my books alone—they took years. But when I found the right who—someone who could bring their gifts to my vision—the process flowed.

When I ran my business alone, making every decision and solving every problem, growth was slow. But when I surrounded myself with people better than me in areas where I struggled—everything accelerated.

The shift was simple but profound: When I stopped believing I had to do it all, everything I wanted started moving faster.

Why We Resist Asking 'Who'

Even knowing this, there is resistance.

There is a voice inside me that still whispers:

You should be able to figure this out. You should already know how to do this. You shouldn't need help.

Where does that come from? Pride? Fear? The need to prove myself?

I know this much: Asking 'who' requires vulnerability. It requires me to admit that I don't have all the answers. It requires me to trust.

And trust is hard. Trust means I might get hurt. Trust means I might be disappointed. Trust means I have to let go.

But trust also means... I open myself to possibilities I never even imagined.

What Becomes Possible When I Let Go?

I breathe in the question:

What happens when I stop trying to figure out how... and instead ask who?

And I already know the answer: Everything expands.

My vision expands. My energy expands. My reach expands.

I am no longer trapped inside my own limitations. I am free to create without the weight of how slowing me down. I am free to focus on what truly matters.

The Call to Action

So today, I let go.

I release the need to figure it all out myself. I open my heart and my mind to collaboration, partnership, and shared creation.

I ask:

Who sees what I do not see? Who holds the key that I do not have? Who can walk with me?

And in that question, I find my answer. I find my freedom.

Because the most powerful question isn't how. It's who.

And the most powerful answer isn't a strategy. It's a person.

Sometimes, that person is me—the parts of me I've been hiding, the wisdom I've been ignoring, the strength I've been denying.

And sometimes, that person is someone else—waiting to be invited, waiting to share, waiting to walk alongside me.

Either way, the answer has always been who.

Chapter 109. The Art of Release - The Inner Work of Letting Go

There is a part of me that still wants to hold on. To control. To strategize. To grip tightly onto the edges of what I think should be, rather than surrendering to what is.

But life is teaching me something different.

Letting go is not passive. It is not weakness. It is not giving up.

Letting go is an act of courage. It is the conscious decision to stop carrying what no longer serves me. To stop gripping so tightly onto a version of myself, a story, a struggle that is ready to be released.

The Fear of Surrender

There is a fear that lingers at the edge of surrender: If I let go, will I still be me?

For so long, I have defined myself by the struggle. By the effort. By the need to prove something to myself, to others, to the world.

If I release that—if I stop identifying with the grind, the overcoming, the striving—what's left?

The Weight I'm Ready to Put Down

I close my eyes and ask: What am I holding onto that no longer belongs to me?

I see it. The expectations I've placed on myself. The old wounds I still protect. The false belief that I must always know the next step before taking it.

And I exhale.

Because I don't have to carry this anymore.

Trusting the Space

Letting go isn't just about releasing what's heavy. It's about trusting that something new will take its place.

It's about trusting that space itself is not emptiness—it is potential.

I don't have to know what will come next. I don't have to control what fills the space.

I only have to trust that the release itself is enough.

The Question I Hold Now

If I put this down—if I stop gripping so tightly—who might I become?

I am ready to find out.

So today, I release. Not with fear but with faith. Not with resistance but with reverence. Not as a loss but as an opening.

Because the act of letting go is not the end of something. It is the beginning of everything.

Chapter 110. A Taste of Truth

There is a process unfolding inside me—inside all of us. It is not a final destination, not a finish line to be crossed. It is movement. A spiraling, expanding current that carries us deeper into the raw experience of being fully alive.

I have lived enough life to understand something that once eluded me: The good life is not a place you reach. It is a direction you choose—again and again.

And what is that direction?

It is the path of openness. It is the shedding of defenses. It is the art of becoming so deeply attuned to life that nothing is rejected, nothing is forced, and nothing is twisted to fit an old story.

To live fully is to let life touch you—without armor, without manipulation, without the illusion that you are anything but presence, awake and alive, moving through this moment.

Openness to Experience

For years, I saw only what I was willing to see. I shaped the world through my defenses, filtering reality through the lens of old wounds and unmet needs. It was like wearing armor I had long since forgotten was there—keeping certain truths at bay, distorting others, protecting me from the very pain that needed to be met.

But the work—the real work—has been in the slow, deliberate unfastening of that armor.

To step out of it and feel the raw air on my skin. To experience what is actually here, not what I wish was here. To let go of the need to shape life—and instead, allow life to shape me.

And I have learned this: The taste of truth is not always sweet.

It burns. It dissolves illusions. It humbles.

But it also frees.

Because the moment I stop defending against life, I begin to truly live it.

The Presence of the Moment

I have spent so much of my life planning—strategizing, projecting forward, and creating structures that would make the future feel certain, predictable, and safe.

But there is no safety in controlling tomorrow.

There is only presence in today.

To live existentially—inside this moment—is to let go of the demand that life fit my plans and instead allow each moment to shape me.

It is to become both the observer and the participant— To feel the full force of what is happening without reducing it to a story. To allow life to move through me, rather than forcing it into my expectations.

Most of us resist this. We enter life with preconceived structures, fixed identities, rigid ideas of who we are and what must be. And then we become frustrated when life refuses to fit inside those lines.

But what if, instead of trying to bend life to fit me, I let life show me who I am?

What if I stepped into each moment with no agenda— but to listen, to feel, to respond with integrity?

This, I believe, is the essence of truly living. Not imposing structure on the experience but discovering the structure within the experience itself.

To surrender to the intelligence of the present moment.

Trusting the Inner Knowing

There was a time when I looked outward for the answers. Books, mentors, philosophies—I sought wisdom from all of them.

And they helped. They shaped me. They gave me tools.

But at some point, the path turned inward.

I began to realize that the truest guidance does not come from external principles or systems.

It comes from the deep, unshakable knowing inside me.

To trust one's own organism— To trust the felt sense of what is right, what is true, what is aligned— That is the highest form of wisdom.

Not because it is perfect. Not because it is infallible.

But because it is alive.

Rules can be broken. External systems can fail. Even wisdom that was once true can become outdated.

But the body knows. The nervous system, the gut, the pull inside that whispers: This way, not that.

When we stop filtering decisions through what others expect, When we stop making choices based on old stories and outdated fears, We begin to move from a place of deep inner coherence.

And that kind of movement—the kind that is guided by presence, not fear— Always leads us home.

The Taste of Truth

So, what does truth taste like?

It is not always sweet—but it is always clean. It is not always easy—but it is always liberating. It is not always comfortable—but it is always real.

To live the good life is to move toward that taste—again and again.

To meet life without defense. To meet the moment without control. To meet myself without pretense.

To trust that whatever emerges from this deep engagement with life will be exactly what is needed.

And to let that be enough.

Because this is the taste of truth. The only question left is—

Are you willing to take it in?

Are you willing to feel the full force of your life? I am trying. Every day, I am trying.

Taste 12. A Taste of Home

The Space Between Seeking and Being

There comes a moment in every journey where the seeking must end. Not because all the questions have been answered or all the wounds have been healed, but because something deeper has been realized—something that was never missing to begin with.

This is that moment.

For years, I believed that growth was a process of becoming—of accumulating wisdom, refining skills, uncovering buried truths, and transcending old limitations. I built my life around that pursuit. I sought knowledge, I sought mastery, I sought understanding. I sought connection, presence, and purpose. And at times, I even sought escape.

But here, in this final section, I step beyond the search.

Because if I listen closely—if I really allow myself to feel the full arc of my own life—I can see that the very thing I was chasing was never somewhere else. It was never in the next realization, the next achievement, or even the next surrender. It was here, in the spaces between. In the quiet pauses. In the moments of tending, not just giving. In the weight of stillness before movement. In the love that does not have to be earned.

What unfolds in these final pages is not another lesson, not another transformation, not another call to action. It is a return. A return to what was always waiting for me beneath the layers of striving and proving. A return to presence. A return to home.

These chapters are the culmination of a lifetime spent in motion—building, creating, searching. But they are also an invitation to rest in what has already been found. To recognize that the real work was never about reaching some final destination but about learning how to fully inhabit the life I have.

This is the final taste of truth. Not the taste of striving but of being. Not the taste of searching but of seeing. Not the taste of becoming but of remembering.

And as I step across this threshold, I no longer ask, *What's next?* Instead, I sit in the quiet certainty of this moment and whisper, *I am already home.*

Chapter III. The Space Between Giving and Tending

I have spent my life in motion.
Building. Creating.
Producing.
Loving in the ways I knew how.
Providing. Supporting. Protecting.

And yet, as I stand here now, at this stage of my life, I see something I had never fully understood before. There is a gap between **giving** and **tending**—a space I never knew existed but one I have lived in my entire life.

For years, I believed that to love someone meant to **give** to them. To show up when needed, to be there when called upon, and to provide in ways that would make their lives easier, better, and more secure. And in so many ways, I did exactly that.

With my daughter, Olivia—I have always been there. Financially, logistically, and even professionally, bringing her into my world, supporting her, and making sure she had what she needed. When she needed tuition, I wrote the check. When she needed guidance in business, I created opportunities. When she needed a safety net, I wove it without hesitation.

But on **ordinary day**s, when no crisis loomed, when no need presented itself—**where was I?**

Did I call just to hear her voice?
Did I ask questions that weren't about solving problems but about knowing her heart?
Did I remember the rhythms of her life when they didn't directly intersect with mine?

That's the tending I missed.

And that was the wound Olivia named when she asked me:
"Dad, do you actually want a relationship with me?"

Not a transactional one. Not one based on support and provision. But a real one. One where she felt **tended to, not just taken care of.**

The Unseen Pattern

As I let this land in me, I saw something I hadn't been willing to see before.

This wasn't just about Olivia.
This was a **pattern** that had shaped my relationships for decades.

It was there with the women I had been with—many of whom I had, in one way or another, **paid to be in relationship with me.** Not always explicitly, not always in ways that were obvious. But I had created an arrangement, an exchange, a way to keep things clean—to keep my window of toleration from being challenged.

And it worked.
Until it didn't.

Because when the **money stopped**, so did the relationship. And I would feel the sting of that as if I had been used—when, in reality, **I had set it up that way**.

I had created a structure that allowed me to engage **without tending**, to be present **without being deeply connected.**

I see now **why I did it.**

I see how my own childhood and my own history played a role in this.

I see the way my mother—an alcoholic, lost in her own needs—used me for her moments of pleasure or necessity, then **discarded me** until she needed something again. There was no consistency, no reliability, and no gentle continuity of care. There were only **moments of intense connection followed by vast deserts of absence.**

There was no tending to me in between. No warmth, no nurture, no steady presence.

And so I learned.

I learned that relationships existed in those **peaks of intensity**—the moments of need, the moments of giving, the moments where something was exchanged.

But in the between spaces?
Nothing.
Silence.
Absence.

And now, I see the way I unknowingly **recreated that model in my own life.**
I see how I have, in many ways, **loved others the way I was loved**—through provision, through grand gestures, through moments of intensity, but without the slow, steady tending that creates a relationship that is **truly felt.**

The Courage to Sit in the Discomfort

This is what I am seeing now.
And I'm not trying to **fix it overnight.**

When I spoke with Olivia about it, I asked her if she wanted to go to therapy with me—to start unraveling this together.

And her response was beautiful.

"Let's let this settle first."

She wasn't looking for an **instant fix.**
She wasn't asking me to rush to the solution.

She was asking me to stay in the **space between**—to sit with this, to hold it with her, to allow this tending to begin before we immediately try to fix.

This morning, I reached out to her, not because there was something to solve but **simply to connect.**

No agenda. No solution. Just presence.

This is My Work Now

Not just with Olivia but with **every relationship** in my life.

To stay **present** in the between spaces.T
o **tend, not just provide.**
To **show up, not just when needed, but when not needed.**

I see now that this is what **intimacy actually is.**

Not the **giving.**
Not the **fixing.**
Not the **moments of intensity.**

But the **tending.**

The slow, quiet, patient presence of love—not for what it gives, but for what it is.

This is a taste of truth I had not yet swallowed before now.

And as I stand here, at this threshold, I can feel it in my bones: This is the next step.

Not another **project**.
Not another **acceleration**.
Not another **thing to produce**.

Just **this**.

Just learning how to be with the people I love in the quiet spaces in between.

Chapter 112. The Space Between Transactions

I built my life around relationships.

My entire business, *By Referral Only*, is rooted in the idea that relationships **thrive** not in the moment of **transaction** but in the space between.

I've spent **decades** teaching people how to nurture, tend, and cultivate those in-between moments—how to **be present** for someone when there's no immediate exchange, no sale, no ask.

And I've been damn good at it.
In fact, I might be the **best in the world** at it.

I've built an empire around this principle. I've trained **thousands** of people to master the **art of deep connection**, to create **loyalty and trust**, and to remain **present long after the handshake, long after the deal is done.**

The biggest names teaching referrals today?
They learned it from me.

My fingerprints are on **every major referral-based business strategy** being taught around the world.

And yet—here I am, standing in front of my own mirror, realizing that the **one place I failed to apply this mastery was in my personal life.**

Because when I look at my relationships—the ones that **matter most**—I see a pattern I hadn't fully acknowledged until now:

I haven't been **tending** to them in between.

The Irony of Mastery Without Application

This is the paradox I'm sitting with.

The thing I built my legacy on, the thing I teach others to do with **effortless precision**, is the very thing I struggle to do in my personal life.

I don't tend to people **between the milestones.**

I've provided. I've given. I've supported in ways that were **clear and measurable.**

With Olivia, I made sure she **never lacked financially.**
She always knew she could count on me for **support when she needed it.**

But between those moments?
Between the transactions of giving?

I wasn't **present** in the way I thought I was.

I didn't **tend to her.**
I didn't **nurture the space between.**

And now I see it wasn't just with her.
It was with the **women in my life.**
My **friends.**
Even my **own internal relationship** with myself.

I was showing up when needed, when there was an **ask**, and when there was a **clear role** to play.

But the moments in between?
The **unstructured, quiet, non-transactional spaces?**

That's where I was **absent.**

It makes sense now.

I was so conditioned to **equate presence with provision**, to see value in what I could **give**, that I missed the reality that tending **isn't about giving—it's about being.**

What We Miss in the In-Between

In business, I teach that the **real value** of a referral-based business **isn't in the sale itself,** but in the way, we **nurture relationships between sales.**

That's what **builds trust.**
That's what **keeps people coming back.**

But what happens when we don't apply that same wisdom to our **personal world?**

I see it clearly now—when there's **no tending**, the relationship **quietly erodes.**

It doesn't **explode.**
It doesn't **fall apart dramatically.**
It just **fades.**

The connection thins out until one day, you look up and realize there's **distance** where there used to be **closeness.**

That's what happened with Olivia.
She had to ask me—**Dad, do you want a relationship with me?**

And my answer was, of course, **yes.**

But in that moment, I saw the **gap.**
I saw where I had **left space unattended.**

And I **felt it.**

I felt how my presence had been **consistent** but my attention had been **conditional.**

How I had been **reliable for the big things** but absent for the small ones.

How I had taught thousands to **nurture the spaces between transactions** while **failing to nurture the spaces between moments in my own home.**

The same pattern showed up in my **romantic relationships.**

My history with women has often involved an **exchange**—money, provision, or financial security in return for companionship, intimacy, and presence.

It worked—
Until the money stopped.
And then, so did the relationship.

But now I see that I built those **structures** because they felt **safer** to me than the **complexity of an untended relationship.**

Real Relationships Require Something More

Real relationships—the ones built **in the space between**—require something more.

They require **presence without an exchange.**
They require **tending without a transaction.**
They require **me, not what I can provide.**

The Hardest Thing to Learn at 68

So here I am, at **68**, staring at this revelation.

It's **humbling.**

I am the **expert** on tending to relationships in business.

And yet, in my personal life,
I am a **beginner.**

And I'm okay with that.

Because this is where the **real work** happens—
Not in the **knowing** but in the choosing.

I can see the pattern now.
I can see where I've **defaulted to distance** in between moments of presence.

And now, I get to **choose differently.**

That's all growth really is—
A willingness to choose differently, even when the old pattern is easier.

The Space Between the Next Step

I know how to tend to relationships in business. Now, I get to learn how to tend to them in my personal life.

Not by **giving.**
Not by **fixing.**
Not by **providing.**

But by **being.**

By showing up in **the space between.**
By learning how to hold **presence without needing a transaction to define it.**

This isn't just about Olivia.
It's not just about women.
It's about **me learning how to be** in a way I've **never allowed myself to before.**

And if I can master that?

Well, that will be my greatest accomplishment yet.

Chapter 113. The Space Between the Dance

There is a moment—just before movement—when stillness holds everything.

Not a pause.
Not an absence.
But a space.

The space between the dance.

Where Movement Begins

I've spent my life in motion.

I've built businesses.
Traveled continents.
Pushed my body beyond what men my age dare to attempt.
Competed, performed, produced, provided.

Even in my spiritual work—whether in meditation, plant medicine, or breathwork—there was always a sense of **doing something.**

But dance?
Dance taught me something I had never quite understood before.

The most powerful part of the dance isn't the movement.
It's the space before it.

The moment where the body hesitates, gathers, listens—before it responds.

The space between.

The Tension Between Action and Surrender

I came into dance like I have come into most things in my life—
Ready to **learn, master, perfect.**

But dance doesn't work that way.

It's not something you **conquer.**
It's something you **surrender into.**

For years, I lived in the **rhythm of drive**—always moving toward the next thing, always creating, always forging ahead.

I knew how to lead.
I knew how to push.
I knew how to **command movement.**

But what I didn't know—what dance slowly, patiently revealed to me—was how to **listen** to the space between.

Listening with the Body

Lysa Castro, my dance teacher, once told me:

"Joe, stop trying to move. Just... wait. Let your body hear the music before it reacts to it."

And that changed everything.

Because I realized—
I wasn't just doing that in dance.
I was doing it in **life.**

I was always moving, always responding, always anticipating—but I wasn't listening.

I wasn't feeling the **pause before the next step.**
I wasn't sitting in the **suspension before the motion.**

I was afraid of the stillness.
Afraid that if I stopped moving, if I stopped **driving, creating, producing, giving**, then what?

Would I disappear?
Would I cease to exist?
Would I become... nothing?

It's an old fear.
One that lives in the bones of men like me—men who were taught that their worth is in their **output.**

The Dance of Presence

But dance—dance **insisted** that I let go of that belief.

Because the best dances aren't **forced.**
They aren't **executed.**

They are felt.
They are allowed.
They emerge from the **conversation between movement and stillness.**

It's a relationship, not a transaction.

And isn't that exactly what I've been learning in my relationships?

That **real connection** doesn't happen in the moments of intensity—but in the space between them.

That what makes something **alive** isn't just what is happening—but the pauses that give it breath.

The Space Between Connection

In ecstatic dance, there's a moment—when two people are moving together, sensing each other, but not **grabbing** for control.

No one is leading.
No one is following.
There is only **attunement.**

A shared listening.
A shared waiting.
A shared space between movement.

And I see now—this is what I've been missing in my relationships.

I have known how to **lead.**
I have known how to **provide.**

But I haven't always known how to **listen.**
To wait.
To let things **unfold instead of forcing them forward.**

This Is My Work Now

To dance—not just with my body, but with my life.

To let there be spaces between movement.
To let relationships breathe instead of control them.
To listen before I act.

To stop **reacting to the music** and start **feeling it.**

And in doing that—I am learning something I have never known before.

That the **space between the dance** is just as sacred as the dance itself.

Chapter 114. The Space Between Noise and Silence

There is a kind of silence that isn't empty.
It holds something.

A presence. A waiting. A weight.

I have spent most of my life filling silence.
With words. With work.
With wisdom.With the hum of productivity and purpose.

But now, I find myself drawn to something else.
Not the noise of doing.But the **depth of being.**

The Illusion of Being Present

For decades, I told myself I was a present man.

If someone needed me, I showed up.
If they asked for help, I provided it.If they had a problem, I solved it.

But presence isn't just **being there when called upon.**
Presence is tending to what exists in the spaces between.

It's checking in, not just responding.
It's listening, not just fixing.
It's being with, not just providing for.

And I see now—
I had built an empire on relationships,
but I had not built relationships that could exist without the empire.

What Happens in the Quiet

I spent a lifetime avoiding silence.
Not the external kind—I've always loved solitude.

But the **inner silence.**
The kind that comes when you sit with someone without needing to do anything.
The kind that isn't about proving, achieving, or earning your worth.

With my daughter, Olivia—I was always there when she needed something.
But was I there when she didn't?

Did I call just to say goodnight?
Did I remember the little things, the **unspoken things,**
the details that weren't urgent but were important?

She once asked me,
"Dad, do you actually want a relationship with me?"

And it cut me.
Because I thought I had already given her that.
I thought I had been **present.**

But what I had been was **available.**

Those aren't the same thing.

The Space Between Transactions

I built my entire career around **teaching people how to tend to relationships.**

Not in the moments of transactions,
but in the spaces between them.

I taught real estate agents how to stay connected,
not just when someone was buying a house,
but **when there was no sale on the horizon.**

I taught mortgage brokers how to check in,
not just when someone needed a loan,
but **when there was nothing to ask for.**

I **mastered the art of tending to clients.**
But had I mastered the art of tending to the people I love?

Had I **practiced** what I preached in my own life?

Or had I spent all my energy nurturing professional relationships,
while leaving personal ones to exist in the gaps?

Being Without an Agenda

I realize now, tending isn't about grand gestures.
It isn't about fixing things.

It's about **being willing to exist in the space between.**

Between words. Between calls. Between milestones.

It's texting Olivia **not because she needs something**,
but because I just want her to know I'm thinking about her.

It's sitting with Jody **without needing to prove anything**
or create something or shape the moment into something meaningful.

It's letting there be a pause—without rushing to fill it.

The Hardest Lesson to Learn at 68

This is what I am sitting with now.
That maybe—just maybe—I don't have to keep filling the silence.

That maybe the silence **isn't absence.**
Maybe it's space. Maybe it's an invitation.

And maybe presence isn't something you **give.**
Maybe it's something you **allow.**

Chapter 115. The Weight of the Unlived Life

There are patterns so deeply embedded in us that they don't feel like choices.
They feel like us.

As though they were written into the marrow of our bones long before we took our first breath.

They come down through generations, through blood, through story, through unspoken agreements that whisper:

This is how it is.
This is how we have always been.

And so, without thinking, we step into the rhythm of those patterns, wearing them like second skin.

They are familiar, so we mistake them for truth.

The Gravity of Time

There is a number that hangs in the air now: **82.**
A timestamp on this incarnation.

A limit to what this life will hold.

Fourteen more years.
Not an eternity.
Not a limitless expanse.

Fourteen years to decide—**Will I live differently this time?**

Because if I do nothing, if I continue as I have been,

I will have **fourteen more years of the same patterns.**

Fourteen more years of relationships that flare brightly but fade quickly.
Fourteen more years of being known for what I provide, but not for how I tend.

Or—I could choose another way.

The Unlived Life

There is a life that I have not lived.

A life where I tend, where I stay, where I don't just show up for the big moments, but for the small ones, too.

A life where I don't just support Olivia when she needs something,
but where I send a message **for no reason at all.**
A life where I don't just offer security to women,
but where I offer my attention, without an exchange.

A life where I don't just keep myself busy
to avoid the discomfort of stillness.

A life where I don't **mistake movement for presence.**

The DNA of Habit

It's easy to think of habits as things we build in a lifetime.
Repetitions of action, ingrained through will or neglect.

But some habits go deeper than that.
They are not chosen but inherited.
They are not just personality but programming.

And programming—especially the kind written into the nervous system—doesn't yield easily.

It does not respond to mere recognition.
It responds to **interruption.**

To **resistance.**
To the sheer force of choosing something different, again and again, until the old way **atrophies from lack of use.**

This is not just a lesson in intimacy.
It is a lesson in **defying gravity.**

The gravity of ancestral repetition.
The gravity of cellular memory.
The gravity of an old soul's inclination to repeat its own stories.

And yet—something new is emerging.

The Reckoning

So now, the question sits before me—not as a burden but as a door.

What does it mean to tend to this part of my life?
What does it mean to stand at the edge of an ancestral pattern and refuse to follow it?
What does it mean to take this life—this one life— and live it as though love matters more than legacy?

Not just romantic love.
Not just sexual love.
But the kind of love that requires deep presence, deep tending,
deep surrender to the **immeasurable.**

The Next Fourteen Years

Maybe the lesson isn't about love at all. Maybe it is about **presence.**

Presence with another.
Presence with myself.
Presence with the in-between moments that have, for so long, gone unnoticed.

This morning, I texted Olivia just to say good morning.
Not to solve anything.
Not to give anything.
Not to fix anything.

Just to be present in the space between our last conversation and the next time we speak.

It felt small.
It felt almost insignificant.

And yet—it was a tiny rebellion
against the gravity of inherited absence.

Maybe this is how the cycle ends.
Maybe this is where the new one begins.

Not with grand declarations.
Not with dramatic transformations.

But with small, consistent acts of presence in the spaces I have always left untended.

Fourteen years.

Not to become someone different,
but to become **more fully who I already am.**

A man capable of tending, not just giving.

A man willing to **stay,**
not just show up.

A man ready to be present in the space between.

Chapter 116. The Three Joes

"The music is not in the notes, but in the silence between them." — **Wolfgang Amadeus Mozart.**

I wake up most mornings knowing that I am not just one thing.

There is **Soulful Joe**—the one who is just here for the ride, reveling in the adventure of being human. He doesn't flinch at pain, doesn't resist challenge, and doesn't even ask why. To him, life is an invitation, and the answer is always yes. He is the part of me that feels the heat of the sauna on my skin, the cold plunge that follows. He is the one who dances barefoot in Sebastopol, who loses himself in music, who breathes in deeply just to feel breath itself.

Soulful Joe doesn't question why he's here. He doesn't search for meaning. He doesn't strive for improvement. He simply **experiences**—fully, completely, without reservation. When he dances, there is no separation between the music and his body. When he laughs, there is no holding back. When he connects with another, there is no agenda, no outcome, no purpose beyond the pure joy of connection itself.

Then there is **Wounded Joe**—the teacup with a broken handle. The part of me that has known abandonment, the imprint of my mother's absence, the years spent proving something I couldn't name. He is the one who learned, early on, that attention was conditional, that love could be a transaction, that safety was something you manage, not something you rest in. Wounded Joe carries a quiet sorrow, a low-frequency hum of *not enough*, even when everything on paper says otherwise. He knows how to build. He knows how to create. But does he know how to be held?

Wounded Joe is the architect of my achievements, the engine behind my empire. He built **By Referral Only** not just as a business but as a fortress—a place where he could control the terms of engagement, where his value was clear, and where his worth was measurable. He is the one who crafted relationships where giving was quantifiable, where presence was scheduled, and where intimacy was contained within predictable boundaries.

And then there is **Seeker Joe**—the one who has spent a lifetime refining, improving, transforming. He is the one who sits with therapists, takes the next training, and does the deep work. He is relentless in his pursuit of truth, always asking, *What's next? What's missing?* He is the one who walks into plant medicine ceremonies, faces the shadow, and interrogates his own patterns with the precision of a scientist and the devotion of a monk.

Seeker Joe believes in evolution. He believes in growth. He believes that with enough insight, enough practice, and enough dedication, he can transcend the limitations of his past. He is both the detective searching for clues and the judge weighing the evidence of his own life.

And yet, **Soulful Joe does not search. Soulful Joe witnesses.**

He watches both of them—Wounded Joe, always protecting himself, and Seeker Joe, always trying to fix himself. And he smiles, knowing that neither of them needs to fight so hard.

Because this is it. **Not the next breakthrough. Not the next realization. Not the next evolution of self.**

This moment. The space between the notes.

The Illusion of the Journey

For so long, I believed I was on a journey. A journey toward wholeness. A journey toward understanding. A journey toward healing.

But **what if there is no journey?**

What if the need to seek is the very thing keeping me from seeing? What if healing is not about fixing but about allowing?

I sit with this. I let it land.

Because if nothing is missing, then what am I looking for? And if I stop searching—if I stop trying to heal—then what remains?

The Exhaustion of Seeker Joe

Seeker Joe has been my most devoted ally. He has worked tirelessly to ensure that Wounded Joe is never left behind.

But he is tired. Not in a defeated way. Not in a lost way. But in a way that says, *I have carried this long enough.*

For decades, Seeker Joe has held up the mirror, asking the hard questions and searching for the missing pieces. He has been relentless in his pursuit of growth, understanding, and transformation. He has built systems, found teachers, sat in ceremonies, and pushed himself to the edges of his own consciousness.

And yet, **Soulful Joe has never been searching.** Because there was never anything to find.

The only thing missing was the permission to **be**.

The Gift of Soulful Joe

Soulful Joe does not ask *why*. Soulful Joe does not demand proof. Soulful Joe does not need a process.

He simply **is.**

He watches the seeker, smiles at the wounded, and whispers:

"Live."

Live without the need to prove. Live without the compulsion to fix. Live as if the lesson was never about the suffering but about the sheer brilliance of waking up each day in a body that can taste, touch, laugh, dance, and create.

The Moment of Choice

For years, I have been trying to integrate my parts. To heal Wounded Joe. To calm Seeker Joe. To embody Soulful Joe.

But maybe that's just another game. Maybe there is nothing to integrate. Maybe there is nothing to fix.

Maybe I don't need to master the art of becoming whole. Maybe I only need to recognize that I already am.

And maybe, just maybe, the moment I stop trying to arrive is the moment I realize **I have always been home.**

Chapter 117. Nothing is Missing

I sit with this—the possibility that **nothing is missing.**
That all of it, every layer of me, is whole in its own right.

Soulful Joe delights in the experience of it all—the way the wind moves through trees, the way words come together in a moment of inspiration, the way a glance can hold a universe of meaning. He is the one who laughs at the absurdity of suffering, not out of cruelty, but because he knows—it's all just the dance.

When Soulful Joe walks into a room, he doesn't calculate what he'll get or give. He doesn't analyze the dynamics. He doesn't track the exchange rate of energy. He simply **shows up**, fully present, curious about what will unfold. When he speaks, it's not to impress or protect or achieve—it's to express what's true in the moment, to connect without agenda, to play in the field of what's possible between souls.

But then there's **Wounded Joe**.

Wounded Joe grips at the fractures. He sees the broken handle on the teacup, sees the fault lines running through his life, and he whispers: *See? This is why they can't hold you. This is why it's safer to be alone.*

Wounded Joe is hypervigilant for signs of rejection, for evidence that he is not enough, and for proof that others will eventually leave. He catalogs every disappointment, every abandonment, every moment where connection faltered. He builds fortresses of self-sufficiency, strategic generosity, and calculated distance—all to ensure that the pain of his childhood never finds him again. He would rather be the one who leaves than the one who is left behind.

And then there's **Seeker Joe**.

Seeker Joe has spent decades in the trenches of self-discovery, turning over every stone, chasing every insight, and mapping out every psychological construct. He is the architect of my evolution, but sometimes I wonder—has he built a **cathedral** or a **prison?**

Seeker Joe believes there is always more to learn, more to understand, more to heal. He devours books on psychology, attends workshops on emotional intelligence, and engages in practices that promise transformation. He can explain attachment theory, articulate trauma responses, and identify cognitive distortions with scholarly precision. He is the cartographer of my inner landscape, constantly updating the map, convinced that if he can just discover the right territory, he will finally arrive at wholeness.

And yet, **Soulful Joe does not search. Soulful Joe witnesses.**

He watches both of them—Wounded Joe, always protecting himself, and Seeker Joe, always trying to fix himself. And he smiles, knowing that neither of them needs to fight so hard.

The Space Between Seeking and Being

I see it now—the tension, the war between **seeking** and **being**.

Seeker Joe keeps looking for the **why.**
Wounded Joe keeps believing in the **not enough.**
Soulful Joe just keeps whispering:

"Stop. Just live."

For years, I have believed that my healing was **unfinished.** That my work was **unfinished.** That *I* was unfinished. That if I could just uncover the next realization, the next truth, the next piece of the puzzle, I would finally arrive at wholeness.

But what if I was **never incomplete?**

The Only Thing Missing Was My Awareness

Yesterday, I thought about Olivia. Not in a heavy, nostalgic way. Not with regret or longing. Just in a quiet, steady sort of way—the way you think about someone you love when they cross your mind unexpectedly.

I didn't text her right away. I just sat with the thought and let it linger.

For years, I've wrestled with the distance between us—not just the physical distance between Northern California and Los Angeles, but the emotional space, the years of separation, and the moments I missed when she was growing up.

There were times I thought I had to **fix** it. That there was some perfect conversation, some overdue reckoning, some missing piece that, if I could just find it, would close the gap between us.

But what if nothing was missing?
What if the only thing I ever needed to do was **be here**—available, present, loving, in whatever way I could be, even from a distance?

So, instead of spiraling into analysis, instead of wondering what I could do better or differently, I did something simple. I picked up my phone and sent her a text.

"Thinking of you. No reason. No need to respond. Just love you."

And that was enough.

Not because it solved anything. Not because it suddenly erased all the space between us. But because it was real. Because it was true. Because it was **what I had to give in that moment.**

Maybe the awareness I needed wasn't about finding the perfect way to connect. Maybe it was about realizing I don't have to **earn** love—I just have to **offer it.**

And in that offering, in that moment of simple presence, I see it clearly:

Nothing is missing.

I Was Never Broken

I look around at my life.

I am not lacking **love.** I am not lacking **purpose.** I am not lacking **presence.**

The only thing that has ever been missing was the belief that I was **already here.**

Already whole. Already living. Already complete.

The only thing that has ever been missing... was my **willingness to see that nothing is missing.**

I sip my tea, run my fingers over the crack in the handle, and realize:

I was never broken. Only believing that I was.

And for the first time, I don't try to fix it.

I just let it **be.**

This is the true nature of tending—not trying to **repair** what seems damaged but nurturing what is **already whole.**
Not rushing to fill in the gaps, but allowing the **spaces between** to breathe, to expand, to contain their own kind of wholeness.

Letting It Be Enough

I pick up my phone.

Not to say something profound.
Not to force a moment. Just to send a quiet acknowledgment into the space between us.

"Just thinking of you. No reason. No need to respond."

And then I sit in the quiet certainty that love exists,
not in the grand gestures, not in the profound conversations, not in the perfect responses,
but in the simple decision to be present again and again, in the ordinary moments that make up a life.

Nothing is missing.
Not in her.
Not in me.
Not in the space between us.

Everything is already here.

Chapter 118. The Seat of the Soul

I sit at my altar, the weight of all my lives converging into this singular moment. It is here, in the stillness, that I sense the full arc of my existence—not just this life, but the deeper thread running through all of them.

I imagine the scene before my arrival. A gathering of souls waiting for their assignments. God steps forward and calls for a volunteer:

"I need a boy to be born to an alcoholic mother. He will learn the language of survival before the language of love. He will have eight brothers and sisters, two of whom he will lose—one by his own hand, the other to the violence of nature. He will drown himself in alcohol, only to awaken in a park, the sun rising on the first day of his reckoning. He will be given a choice: the cold bars of a jail cell or the arms of a stranger who will guide him home. He will walk the path of seekers, of wanderers, of warriors who battle their own demons. He will meet a man named Milton, who will walk beside him for a decade before exhaling his last breath, whispering, 'I have done what I came to do.' And in the years that follow, this boy-turned-man will search and search and search, believing that wholeness is something to be found rather than remembered."

I picture myself in that celestial gathering, my soul raising its hand. *"I'll do it. I'll live that life."*

And not just that—I volunteered knowing exactly what it would entail. The pain of abandonment. The struggle for worth. The constant seeking. The brilliance of creation alongside the blindness to what was always present.

I chose this. All of it. Not as punishment, not as a lesson, but as an **experience.** As a journey that was never meant to arrive anywhere but **here**—this moment, this breath, this recognition.

And so here I am, decades later, seated in the same body that once lay broken in a park, the same body that has climbed mountains, built empires, sought truth in a thousand places. Here I sit in what Gary Zukav called **The Seat of the Soul.**

The Soul That Chose This Life

I see it now.

The one who volunteered for this life is still here. He never left.

Soulful Joe—he watches, he marvels, he delights in the game of it all. He does not analyze. He does not repair. He does not seek.

He is the one who knew before I was born that this life wasn't about **getting it right.** It wasn't about **becoming perfect.** It wasn't about **transcending pain or achieving enlightenment.**

It was about experiencing **everything.** The ecstasy and the agony. The connection and the loneliness. The giving and the taking. The showing up and the disappearing.

But then there's **Seeker Joe**, who is relentless. He is the custodian of **Wounded Joe**, tending to the cracks, the bruises, the places that still ache. He has studied, traveled, and asked the hard questions. He has learned the mechanics of healing like a master craftsman.

He can explain why I pull away when intimacy demands consistency. He can trace the neural pathways that light up when abandonment feels imminent. He can articulate the exact ways in which my mother's alcoholism shaped my capacity for trust, my approach to love, and my perspective on tending.

And yet, all his efforts still whisper the same hidden question: *"Am I enough?"*

And then there is **Soulful Joe**, who does not ask. He simply **is**.

He watches the seeker, smiles at the wounded, and whispers:

"Live."

Live **without the need to prove.** Live **without the compulsion to fix.** Live as if the lesson was never about the suffering but about the sheer brilliance of waking up each day in a body that can **taste, touch, laugh, dance, and create.**

The Wisdom of Milton

Milton knew. That's why he left with a breath of completion.

"I have done what I came to do."

That moment stayed with me. Haunted me. Inspired me. Shaped me.

Because if Milton could leave this life with that clarity, could I?

Could I, at the end of it all, breathe out and say, *"I have done what I came to do"*?

And what if the only way to say that—the only way to know I had completed my assignment—was to stop searching for the moment of arrival and realize **I am already living it?**

What if *"what I came to do"* was never about the empire I built, the people I helped, or the wisdom I shared?

What if it was simply about **experiencing this**—all of it—through the unique lens of this particular soul?

What if there was never anything to fix, never anything to heal, never anything to overcome?

What if there was only ever **this**—this body, this breath, this moment, this life, exactly as it is?

The Soulful Choice

I sit with this now. Not as an insight to grasp. Not as another puzzle to solve. But as a truth I am finally allowing to land.

The soul that volunteered for this experience doesn't need a reason to be here. He simply **is**.

And that's enough.

So I let **Seeker Joe** rest.
I let **Wounded Joe** soften.
And I take my seat.

Not as a **seeker.**
Not as a **survivor.**
Not as a **man looking for what's next.**

But as the one who **raised his hand.**

"I'll do it. I'll live that life."

And so I sit in **The Seat of the Soul.**

I reach for my phone. I text Olivia:

"I'm here. Not just when you need me. Not just when there's something to solve. But in the spaces between. In the ordinary moments. In the quiet Sunday afternoons and the busy Tuesday mornings. I'm here, tending to the space between us. Not because I should. Not because I'm trying to fix anything.

But because this – this presence, this attention, this love – is what I came to do."

And then I set the phone down, closed my eyes, and let myself **live.**

Not as a man on a journey toward wholeness.

But as a soul who is **already home.**

Made in the USA
Monee, IL
13 April 2025